INTERNATIONAL CORPORATE LAW: 1

International Corporate Law
Volume 1

Edited by
FIONA MACMILLAN
Murdoch University

·HART·
PUBLISHING

OXFORD – PORTLAND OREGON
2000

Hart Publishing
Oxford and Portland, Oregon

Published in North America (US and Canada) by
Hart Publishing c/o
International Specialized Book Services
5804 NE Hassalo Street
Portland, Oregon
97213-3644
USA

Distributed in the Netherlands, Belgium and Luxembourg by
Intersentia, Churchillaan 108
B2900 Schoten
Antwerpen
Belgium

Hart Publishing Ltd is a specialist legal publisher based in Oxford, England.
To order further copies of this book or to request a list of other
publications please write to:

Hart Publishing Ltd, Salter's Boatyard,
Folly Bridge, Abingdon Road, Oxford OX1 4LB
Telephone: +44 (0)1865 245533 or Fax: +44 (0)1865 794882
e-mail: mail@hartpub.co.uk

British Library Cataloguing in Publication Data
Data Available
ISBN 1 84113–037–0 (cloth)
ISSN 1 469 0594

Typeset by Hope Services (Abingdon) Ltd.
Printed in Great Britain on acid-free paper
by Biddles Ltd, Guildford and Kings Lynn.

Table of Contents

List of Contributors   vii
Members of the Advisory Committee of International Corporate Law   ix
Contributions to the Next Volume of International Corporate Law   xi

PART I

Chapter 1: The Role of the State in Corporate Law Formation   1
GREGORY A MARK

Chapter 2: Public Beginnings, Private Ends—Should Corporate
Law Privilege the Interests of Shareholders?   17
JENNIFER HILL

Chapter 3: Scenes from a Wharf: Containing the Morality of
Corporate Law   37
PETA SPENDER

Chapter 4: Directors' Liabilities to Third Parties   69
MITSUMASA TANABE

Chapter 5: Protecting Minority and Public Interests in Nigerian
Company Law: The Corporate Affairs Commission as a
Corporations Ombudsman   79
AMEZE GUOBADIA

Chapter 6: The Current US Tax Controversy over International
Hybrid Entities   101
KEITH E ENGEL

Chapter 7: Environmental Challenges for Japanese Corporations
in the Twenty-First Century: Aspects of Environmental Risk
Management   125
JUNKO UEDA

Chapter 8: Takeover Bids in Japan   143
MAMI SAKAUE

Chapter 9: Legitimating Global Corporate Power   155
FIONA MACMILLAN

PART II—COUNTRY REPORTS

Chapter 10: Australia: Australia and the UK on the Quest for Best
Corporate Governance Practice   173
FIONA ELLETT

Chapter 11: Japan: Japan's Current Move Toward Corporate
Statutory Reform: Is it a Breakthrough to a New Era?   179
JUNKO UEDA

Chapter 12: Nigeria: Improving Nigeria's Investment Climate   187
C O OKONKWO

Chapter 13: United Kingdom: Recent Developments in UK
Company Law   193
D R MACDONALD

Index   203

List of Contributors

FIONA ELLETT is a recent honours graduate in Law from Murdoch University and an articled clerk at Mallesons Stephen Jaques Solicitors in Perth, Western Australia

KEITH E ENGEL is Assistant Professor of Law at Washington and Lee University, Virginia

AMEZE GUOBADIA is Professor of Law at the Nigerian Institute of Advanced Legal Studies, Lagos

JENNIFER HILL is Associate Professor of Law at the University of Sydney

D R MACDONALD is a member of the Department of Law at the University of Dundee

FIONA MACMILLAN is Associate Professor of Law at Murdoch University, Western Australia

GREGORY A MARK is Professor of Law at Rutgers Law School, Newark, and a Member of the Graduate Faculty in History at Rutgers University, Newark

C O OKONKWO is Professor of Law at the University of Nigeria, Enugu

MAMI SAKAUE is Associate Professor of Law at Shimane University

PETA SPENDER is a Senior Lecturer in Law at the Australian National University, Canberra

MITSUMASA TANABE is Professor of Law at Nagoya University

JUNKO UEDA is Associate Professor of Law at Sugiyama Jogakuen University, Nagoya

Members of the Advisory Committee of International Corporate Law

Contributions to the Next Volume of International Corporate Law

Contributions for consideration for publication in the next volume of International Corporate Law are invited.

Contributions for Part I should be between 7,000 and 12,000 words including footnotes and should relate to one or more of the following general areas:

- international or comparative aspects of corporate law;
- theoretical or jurisprudential perspectives on corporate law;
- domestic or regional issues in corporate law which would be of interest to an international readership.

Contributions for Part II should be between 1,000 and 3,000 words including footnotes and should relate to recent developments in corporate law in one or more jurisdictions or regions.

Contributions should be sent to the editor at the following address:

Associate Professor Fiona Macmillan
School of Law
Murdoch University
Murdoch
Western Australia 6150

F.Macmillan@murdoch.edu.au

1

The Role of the State
in Corporate Law Formation

GREGORY A. MARK[1]

Corporate entities have been the object of concern, hence study, for the greater part of the millennium. Business corporations have dominated the attention of those concerned with corporate entities for most of the last two centuries of the millennium.[2] As the dominant form of the entity has changed, the mix of methods for addressing the concerns raised by the entity has changed. In the days when the Church was the corporate entity central to society, the natural mode of inquiry was theological, with history enlisted to buttress arguments about the legitimacy of organised hierarchy.[3] During the seventeenth and eighteenth centuries corporate entities were primarily political tools, serving the expansionist aims of imperial powers, securing colonies and trade abroad and facilitating consolidation domestically by controlling currency, finance and infrastructure.[4] The nineteenth century saw the corporate entity further evolve, adapting and emphasising the economic ends of corporate existence while nonetheless retaining an essential political component.[5] As adaptations raised political concerns of concentrated and autonomous economic power political arguments were deployed, as had been their theological predecessors, to understand and debate the corporation's place in society.[6] Again, the history of the

---

[1] An early version of this chapter was presented at the 1998 Annual Meeting of the Law and Society Association. I am grateful to Professor Robert Gordon for his comments on the chapter, to members of the panel and audience for comments and questions, and to Amy L Miller for her assistance in preparing the chapter.

[2] See A F Conard, *Corporations in Perspective* (Minolta, Foundation Press, 1976), at 135.

[3] See A A Berle and G C Means, 'Corporation', in *The Encyclopædia of the Social Sciences* (1931), iv, at 414, 414–5.

[4] See J S Davis, *Essays in the Earlier History of American Corporations* (Harvard University Press, 1917, reprinted Russell & Russell, Inc., 1975), i, at 87–103. See also Berle and Means, *supra* n.3, at 415–6.

[5] The literature making this point is voluminous. Still the best work on the United States is J W Hurst, *The Legitimacy of the Business Corporation in the Law of the United States 1780–1970* (Charlottesville, University Press of Virginia, 1970), at 13–57.

[6] *Ibid.*, at 58–111.

corporate entity was invoked largely to legitimate its roll and to quell fears that the entity had become too autonomous.[7]

In the twentieth century, the corporation has largely shed its overt political character, at least in the United States, and its economic role has been emphasised.[8] Not surprisingly, by the late twentieth century the dominant tool for understanding the corporation has become economics,[9] and history is again being deployed to buttress the dominant economic perspective. Unlike the transition from religiosity to politics, however, the transition from politics to economics is accompanied by what appears to be a completely revisionist explanation of the roots of the business corporation.[10] That is, many analysts of the business corporation have propounded or accepted an explanation—including an historical explanation—that leaves a principled political role out of the explanation altogether.[11] Others have adopted an understanding of the evolution of the corporation that is phrased in the vocabulary of economics, treating political considerations as mere stimuli that set the evolution off in one direction or another.[12] The first explanation depends on application of rent-seeking theory to an explanation of the firm.[13] The second explanation adapts a theory of institutional inertia developed by economic historians, notably Douglass North, known as path-dependency.[14]

In this chapter, I will address the first explanation, the one which has read politics and the state out of corporation history. First, two observations: modern neo-classical economics supposes that individuals are rational actors seeking to maximise gain and uses that insight as the basis for its analytic force. This monocausal approach is characteristic of the modern social sciences which seek—as a matter of their science—to isolate individual explanatory variables in social phenomena. Of course, there is nothing wrong—and much that is useful—about that, especially in so far as economic man is descriptively accurate for players in the modern market. The analytic techniques of modern social science, economics included, are, however, usefully applicable to different historical eras only in so far as their underlying assumptions are descriptively accurate in those eras. Thus, (1) the neo-classical assumption shifts the analytic focus for

---

[7] See G A Mark, 'The Personification of the Business Corporation in American Law' (1987) 54 *University of Chicago Law Review* 1441, at 1462–3.

[8] See Hurst, *supra* n.5, at 69–75.

[9] See R Romano, *Foundations of Corporate Law* (New York, Oxford University Press, 1993), at p.v.

[10] See G A Mark, 'Some Observations on Writing the Legal History of the Corporation in the Age of Theory' in L E Mitchell (ed.), *Progressive Corporate Law* (1995) 67, at 72–3.

[11] See, e.g., J R Macey and G P Miller, 'Toward an Interest Group Theory of Delaware Corporate Law' (1987) 65 *Texas Law Review* 469.

[12] See, e.g., M J Roe, 'Chaos and Evolution in Law and Economics' (1996) 109 *Harvard Law Review* 641, at 643–62.

[13] See, e.g., R Romano, 'The Political Economy of Takeover Statutes' (1987) 73 *Virginia Law Review* 111.

[14] See, e.g., D C North, *Institutions, Institutional Changes and Economic Performance* (New York, Cambridge University Press, 1990).

purposive economic activity from the state to the individual, (2) in so doing it reverses our political—indeed our moral—presumptions about such behaviour by recasting corporate gain from being a matter collectively agreed upon to a product of individual desires. Historiographically, this has meant a shift of attention from the creative role of the state to the creative role of the individual. Furthermore—and my use of the term creative was deliberate—it has changed our attitude about corporators from presumptive monopolists to entrepreneurs. The revisionist overtones are obvious. The question is, are they correct, or even novel?

What follows is not itself an exercise in writing corporate legal history. Rather, it is an exercise in caution, caution against a too-facile application of theory to history. The chapter first sets out the traditional (American) story of the role of the state in corporate law formation. In telling that story it makes the point that the story is generally one of state policy, not a story about who or what is primarily responsible for the formation of capitalised entities. It then sets out the challenge that neo-classical economics poses by examining one of the leading articles that claims to refute the traditional story. Finally, it suggests that the refutation is not nearly so decisive as is claimed. First, the refutation is aimed at a claim the traditional story rarely makes—few, if any, historians have claimed that the state is responsible for the actual bringing together of corporators and capital. The traditional story is rather one of facilitation tempered by regulation. Secondly, to the extent that historians have focused on corporators, the scholars have acknowledged those entrepreneurs as the motive force behind capitalised enterprises. Thirdly, sophisticated historians have made, and tempered, virtually all the claims in the challenge to the traditional story—from the claim that the role of limited liability is overstated to the claim that entrepreneurs understood corporate formation as a species of contract. Fourthly, and finally, much more is required by way of exploration of historical evidence, and much more sophistication in understanding the intellectual history of economic theory, risk and comparative political systems, before we can assume that modern American market assumptions carry over wholesale into earlier eras or that evidence from foreign experience has universal applicability.[15]

Application of economic techniques to the legal history of the business corporation has at least two potentially salutary consequences and at least two dangers. The first important benefit is that it keeps the historian's feet planted firmly on the ground by focusing inquiry directly on the incentives each actor in corporate history had for every act taken. Such an approach makes at least some sweeping claims of high political theory problematic. Of course, historians might note—correctly, in my view—that the ground is where their feet have

---

[15] Indeed, the question whether any given advanced industrial state has a superior system of corporate governance and the related question whether aspects of those systems are freely transferable is the subject of intense debate in both legal and economic literatures: see W W Bratton and J A McCahery, 'Comparative Corporate Governance and the Theory of the Firm: The Case Against Global Cross Reference', 34 *Colom. J. Transnat'l L.*, 1999.

always been. But, most historians, coming to the corporation from the vantage point of traditional political and legal history, have focused on the legislatures and the courts and have taken, usually at face value, the word of the courts about the role of the state as an actor, on the one hand, and analysed legislative acts within the context of partisan politics on the other.[16] In virtually none of the studies by such scholars is the focus, even fleeting, on economic incentives, especially the incentives of the corporators.[17] Thus, the second valuable feature of the economic perspective is its focus on corporators—those individuals who actually owned, and usually ran, the corporations created by the legislature. And surely that is a good thing. We ought to know more about what investors and entrepreneurs needed and desired, what legal forms were preferred over others, and why.

There lies, however, in what is unfortunately a lacuna in the historical profession, a rich group of studies dealing with entrepreneurs. The focus of most of these studies is the enterprise builders of the late nineteenth and early twentieth centuries. Indeed, it was Alfred Chandler's complaint that business historians had too long dealt with prominent entrepreneurs and too little with the enterprises they built. Moreover, he complained, they did so at first to attack such men—they were the robber barons—or to rescue them from infamy—they were industrial statesmen.[18] While such studies often highlighted motives which were vulgar and thus were reductionist in their focus on gain, or were simply hagiographic at the other extreme, they also served to suggest, first, that motives were rarely mixed or fluid and, more importantly, that all gain-seekers were alike in motive and untempered by other concerns.

Unfortunately, the focus of neo-classical scholars does not really provide us with much more information about either corporators or their incentives. Instead, it presumes that corporators have precisely the same desires, needs and incentives as are *presumed* for actors in modern American markets.[19] This presumption has two potential problems, either or both of which may serve to undermine the genuine contributions a neo-classical viewpoint may have for historical inquiry. First, it presents the problem of anachronism. No one would deny, I assume, that human beings have an element of rational gain-seeking about them and, I also assume, no one would deny that it has been an element of human behaviour for all of recorded history. Nonetheless, the particular manifestations and costs of selfish rationalism in any given era may elude

---

[16] This must be due at least in part to the relatively greater accessibility of reported cases, statutory law and newspapers than records of lawyers and their clients, legislative and committee debates and activities, and corporate records. The focus may also result from the tradition in history of studying great men and politics which, when supplanted, was supplanted by social history far more than the study of economic and legal institutions.

[17] A P Chandler, *The Visible Hand: The Managerial Revolution in American Business* (Cambridge, Massachusetts, Harvard University Press, 1977), at 4–5.

[18] *Ibid.*, at 5.

[19] I am unaware of any scholar in law and economics who imports an understanding of politics and ideology to the historical study of the market with the sophistication of a scholar such as Joyce Appleby, for example.

analysts who assume that it looks the same all the time. Different ends about which individuals may rationally be selfish can vary, and have, over time. Put differently, different ends have different valuations placed on them at different times, and this phenomenon is as likely to be true for individuals as for collectivities.

Secondly, and not completely separate from the first point, a single-minded focus on rational selfishness needlessly narrows the focus of historical inquiry, even when addressing economic phenomena, including the business corporation. Here I do not mean simply that some motivations and mindsets are not susceptible easily to monetisation or quantification, though I believe that to be true. Individuals, even individuals who own or manage corporations, may be or may have been motivated in their actions by incentives unrelated to rational selfishness. More importantly, those in a position to act upon corporations, including members of legislatures and courts, may have been so motivated.[20] That is, not every legislator or putative regulator should be assumed to have been a closeted rent-seeker. Hence, even if all corporators have always resembled in every meaningful way the stereotypical economic man of neo-classical economics, they have had to contend with others bearing little resemblance to such a creature. Thus, any story about the evolution of the business corporation in law, while enriched by the focus on corporators, tells an incomplete story if it assumes that political and legal actors were either essentially passive or merely obstructionist in manifesting their own rational selfishness.

What does all this abstract discussion about thought about the business corporation actually have to do with understanding the history of the corporation? A great deal, actually, as I hope to suggest. The most developed historical scholarship of legal scholars who have adapted economic tools to the study of corporate history deals with the role of the state in corporation and corporate law formation. That scholarship seems, therefore, a fruitful place to begin in asking what the insights and drawbacks of the approach have been.

The traditional story of the rise of the business corporation has emphasised the powers of the state in the creation of corporations.[21] The first important monographical work on American business corporations was written by Joseph Davis, an economic historian at Harvard, and published in 1917.[22] His *Essays in the Earlier History of American Corporations* dealt with the creation of corporations in this country from the colonial through the very early national period. His scholarship emphasised several aspects of early American corporations that have been repeated, rediscovered and emphasised by most historians ever since. He noted that American corporations were utilities or performed public service

---

[20] The most recent and quite excellent contribution here is W J Novak, *The People's Welfare: Law & Regulation in Nineteenth-Century America* (Chapel Hill, University Of North Carolina Press, 1996), at 83–133.

[21] This emphasis should not be mistaken for the belief that the state acted in all, or even in most, cases to create an entity *without* a co-ordinate or pre-existing body of corporators who sought the assistance and approval of the state.

[22] See Davis, *supra* n.4.

functions analogous to those of utilities.[23] That is, early American corporations ran roadways, canals and other infrastructure projects; they were banks and insurance companies; and, very rarely, they engaged in manufacture and commerce. He also noted that these corporations obtained charters granted by the states. Many of these corporate charters also contained special favours from the state, usually monopoly or limited monopoly rights, and subsidies that usually took the forms of grants of land, power to obtain land cheaply or direct capital infusions by the state.[24] Along with these advantages came some, though not necessarily all, of the modern attributes of corporateness—such as legal identity, internal structure governed by fiat, not contract, and limited liability.[25] And, since both popular and scholarly wisdom was that corporate property was inherently less efficiently managed than personal property because no man would attend to corporate property with the diligence paid to personal property,[26] these special powers and subsidies were thought necessary to entice corporators into risking their capital and time in ventures that the state found useful.[27] Obviously the state and its interests—especially its developmental interests—were at the centre of the story that Davis and subsequent scholars told. And, if one judges by language of prominent case law in the period, all of these assumptions are borne out. The Supreme Court in *Dartmouth College*,[28] for example, while acknowledging the interests of the founders and members of Dartmouth College, placed special emphasis on protecting the rights accorded to the corporation from the state so that the corporation might best fulfill the purposes for which it was chartered.[29] That case explicitly emphasises how difficult it can be to get individuals to organise themselves for important activities without the enticements offered by the state.[30] It is significant that virtually all of the cases dealing with corporations that reached the Supreme Court before the middle of the nineteenth century dealt with corporations that had the attributes Davis mentioned: consider only the most prominent—*Bank of United States* v. *Deveaux*,[31] *McCulloch* v. *Maryland*[32] and, of course, *Charles River Bridge* v. *Warren Bridge*.[33]

Those who took up where Davis left off authored a remarkable series of state studies that reinforced the views propounded by Davis, carrying them forward well into the history of the nineteenth century. Consider, for example, Joseph Blandi's work on Maryland, published in 1934,[34] William Miller's article on

---

[23] See Davis, *supra* n.4, at 3–33.

[24] See Hurst, *supra* n.5, at 21and 23.

[25] *Ibid.*, at 19–20, 21–2.

[26] See Mark, *supra* n.7, at 1448.

[27] See Hurst, *supra* n.5, at 10.

[28] *Dartmouth College* v. *Woodward*, 17 US 518 (1819).

[29] *Ibid.*, at 663, 665.

[30] *Ibid.*, at 665.

[31] 9 US 61 (1809).

[32] 17 US 316 (1819).

[33] 36 US 420 (1837).

[34] J Blandi, *Maryland Business Corporations 1783–1852* (Baltimore, The John Hopkins Press, 1934).

Pennsylvania, published in 1941,[35] Joseph Cadman's remarkable work on New Jersey, published in 1949,[36] and, of course, the more expansive works by Louis Hartz on Pennsylvania[37] and the Handlins on Massachusetts.[38] More recent studies, notably Harry Scheiber's *Ohio Canal Era*[39] and especially Ronald Seavoy's study of New York, tellingly subtitled 'Broadening the Concept of Public Service During Industrialization,',[40] do nothing to belie Davis' observations. What they emphasise in taking the story of corporate and corporate law formation into the nineteenth century, however, is an evolution of the corporation's legal form.

The nineteenth century, they all argue, witnesses, most importantly, a huge increase in the number of charters granted.[41] With that increase comes a regularity in form marked by a decline in active legislative consideration of charters and an increase in what amounts to an administratively granted charter—usually by a department within the executive branch of the state government.[42] Regularisation meant declines in privilege—grants of monopolies, never highly regarded, soon became much rarer and played only a peripheral and tiny role in corporation law as the century progressed.[43] Moreover, with the important exception of the railroads, subsidies declined and direct investment by public bodies nearly disappeared, casualties of public disaffection with state investment in enterprises gone sour—notably canals.[44] And, as the corporate form grew common, the efficacy of agent-managed capital, rather than personally managed capital, became apparent.[45] Not that agent management was not still viewed with suspicion—witness the codes embodying restrictions on the issue of dividends (a protection for creditors),[46] and strict conflict of interest rules created by the courts (a protection for passive investors).[47]

The role of the state, however, is still central in the telling of this story. The state provided the legal framework enabling individuals and capital to join

---

[35] W Miller, 'A Note on the History of Business Corporations in Pennsylvania, 1800–1860' (1940–1) 55 *Quarterly Journal of Economics* 150.

[36] J W Cadman, *The Corporation in New Jersey: Business and Politics 1791–1875* (Cambridge, Massachusetts, Harvard University Press, 1949).

[37] L Hartz, *Economic Policy and Democratic Thought* (Cambridge, Massachusetts, Harvard University Press, 1948).

[38] O Handlin and M Flug Handlin, *Commonwealth* (Cambridge, Massachusetts, Harvard University Press, 1947).

[39] H N Scheiber, *Ohio Canal Era: A Case Study of Government and the Economy, 1820–1861* (Athens, Ohio, Ohio University Press, 1968).

[40] R E Seavoy, *The Origins of the American Business Corporation, 1784–1855: Broadening the Concept of Public Service During Industrialization* (Westport, Greenwood Press, 1982).

[41] See G H Evans, *Business Incorporations in the United States 1800–1843* (New York, Bureau of Economic Research, 1948).

[42] See Mark, *supra* n.7, at 1454.

[43] See *ibid.*, at 1453.

[44] See Scheiber, *supra* n.39, at 135, 176–7, 297–8, 358–9; Hartz, *supra* n.37, *passim*.

[45] See Mark, *supra* n.7, at 1472–3 (noting that by the end of the 19th century corporations were identified with their managers and not their owners).

[46] See Hurst, *supra* n.5, at 51.

[47] See H Marsh, 'Are Directors Trustees? Conflict of Interest and Corporate Morality' (1966) 22 *The Business Lawyer* 35.

together[48]; it provided mechanisms to protect the inactive investor who risked capital and the insufficiently informed creditor who treated with the corporation.[49] With limited liability preventing direct access to investors' pockets on default, the law at least attempted to ensure that creditors did not suffer losses due to managerial cupidity by requiring reserves of paid-in capital.[50] Why all this effort to ensure investment and trust in aggregated capital? The state had its aims—in the nineteenth century, as before, the state wanted the economy to develop. Having failed with state enterprise, such as canals, the state nonetheless kept a directional handle on development for much of the nineteenth century, specifying some of the terms to be embodied in charters industry by industry—mining company charters differed from those issued for banks, which in turn differed from those issued for plank roads, which in turn differed from land development companies, and so on.[51] Some industries required greater enticements to bring people together, others required more regulation to prevent exploitation of the public. Real general incorporation law nominally took hold only mid-century and, in reality, played a significant role in corporate organisation only at the century's end.

Note the focus of this traditional story. The state, through the legislature first, and later the administrative bureaucracy, is the law-giver. And, while the move to general incorporation laws has an element I have left out—part of the emphasis in the traditional story is corruption, such as bribery, in the obtaining of corporate charters (which turns out to have been largely mythic)[52]—otherwise the corporators themselves play no part, or at best an extremely peripheral part, in the development of corporate law. Since those concerned with telling the story saw it as an essentially political history—a history of developmental *policy* and the governmental and legal mechanisms designed to carry out that policy,[53] that focus should hardly be surprising. Even Cadman's study, after all, is subtitled 'Business and Politics'.

We might legitimately ask whether the focus changed when the late Willard Hurst brought his interpretive framework to bear on the corporation. The answer is yes—and no. In *Law and the Conditions of Freedom*,[54] his great essay published in 1956, he argued that the state was still the party responsible for economic progress, but usually by letting go of, as opposed to hanging on to, the economic reins.[55] The state was a facilitator of private aims, aims congruent with public developmental aims.[56] The state released land for development,

---

[48] See Mark, *supra* n.7, at 1473.
[49] See Hurst, *supra* n.5, at 53 (limited liability was itself the protection for the inactive investor).
[50] *Ibid.*
[51] See, e.g., Cadman, *supra* n.36, *passim*.
[52] See Hurst, *supra* n.5, at 136–9.
[53] One can speculate about the reasons for the lack of focus: see *supra* n.15.
[54] J W Hurst, *Law and the Conditions of Freedom in the Nineteenth-Century United States* (Madison, University of Wisconsin Press, 1956).
[55] *Ibid.*, at 3–32.
[56] *Ibid.*, at 33–70.

provided mechanisms to secure property rights and otherwise organised society as the population rolled west, underwrote the development of educational institutions that provided a cadre of practically minded individuals to manage development, and the like.[57] And, when some 15 years later, Hurst produced his seminal *The Legitimacy of the Business Corporation in the Law of the United States*, he simply narrowed the discussion in *Law and the Conditions of Freedom* to the corporate entity. The title itself is revealing. Hurst was concerned with the legitimacy of the institution of aggregated capital[58]—to read a presentist concern into his work is almost overwhelmingly tempting, given the scrutiny under which American institutions found themselves in the late 1960s (the work was originally a set of lectures delivered in 1969), until one realises how consonant it is with the rest of his work.

Throughout the brief book, Hurst sets out the changing balance between corporations as entities facilitative of the desires of businessmen and corporations as expressions of the developmental policy of individual states. In short, corporate law was the imprimatur the state put on organised capital. In Hurst's story, as in the traditional story, the state grew ever more facilitative as the century progressed. Nonetheless, despite the willingness to leave economic development in private hands, in his words, despite having granted businessmen 'a free hand in adapting the corporate instrument to their will' we 'at the same time . . . showed disquiet at the growth of the practical power and impact of big corporations'.[59] With that disquiet came the regulatory state. The role of the state thus remained central, if more implicit, in the Hurstian story, even in the twentieth century.

Against this near century-long historiographical tradition of state-centred study of the corporation has been deployed a powerful revisionist argument, or, at least, what appears to be a powerful revisionist argument. While several scholars, including Henry Butler,[60] have made such contributions, Gary M Anderson and Robert D Tollison[61] are the clearest and most emphatic proponents of the revisionist neo-classical view. It is on their work I will focus. In 1983 they published an article now regarded as most compelling by neo-classical scholars. It is provocatively entitled 'The Myth of the Corporation as a Creation of the State'. In their brief article they sum up all prior scholarship in a paragraph, concluding: '[i]n short, the evolution of the modern corporate form is believed to have been crucially dependent on legislation favoring this type of business organization. Therefore, the corporation was a creature born of government intervention.'[62] Two pages later, however, they claim, 'the corporation

---

[57] *Ibid*.

[58] See Hurst, *supra* n.5, *passim*.

[59] See *ibid*., at 13.

[60] H A Butler, 'Nineteenth-Century Jurisdictional Competition in the Granting of Corporate Privileges' (1985) 14 *Journal of Legal Studies* 129.

[61] G M Anderson and R D Tollison, 'The Myth of the Corporation as a Creation of the State' (1983) 3 *International Review of Law and Economics* 107.

[62] *Ibid*., at 107.

developed in its modern outlines in a legal environment which was at worst hostile and at best uncertain'.[63] A scant seven pages later they conclude, '[o]ur point is that this evolutionary process was not dependent in any important way on government'.[64] So much for a century of scholarship.

Before assessing their historical claim, however, we would do well to note the claim's normative counterpart, for it might provide some insights into the aggressiveness with which the putative revisionism is put forward. About four years before Anderson and Tollison published their article, Robert Hessen published a short book entitled *In Defense of the Corporation* which contained a ten-page chapter that, while not explicitly historical, anticipated much of Anderson's and Tollison's article.[65] Unlike Anderson and Tollison, however, Hessen concluded the chapter with an explicitly normative conclusion:

> [T]he entity concept serves no valid purpose. Like the idea that corporations are creatures of the state, it is a vestige of medieval mentality and should be discarded. The proper alternative is the inherence theory of corporations — the idea that men have a natural right to form a corporation by contract for their own benefit, welfare and mutual self-interest. *It is the only theory of corporations that is faithful to the facts* and philosophically consistent with the moral and legal principles of a free society.[66]

Anderson and Tollison cite Hessen.[67] Their aim was to supply the historical facts to which their theory of the corporation could be faithful. How good are those facts? Are these economists good historians? Not really, though, as it turns out, that does not matter very much. Historians would do well nonetheless to pay attention to their arguments.

Anderson and Tollison argue that firms, in the Coasian sense of firms, that is, organisations of individual and capital in which internal organisational decisions are made by fiat rather than contract, would have arisen in the United States whether or not the states had created corporate codes.[68] They go a step further and suggest that limited liability conferred by statute is irrelevant to the history of corporation formation.[69] In support of the first proposition, they turn to the history of England and Scotland, noting that in both jurisdictions the mainstay of firm activity was not the chartered corporation, but the unincorporated joint stock company.[70] From this experience they implicitly suggest that the same regime could have easily taken hold in America in the nineteenth century.[71] As for limited liability, they note, first, it was an implicit feature of the

---

[63] G M Anderson and R D Tollison, 'The Myth of the Corporation as a Creation of the State' (1983) 3 *International Review of Law and Economics* 107 at 109.

[64] *Ibid.*, at 116.

[65] R Hessen, *In Defense of the Corporation* (Stanford, Hoover Institute Press, Stanford University, 1979), at 14–22.

[66] *Ibid.*, at 22.

[67] See Anderson and Tollison, *supra* n.61, at 116–20 and nn.2, 9, 52.

[68] *Ibid.*, at 107 (by inference), 110 (by example), 116 (explicitly).

[69] *Ibid.*, at 113–5.

[70] *Ibid.*, at 109–11.

[71] See *supra* n.68.

joint stock company, accomplished at common law before the Bubble Act and after by contract, either included in articles of association or by equivalent terms in contracts with creditors.[72] As for 'liability for torts, which inspires so much contemporary controversy', they argue that such liability was 'unheard of in the eighteenth century in relation to the operation of firms'.[73] Secondly, they note that it 'is analytically misleading' to assume that limited liability 'lowered the cost of capital to early firms' by providing safety in ownership to investors.[74] The rationale is purely neoclassical and worth quoting:

> Credit markets are a Coasian world of face-to-face transactions. Real interest rates negotiated by lenders and borrowers in this setting accurately reflect the underlying risk-return relationship posed by the firm. Firms cannot hide behind the veil of limited liability. If they choose limited liability and thereby offer less collateral to the lender, the borrowing rate will rise. It only takes a simple hypothesis about the efficiency of the capital market to see that limited liability would not have altered the real cost of capital to early joint-stock firms, incorporated or otherwise. . . . Limited liability is a form of investor asset insurance which, due to transaction costs, is usually more efficient for the firm to provide than for individual investors to provide themselves. The market provided such insurance efficiently long before government made it generally available. In those cases where firms refrained from adopting limited liability provisions contractually, individual shareholders perceived that the cost of this insurance exceeded its benefits.[75]

Since the advantages of incorporation were available without the effort (and they were not such great advantages to begin with) and since the 'government sought to maximize its revenue from the sale of corporate rights'[76] associated with monopoly grants, no rational corporator would seek incorporation until it was so cheap as to obviate the need for the contractual terms desired, as eventually happened by Parliamentary enactment in 1844.[77]

Now this is a powerful critique, at least at first glance. First, however, the historian's criticisms. Anderson and Tollison did not write a history that historians would recognise as having broken any new evidentiary ground. Every source they relied on was a secondary source, and they relied on very few of them. Even if one counts law review articles as secondary works of history, they cite no more than a dozen secondary works, the majority of which they cite but once. Curiously, however, even though they seek to challenge 'the schema commonly advanced by economic and legal historians regarding the evolution of the corporate form of business organization'[78] they cite none of the works listed

---

[72] See Anderson and Tollison, *supra* n.61, at 114.
[73] *Ibid.*, at 115.
[74] *Ibid.*, at 114.
[75] *Ibid.*, at 114–5.
[76] *Ibid.*, at 116.
[77] *Ibid.*
[78] *Ibid.*, at 107.

among the traditional histories I have mentioned. Nonetheless, I take those traditional histories to be among their targets. Even more curiously, since 'the schema commonly advanced' is an interpretation advanced about the history of American corporations—not English or Scottish companies—secondary histories of England and Scotland dominate. No more than a couple of their sources deal with America. On the other hand, despite their general claim, as I have suggested, they are really reinterpreting the English and Scottish experience and making a counterfactual suggestion about America, so the absence of sources dealing with this country can be explained.

What is harder to explain, however, is their failure to deal with the actual stories told by those secondary sources, all of which are thoroughly traditional. Anderson and Tollison are remarkably selective in the data and the examples they mine. Since the authors of the secondary works have read the original sources—the Acts of Parliament, the company records, the papers of the principals, and the like—and since they have more than a passing familiarity with English and Scottish legal and political culture (or at least I would be unwilling to second guess someone like Holdsworth on such matters, for example, and he is one of their sources) we might well want to pause and think long and hard before accepting such revisionism.

Nonetheless, as I have noted, they may be mediocre historians and may still be right. While it would have been helpful if they had engaged the primary sources—the legislative record, the petitions for incorporations, the archives of businesses, and so on—that may be neither possible nor necessary. Hurst, after all, knew of the existence of unincorporated businesses on both sides of the Atlantic, but in an uncharacteristically elliptical claim, suggested that there might not be enough evidence to explore their history.[79]

Even so, it seems to me that Anderson and Tollison may simply replicate an interpretive error committed by the traditional, state-centred, histories. That is, just as in Hurst's assertion that the states gave businessmen a 'free hand in adopting the corporate instrument to their will'[80] by the twentieth century, without ever asking what that will—or, more likely, multiplicity of wills—might have been, Anderson and Tollison, while asserting the primacy of an entrepreneur driven market in shaping the corporate form,[81] never suggest what precisely the entrepreneurs wanted and the market gave. That is an especially odd omission in their case, given their underlying claim that the state's creative role is 'mythic'. Thus, even if they are right and the state's role was passive or negative, we ought to be treated to some suggestion of the creative role of the corporators and not be left simply to assume, or to guess.

Implicit in their approach, however, is an assumption—precisely the reversal of traditional presumptions, as I suggested at the outset. The corporators have

---

[79] See Hurst, *supra* n.5, at 14 ('We lack evidence to compare the use of the corporation to its nearest informal analogue, the joint stock company').

[80] *Ibid.*, at 13.

[81] See Anderson and Tollison, *supra* n.61, at 116.

gone from individuals who had to be enticed into committing capital and energy into productive developmental projects and whose atavistic urges had then to be carefully policed, to creative economic heroes, at least implicitly. The vision of the state, too, has changed, from the vessel for the commonwealth to rent-seeking entity, hampering the development of the economically creative.

Surely both pictures are wrong. Hurst noted more than a quarter of a century ago that by the beginning of the nineteenth century, businessmen were, in fact, the motive force behind the creation of corporations.[82] And he suggested quite explicitly that the role of limited liability had been overstated.[83] But, he claimed, the state did facilitate entrepreneurial endeavour.[84] And, unlike Anderson and Tollison, he was sensitive to changing economic and political dynamics over time.

What is surely true is that both corporators and the state—or, more properly, in this country at least, the states—had multiple desires, desires informed by different levels of knowledge, different revenue needed and different understandings about how to meet those needs. And, just as surely, the bureaucracies of state government had their own imperatives. Nor were entrepreneurs and investors models of perfect knowledge and clear thinking. They, too, existed in a great fog of mixed motives and imperfect knowledge.

The states existed within a constrained ideology masked by partisan politics and bureaucratic imperatives. Thus, the legislative motives for corporate chartering are likely to have been far more complex than we have imagined. First, a revolutionary perspective is likely to have led to a complex understanding about the role of corporations, even business corporations, in the political economy, as Pauline Maier recently suggested.[85] Secondly, as revolutionary experience led to multiple charterings, patterns developed. In a federal system, marked by mercantile and nationalist economic ambitions on the one hand, and business localism and political parochialism on the other, those patterns manifested themselves in state chartering patterns and litigation in federal courts setting the boundaries of state power, as I have recently noted.[86] Nationalists wanted an integrated economy; mercantilists wanted an economy in service to the state; the states wanted to localise the wealth created and to control its development. Thus, if one looks at rates of incorporation, they differ markedly by state and region—but in states where incorporation rates were comparatively low, contra

---

[82] See Hurst, *supra* n.5, at 11 ('It was businessmen who developed the goals, organization, and procedures of corporations') and 14.

[83] *Ibid.* at 26 ('Tradition assigns as a prime limited-commitment inducement to use of the corporation the limited liability of shareholders to outsiders for debts of the enterprise. The tradition has substance and has gained more substance with time. But the record requires qualification') and 27–8 (elaborating).

[84] *Ibid.*, at 22–6.

[85] P Maier, 'The Revolutionary Origins of the American Corporation' (1993) 50 *William and Mary Quarterly* 51.

[86] G A Mark, 'The Court and the Corporation: Jurisprudence, Localism, and Federalism' [1997] *Supreme Court Review* 403.

Anderson and Tollison, unincorporated enterprise did not pick up the slack,[87] at least to judge by aggregate economic data. Furthermore, as America expanded westward in the nineteenth century, states did not adopt corporate codes as a matter of competing with one another for corporations—rather, in a pattern manifest in state law from constitutional provisions to lowly legislation, they simply copied one another. This suggests that state legislatures had motives other than rent-seeking in mind, for rent-seeking would inspire competition, not emulation. Or, at a minimum, it suggests that legislators felt they could maximise their political utility in areas other than corporate law. Finally, as Hovenkamp has suggested in a different context, economic knowledge was sufficiently undeveloped for much of the nineteenth century such that even if legislatures had wanted to fine-tune their chartering policies to maximise net revenue, they would not have been able to do so, at least by design.[88]

If, however, Anderson and Tollison really point us toward a new focus on corporators in the development of corporate law then, just as we need a richer description of state acts, we need a richer description of the economic rationality of corporate actors. Several examples might be suggestive. Anderson and Tollison suggest that the unincorporated associations jumped at the chance to formalise their existence after the mid-century passage of the Companies Act.[89] Why? They claim, '[t]he legislative availability of cheap and simple incorporation was not the stimulus to the expansion of the corporate form, but merely a response to previous developments. In effect, corporate chartering was deregulated because it was no longer feasible to regulate it.'[90] But, their source, Hunt, claimed that the Companies Act was designed 'to afford protection to the public'.[91] Given the traditional view, no surprise there, except, of course, that it does not support Anderson's and Tollison's claim. If one peruses Evans, another of their sources, something surprising pops up. In his study of English corporate finance it appears that women were significant shareholders of *incorporated* entities before the Companies Act.[92] One can speculate that access to this source of capital required the superintendence of the state—given the sensibilities of the time—and thus regulation via incorporation and facilitation of a corporate aim (access to capital) were congruent, not conflicting. But, even speculation depends on a clear understanding that economic rationality is itself culturally

---

[87] Hurst, *supra* n.5, at 14 ('[T]here is no solid evidence that . . . unincorporated [joint stock companies] set the norm for associated enterprise or that corporate charters merely copied what private contract had thus already accomplished. Given a simple economy, the inference is rather that . . . corporate charters represented the main type of the most ambitious and sophisticated business associations of the time. This inference fits the later record, which shows no broad use of the unincorporated joint-stock company') (citation omitted).

[88] See H Hovenkamp, *Enterprise and American Law 1836–1937* (Cambridge, Massachusetts, Harvard University Press, 1991), at 187–91.

[89] See Anderson and Tollison, *supra* n.61, at 116.

[90] *Ibid.*

[91] *Ibid.*, at n.50, citing B C Hunt, 'The Joint-Stock Company in England, 1830–1844' (1935) 43 *Journal of Political Economy* 331.

[92] G H Evans, *British Corporation Finance, 1775–1850* (Baltimore, John Hopkins Press, 1936).

situated. Recent work by Nelson on the twentieth-century history of fiduciary duty in New York suggests a judiciary highly attuned to the politics of economic development, which again suggests that, even if we adopt a rent-seeking model for all political actors, we must understand that different groups of individuals, differently situated, maximise their utilities in ways not necessarily in keeping with a pure profit maximisation model.[93] Not everything monetises, in other words, or at least not easily.

The claims of those who would debunk the traditional story may also be subject to criticism on theoretical grounds, as well as historical grounds. First, it is not clear that the experience of England and Scotland is directly transferable to other countries, even the United States. Even if we put aside unique governmental structures, such as federalism and judicial review in the United States, and even if we ignore cultural considerations such as America's relatively more informal class structure, the political role of industry in America has been different from that in England or Scotland. Because it is unclear whether governance structures in a modern integrated world economy are freely transferable, the inference should be that experience of corporators in England and Scotland in the nineteenth century and earlier is even less likely to be replicable.

Secondly, the historical application of the theories and experience of market efficiency is itself problematic. For example, in their discussion of limited liability Anderson and Tollison argue—and they use the present tense, not the historical past tense—that credit markets are 'face-to-face transactions'.[94] As for modern capital markets, they surely cannot mean that literally. Even if we understand them to mean that financial intermediaries deal 'face to face' with commercial borrowers the 'negotiation' between 'lenders and borrowers' depends not on being 'face to face' but on a host of informational inputs antecedent to and concurrent with those negotiations. Their 'simple hypothesis about the efficiency of the capital markets'[96] must be that the 'real interest rates negotiated' and ancillary protection for lenders, such as collateral, reflect such informational input and the parties' ability to evaluate such inputs. If we remember that the earliest of credit agencies, such as Dun and Bradstreet, had only begun to get going in the nineteenth century, and that much of their reporting amounted to gossip, we have some inkling of the quality of informational inputs available. Moreover, if we also remember that the capacity systematically to evaluate 'the underlying risk-return relationship'[97] depended on the lender's ability to understand risk, the idea that each lender could effectively negotiate rates and protection effectively is even more problematic. As Peter Bernstein has shown in his most recent work, the capacity to understand and

---

[93] See W E Nelson, 'The Integrity of the Judiciary in Twentieth-Century New York' (1999) 51 *Rutgers Law Review* 1.
[94] Anderson and Tollison, *supra* n.61, at 114.
[95] *Ibid.*
[96] *Ibid.*
[97] *Ibid.*

evaluate risk has its own history. As he suggests, '[e]ven well into the Great Depression, the notion persisted that economic fluctuations were accidents of some kind rather than events inherent in an economic system driven by risk-taking'.[98] Under these conditions any universal claim about whether parties themselves or a legal default rule is the more efficient is open to question and the variegated rules embodied in statutes, the common law, and contracts themselves make much more sense. In an era when lenders had difficulty measuring risk across a broad array of borrowers a default rule that limited investor risk to a stated multiple of investment, for example, limited investor risk and provided lenders with a higher degree of protection while reducing the high transaction costs of evaluating risk borrower by borrower in a world of limited information and incomplete ability to evaluate the information. The other default rules of state charters may well have provided similar advantages. We do simply not know without looking, and we should avoid making assumptions that stop us from looking.

The study of the corporation, including historical study, gains little by narrowing rather than expanding the understanding of the interactions of individual corporators and the state and its many conflicting constituencies. The rhetorical tradition of legal history has emphasised the role of the state, but the corporators were always in the picture. No one ever seriously claimed that the impetus for the vast majority of corporate charters granted came from the state. In legal history our understanding of the role of corporators may have been underdeveloped, but it was hardly non-existent. Moreover, many stories of corporate entrepreneurs have been told in the literature of business history and are waiting to be discovered by legal historians and integrated with legal history. The debates in business history belie any monocausal understanding of entrepreneurial and managerial action.[99] To the contrary, entrepreneurs and managers exhibited the broad range of human motivation. State legislators and judges exhibited a similarly broad range of aspirations and fears, self-interest and altruism. They were not all rent-seekers all the time.

The economic perspective has, I hope, made us at long last focus as closely on the corporators as on the state. But it should not blind us into a constricted understanding of either the state's role *or* the corporators' role in the development of corporate law. Rather, to borrow the language of economics, that development is best characterised as a dynamic equilibrium in which the interests of the state and the corporators were constantly recalculated and rebalanced and one in which, given the way things have turned out thus far, unincorporated status is—or was—at most a second-best world.

---

[98] P L Bernstein, *Against the Gods: The Remarkable Story of Risk* (New York, John Wiley & Sons, 1996), at 193.

[99] See R R John, 'Elaborations, Revisions, Dissents: Alfred D. Chandler, Jr.'s, *The Visible Hand* After Twenty Years' (1997) 71 *Business History Review* 151, 160 n.27 (wryly noting Chandler's comment in correspondence: 'Don't use "the" when you can use "a",' in discussing reasons for the rise of managerial capitalism).

2

Public Beginnings, Private Ends— Should Corporate Law Privilege the Interests of Shareholders?

JENNIFER HILL[1]

INTRODUCTION

In its relatively brief floriat,[2] the corporation has demonstrated an impressive capacity to reinvent itself. Successfully discarding its restrictive nineteenth-century 'public' beginnings, the corporation and its shareholders nonetheless managed to retain the benefits of limited liability.[3] In recent times, the law and economics nexus of contracts model of the corporation has bolstered, and attempted to legitimate, a private conception of the corporation, in which shareholder interests are preeminent. This model of the corporation also underlies Australia's current Corporate Law Economic Reform Program.

This chapter questions whether preeminence of shareholder interests inherent in a nexus of contracts model of the corporation is justified in the late twentieth century. First, the chapter considers the extent to which such a model accurately reflects commercial reality, through an examination of some contemporary trends in corporate finance and in labour law. Secondly, the chapter discusses the normative issue of whether the privileging of shareholder interests is desirable from a policy perspective. This section of the chapter focuses on current political models of the corporation, which advocate shared governance by

[1] I am grateful to Theresa Kelly and Robert Apps for their research assistance and to those who discussed some of the issues in this chapter with me, including Joanna Bird, Andrew Lumsden, Christos Mantziaris, Ron McCallum, Robert Thompson and Richard Vann, as well as the students in my Modern Corporate Governance class. An earlier version of this chapter was published in (1998) 9 *Australian Journal of Corporate Law* 21. Financial assistance for this research was provided by the Australian Research Council.

[2] Adam Smith, e.g., viewed the corporation as having little future: see R L Heilbroner, *The Worldly Philosophers* 6th edn. (New York, Simon & Schuster, 1986) 71.

[3] In recent times, however, limited liability has to some extent been under attack. See generally, J Hill, 'Corporate Groups, Creditor Protection and Cross Guarantees: Australian Perspectives' (1995) 24 *Canadian Business Law Journal* 321, at 325–30.

institutional investors and management, and the trend towards 'collectivisation' of the interests of shareholders and managers.

The chapter argues that, in spite of widespread acceptance of corporate models which assume shareholder pre-eminence,[4] there are a number of problems and dangers, both from a commercial and policy perspective, in privileging shareholder interests in this way. The chapter concludes that at a theoretical level, more regard needs to be paid to the corporation as an autonomous enterprise, combining and balancing a wider range of interests than those merely of its shareholders. This, however, is not to deny shareholders an important position in corporate governance. It is in the interests of all corporate stakeholders to prevent managerial self-interest and shareholders, particularly strong institutional investors, may be in a unique position to constrain such conduct for the benefit of the enterprise as a whole.

PUBLIC BEGINNINGS, PRIVATE ENDS

The corporation had very 'public' origins indeed. Occupying an ambiguous position within liberalism's state/individual dichotomy,[5] the early phases of the corporation were characterised by quasi-public functions and by the state's involvement in corporate goals through the granting of charters.[6] This was followed by a period of struggle, in which the corporation fought to transfigure itself into an autonomous entity, possessing private rights and freedom of association.[7] This transition effectively created a schism for much of this century between corporations, which were classified as 'private', and government institutions, which were treated as public bodies subject to administrative law principles.[8] This contributed to viewing corporations in isolation, rather than within a broader matrix of associations,[9] and disguised the plurality and flexibility of organisations and their structures.[10]

[4] See generally D G Smith, 'The Shareholder Primacy Norm' (1998) 23 *Journal of Corporation Law* 277.

[5] G E Frug, 'The City as a Legal Concept' (1980) 93 *Harvard Law Review* 1057; G A Mark, 'The Personification of the Business Corporation in American Law' (1987) 54 *University of Chicago Law Review* 1441, at 1445; P Selznick, *Law, Society and Industrial Justice* (New York, Russell Sage Foundation, 1969), at 37–8.

[6] G A Mark, 'Some Observations on Writing the Legal History of the Corporation in the Age of Theory' in L E Mitchell (ed.), *Progressive Corporate Law* (Boulder, Westview Press, 1995), at 67 and 68–9; D Millon, 'Theories of the Corporation' [1990] *Duke Law Journal* 201, at 206*ff*; D P Sullivan and D E Conlon, 'Crisis and Transition in Corporate Governance Paradigms: The Role of the Chancery Court of Delaware' (1997) 31 *Law and Society Review* 713, at 727; Smith, *supra* n.4, at 291.

[7] See Mark, *supra* n.5; G Teubner, 'Enterprise Corporatism: New Industrial Policy and the "Essence" of the Legal Person' (1988) 36 *American Journal of Comparative Law* 130; M J Horowitz, '*Santa Clara* Revisited: The Development of Corporate Theory' (1985) 88 *West Virginia Law Review* 173; Sullivan and Conlon, *supra* n.6, at 728–9.

[8] See Frug, *supra* n.5.

[9] See, e.g., H Hansmann, *The Ownership of Enterprise* (Cambridge, Mass., The Belknap Press of Harvard University Press, 1996), at 1–8; E Orts, 'The Future of Enterprise Organization' (1998) 96 *Michigan Law Review* 1947; R B Stewart, 'Organizational Jurisprudence' (Book Review)

At the end of the twentieth century, the wheel has to some extent come full circle, with the trend towards privatisation of government business enterprises (GBEs) creating a new, overt convergence between public institutions and corporations.[11] Tension created by such convergence is reflected in the recent debate on corporate philanthropy, fostered by the attempts of government to shift responsibility for an increasing range of social services and welfare into the private sector,[12] and the efforts of some activist shareholders to resist the trend.[13] A number of scholars have argued that securing private rights for large corporations is today less important than ensuring responsibility and accountability for their acts,[14] which may have significant social consequences.[15] One possible effect of this convergence might have been to infuse corporate law with some of the administrative principles from beyond the public divide.[16] The reality however seems to be quite the reverse—corporate law has trumped administrative law in the dissolution of traditional boundaries.[17] The strength of the 'private' conception of the corporation is, if anything, more assured today under a contractual model of the corporation than in the past.[18] This is paradoxical, since the justifications for an exclusively private conception of the corporation have been greatly eroded in the modern public corporation.[19]

(1987) 101 *Harvard Law Review* 371; Z Chafee, 'The Internal Affairs of Associations Not for Profit' (1930) 43 *Harvard Law Review* 993; Selznick, *supra* n.5, ch.2.

[10] See P F Drucker, 'Management's New Paradigms', *Forbes Global Business and Finance*, 5 Oct. 1998, at 52.

[11] See M Allars, 'Private Law But Public Power: Removing Administrative Law Review from Government Business Enterprises' (1995) 6 *Public Law Review* 44; M Allars, 'Administrative Law, Government Contracts and the Level Playing Field' (1989) 12 *University of New South Wales Law Journal* 114; C Sampford, 'Law, Institutions and the Public/Private Divide' (1991) 20 *Federal Law Review* 185. From the corporate side of the divide, see S Bottomley, 'From Contractualism to Constitutionalism: A Framework for Corporate Governance' (1997) 19 *Sydney Law Review* 277.

[12] J E Fisch, 'Questioning Philanthropy from a Corporate Governance Perspective' (1997) 41 *New York Law School Law Review* 1091, at 1092.

[13] See comments by C Elson, 'Transcript of Proceedings—Corporate Charity: Societal Boon or Shareholder Bust?' (1998) 28 *Stetson Law Review* 52, at 53.

[14] P I Blumberg, 'The Corporate Entity in an Era of Multinational Corporations' (1990) 15 *Delaware Journal of Corporate Law* 283, at 285; C D Stone, 'The Place of Enterprise Liability in the Control of Corporate Conduct' (1980) 90 *Yale Law Journal* 1.

[15] See J E Parkinson, *Corporate Power and Responsibility: Issues in the Theory of Company Law* (Oxford, Clarendon, 1993), ch 1; P I Blumberg, 'The Politicalization of the Corporation' (1971) 26 *The Business Lawyer* 1551; R M Buxbaum, 'Corporate Legitimacy, Economic Theory, and Legal Doctrine' (1984) 45 *Ohio State Law Journal* 515, at 517–8.

[16] See, e.g., Allars, 'Private Law But Public Power: Removing Administrative Law Review From Government Business Enterprises', *supra* n.11 and Bottomley, *supra* n.11, recommending such an approach.

[17] See, e.g., *Report of the Independent Committee of Inquiry on National Competition Policy* (Hilmer Report) (1993), at 296. For tensions in the convergence, however, see C Mantziaris, 'When the Minister Leans on the Board: The Forced Resignation of the Managing Director of the Overseas Telecommunications Commission' (1997) 19 *Asian Journal of Public Administration* 157.

[18] See W W Bratton, 'The "Nexus of Contracts" Corporation: A Critical Appraisal' (1989) 74 *Cornell Law Review* 407, at 439–40; Millon, *supra* n.6, 229–31.

[19] See Frug, *supra* n.5, at 1129*ff*. See also A Wolfe, 'The Modern Corporation: Private Agent or Public Actor?' (1993) 50 *Washington and Lee Law Review* 1673, at 1676, claiming that the nexus of

A corollary of the private conception of the corporation has been the privileging of shareholder interests within the corporation. Indeed, in the majority of diverse theories of the corporation which have prevailed since the nineteenth century, pre-eminence of shareholder interests is assumed.[20] It has also generally been assumed in corporate doctrine, in terms of the meaning of the duty of directors to act *bona fide* for the benefit of 'the company as a whole'.[21] Nonetheless, while treating shareholder *interests* as paramount, most corporate theories also assume that shareholder *participation* in corporate governance is either impossible,[22] unnecessary,[23] or positively undesirable.[24] Yet even this assumption has been challenged with the rise of institutional investors, and the influence of recent shareholder-centred political models of the corporation, which advocate protection of shareholder interests through increased shareholder participation in governance.[25]

In contrast to shareholder-centred theories of the corporation, a competing model viewed the corporation as essentially a system of private government.[26] In recent years, communitarian scholarship has arisen in the USA within this general tradition, as a strong counterpoint to the economic nexus of contracts model of the corporation and its assumption of shareholder primacy. Grounded in sociology and notions of the corporation as community, communitarianism focuses on vulnerability of non-shareholder constituencies and challenges the individualistic premises of the economic theory of the corporation.[27] A central question in communitarianism is 'who says that shareholder primacy should now and in all settings be the central norm in corporate law, and by what

contracts model of the corporation does not reflect reality, but rather constitutes a normative prescription.

[20] See generally J Hill, 'Changes in the Role of the Shareholder' in R. Grantham and C. Rickett (eds.), *Corporate Personality in the 20th Century* (Oxford, Hart Publishing, 1998), 175 (forthcoming, *American Journal of Comparative Law*).

[21] See generally, D Heydon, 'Directors' Duties and the Company's Interests' in P D Finn (ed.), *Equity and Commercial Relationships* (Sydney, Law Book Company, 1987), 120; I A Renard, 'Commentary', *ibid.*, 137.

[22] See A A Berle, 'Corporate Powers as Powers in Trust' (1931) 44 *Harvard Law Review* 1049; J L Weiner, 'The Berle-Dodd Dialogue on the Concept of the Corporation' (1964) 64 *Columbia Law Review* 1458, n.8.

[23] On the basis that the market and contractual constraints will force managers to act in the shareholders' best interests. See generally H N Butler, 'The Contractual Theory of the Corporation' (1989) 11 *George Mason University Law Review* 99.

[24] See F H Easterbrook and D R Fischel, 'Voting in Corporate Law' (1983) 26 *Journal of Law and Economics* 395.

[25] See e.g., J Pound, 'The Rise of the Political Model of Corporate Governance and Corporate Control' (1993) 68 *New York University Law Review* 1003; J Pound, 'The Promise of the Governed Corporation' [1995] *Harvard Business Review* 89.

[26] See, e.g., E Latham, 'The Body Politic of the Corporation' in E S Mason (ed.), *The Corporation in Modern Society* (Cambridge, Mass., Harvard University Press, 1960), 218; Steinmann, 'The Enterprise as a Political System' in K J Hopt and G Teubner (eds.), *Corporate Governance and Directors' Liabilities: Legal, Economic and Sociological Analyses on Corporate Social Responsibility* (1985), 401; Bottomley, *supra* n.11. See generally Hill, *supra* n.20, at 185*ff*.

[27] D Millon, 'Communitarianism in Corporate Law: Foundations and Law Reform Strategies' in Mitchell, *supra* n.6, 1.

authority do they speak?'[28] This issue is by no means a new concern in corporate law,[29] but it is an important one.

Paradoxically, some contemporary scholarship reflecting communitarian concerns itself accepts and relies upon a contractual model of the corporation,[30] in which the corporation can be deconstructed into a set of agreements between stakeholders. In this contractual version of the corporation, however, the deconstruction process ultimately maintains a wider range of interests than those merely of shareholders. The underlying aggregate theory of the corporation in both these contractual approaches contrasts with organisational models of the corporation, which assert that modern corporate law needs to give greater recognition to organisations themselves as legal persons, corporate actors[31] and even, potentially, moral agents.[32]

CORPORATE FINANCE—THE BLURRING OF THE BOUNDARY BETWEEN DEBT AND EQUITY

One of the earliest models of the corporation to assume shareholder primacy was the nineteenth century aggregate or partnership model of the corporation, which viewed shareholders as 'owners' of the corporate enterprise. Under this model, the role of directors was to carry out the will and pursue the interests of shareholders.[33] Corporate doctrine at that time followed suit, assuming that, within standard principles of agency law, shareholders had a formal right to control their agents and the ability to overrule board decisions.[34]

With the notable exception of the Australian High Court decision in *Gambotto* v. *WCP Ltd*,[35] it is generally accepted that any vision of shareholders as corporate owners with full-blown proprietary rights is now obsolete.[36]

---

[28] L Johnson, 'New Approaches to Corporate Law' (1993) 50 *Washington and Lee Law Journal* 1713, 1719.

[29] The polarity today between the nexus of contracts and communitarian models of the corporation is a modern reflection of the Berle/Dodd debate more than 50 years ago. See Berle, *supra* n.22; E M Dodd, 'For Whom Are Corporate Managers Trustees?' (1932) 45 *Harvard Law Review* 1145; A A Berle, 'For Whom Corporate Managers *Are* Trustees: A Note' (1932) 45 *Harvard Law Review* 1365.

[30] See Millon, *supra* n.27, at 16*ff*; Wolfe, *supra* n.19, at 1690–1.

[31] See, e.g., Teubner, *supra* n.7.

[32] See, e.g., Stewart, *supra* n.9; P E Wilson, 'Barring Corporations From the Moral Community—The Concept and the Cost' (1992) 23 *Journal of Social Philosophy* 74; Wolfe, *supra* n.19.

[33] See V Brudney, 'The Independent Director—Heavenly City or Potemkin Village?' (1982) 95 *Harvard Law Review* 597, at 602.

[34] *Isle of Wight Rly Co* v. *Tahourdin* (1883) 25 Ch D 320.

[35] (1995) 69 ALJR 266.

[36] See, e.g., E S Mason, 'Introduction' in Mason, *supra* n.26, 5–6; W S W Leung, 'The Inadequacy of Shareholder Primacy: A Proposed Corporate Regime that Recognizes Non-Shareholder Interests' (1997) 30 *Columbia Journal of Law and Social Problems* 587, at 591–2; M M Blair, *Ownership and Control: Rethinking Corporate Governance for the Twenty-First Century* (Washington, Brookings Institution, 1995), at 223–5. See also comments by M M Blair in 'Transcript of Proceedings—Corporate Charity: Societal Boon or Shareholder Bust?' (1998) 28 *Stetson Law Review* 52, at 66–7.

Certainly, the concept of shareholders as corporate 'owners' is alien to a modern contractual model of the corporation, where shareholders are viewed as merely one of a group of resource holders, *prima facie* on equal footing with other groups such as managers, creditors, employees and customers.[37] Yet this apparent difference is ultimately insignificant, since the economic contractual model's focus on 'profit maximisation'[38] has the effect of resurrecting shareholder interests to pre-eminence (though deflating the participation rights, which were assumed under an ownership model).[39] Both are simply variants of a shareholder-centred aggregate theory of the corporation.[40]

Traditionally, most shareholder-centred theories of the corporation have assumed that shareholder interests are distinct, and inherently different, from the interests of other groups associated with the corporation, such as creditors. Law and economics scholarship, for example, generally assumes both a clear economic demarcation between debt and equity, and policy justifications for their different treatment by law.[41] Shareholder interests are treated as pre-eminent on the basis that shareholders are residual claimants in the enterprise,[42] bear the greatest risk in the enterprise,[43] have the greatest incentives to maximise the firm's value,[44] and are less able to protect their interests by contract than other corporate constituencies.[45]

Contemporary corporate finance, however, presents a rather different picture of debt and equity from that accepted under shareholder-centred aggregate theories of the corporation. First, modern corporate finance erodes the mystique of share capital, by suggesting that, in economic terms, share capital may be relatively unimportant in large public companies, depending upon the commercial climate.[46]

---

[37] Butler, *supra* n.23, at 107; Easterbrook and Fischel, *supra* n.24, at 396.

[38] See, e.g., J R Macey, 'An Economic Analysis of the Various Rationales for Making Shareholders the Exclusive Beneficiaries of Corporate Fiduciary Duties' (1991) 21 *Stetson Law Review* 23.

[39] See generally Bratton, *supra* n.18, at 427ff; L Dallas, 'Two Models of Corporate Governance: Beyond Berle and Means' (1988) 22 *University of Michigan Journal of Law Reform* 19; Millon, *supra* n.6, at 229–31; L E Mitchell, 'Groundwork of the Metaphysics of Corporate Law' (1993) 50 *Washington and Lee Law Journal* 1477, at 1477–8.

[40] W W Bratton, 'The New Economic Theory of the Firm: Critical Perspectives from History' (1989) 41 *Stanford Law Review* 1471, at 1472–3.

[41] See, e.g., H Kanda, 'Debtholders and Equityholders' (1992) 21 *Journal of Legal Studies* 431.

[42] See Kanda, *ibid*, at 445; J R Macey, 'Externalities, Firm-Specific Capital Investments, and the Legal Treatment of Fundamental Corporate Changes' [1989] *Duke Law Journal* 173, at 175.

[43] Easterbrook and Fischel, *supra* n.24, at 416; Butler, *supra* n.23, at 107. For the origins of a view of shareholders as having the 'entrepreneurial mantle' and status of 'adventurer', see W W Bratton, 'Corporate Debt Relationships: Legal Theory in a Time of Restructuring' [1989] *Duke Law Journal* 92, at 103.

[44] *Cf* L Dallas, 'Working Toward a New Paradigm' in Mitchell, *supra* n.6, 35, at 47.

[45] Macey, *supra* n.38, at 25; Kanda, *supra* n.41, at 435; O E Williamson, 'Corporate Governance' (1984) 93 *Yale Law Journal* 1197, at 1210.

[46] Dallas, *supra* n.44; L A Stout, 'The Unimportance of Being Efficient: An Economic Analysis of Stock Market Pricing and Securities Regulation' (1988) 87 *Michigan Law Review* 613, at 644ff, who argues that equity issues provide a 'negligible fraction' of corporate fundraising (at 647).

Empirical research in both the USA[47] and Australia[48] has shown that, in the hierarchy of sources of corporate finance, equity issues have tended to rank as the choice of last resort, with companies preferring internally generated cash, intragroup loans and debt to fund projects. The derogation of share capital within corporate finance has become more evident in Australia in recent times as a result of the increased diversity and depth of debt sources and greater access to international markets.[49]

Secondly, debt and equity providers have tended to be structurally distinct in countries such as Australia[50] and the USA,[51] where legal rules or guidelines either prevented or discouraged banks from taking strong equity positions in companies. This was in contrast to the position adopted by banks in jurisdictions such as Germany and Japan.[52] This structural division between debt and equity providers in Australia is now breaking down. Institutional investors have adopted dual roles as debt and equity holders. There has also been a policy retreat from previous political resistance to banks holding shares.[53] This greater market fluidity in Australia will only accelerate in the wake of the Wallis Committee recommendations.[54]

Thirdly, the concepts of debt and equity have become increasingly ambiguous in modern corporate finance.[55] It has long been recognised that preference shares, while classified as equity, are often functionally equivalent to debt.[56] Nonetheless, the blurring of the boundary between debt and equity, exemplified by preference shares, has been exacerbated by financial innovation and engineering in recent years.[57] The distinction between 'debt' and 'equity' is

---

[47] G Donaldson, *Corporate Debt Capacity* (Boston, Graduate School of Business Administration, Harvard University, 1961), at 69.

[48] D E Allen, 'The Determinants of the Capital Structure of Listed Australian Companies: The Financial Manager's Perspective' (1991) 16 *Australian Journal of Management* 103, at 108–10.

[49] R Bruce (ed.), *Handbook of Australian Corporate Finance* (5th edn., 1997), at 12; Wallis Committee, *Financial System Inquiry Final Report* (1997), 'The Financial System: Towards 2010', Overview, at 6.

[50] See Martin Committee, '*A Pocket Full of Change: Banking Deregulation; The House of Representatives Standing Committee on Finance and Public Administration*' (1991), at 172.

[51] M J Roe, 'A Political Theory of American Corporate Finance' (1991) 91 *Columbia Law Review* 10; B S Black, 'Shareholder Passivity Re-examined' (1990) 89 *Michigan Law Review* 520.

[52] See M J Roe, 'Some Differences in Corporate Governance in Germany, Japan and America' in T Baums, R M Buxbaum and K J Hopt, *Institutional Investors and Corporate Governance* (New York, W. de Gruyter, 1994), at 23; T Baums, 'Corporate Governance in Germany: The Role of the Banks' (1992) 40 *American Journal of Comparative Law* 503.

[53] Reserve Bank of Australia, 'Equity Investments by Banks' (1995) 95 *Reserve Bank of Australia Bulletin* 20; Reserve Bank of Australia, 'Banks' Association with Non-Banks', Prudential Statement G1, Dec. 1995, cited in N L Scheinkestel, 'The Debt-Equity Conflict: Where Does Project Financing Fit?' (1997) 8 *Journal of Banking and Finance Law and Practice* 103, at 119, n.101.

[54] Wallis Committee, *Financial System Inquiry Final Report* (Canberra, Australian Government Publishing Service, 1997).

[55] See A O Emmerich, 'Hybrid Instruments and the Debt-Equity Distinction in Corporate Taxation' (1985) 52 *University of Chicago Law Review* 118.

[56] See generally J Hill, "Preference Shares" in R P Austin and R Vann (eds.), *The Law of Public Company Finance* (Sydney, Law Book Company, 1986), 139.

[57] See generally P F Pope and A G Puxty, 'What is Equity? New Financial Instruments in the Interstices between the Law, Accounting and Economics' (1991) 54 *Modern Law Review* 889, at 903–9; A C Warren, 'Financial Contract Innovation and Income Tax Policy' (1993) 107 *Harvard Law Review* 460.

important historically, legally and commercially in risk assessment through gearing ratios.[58] However, with the rise of more complex funding instruments, the traditional distinction between debt and equity fails to accord with economic reality[59] and looks artificial, arbitrary and increasingly passé.

Fourthly, even the distinctive status of shareholder as residual claimant and ultimate risk bearer under a nexus of contracts model of the corporation[60] is compromised by innovation in financial instruments. Traditional instruments continue to be the building blocks for recent financial engineering. However, processes of disaggregation and recombination have facilitated a mix-and-match approach to their constituent parts to create new forms of financial contract.[61] Specifically, this trend has enabled the marketing of disaggregated equity, in which the control and risk components of shares may be separated.[62] Against this backdrop, it cannot be regarded as axiomatic that the shareholder is residual claimant and risk bearer in the corporation.[63] At an even more fundamental level, it has been claimed that risk itself has been undermined, through advances in computer technology which have allowed corporations to engage more freely in judgment proofing strategies, resulting in 'the death of liability'.[64]

Fifthly, even where no ambiguity exists in financial instruments themselves, background factors may blur or reorder the interests of shareholders and creditors in corporate governance.[65] Where, for example, a company is insolvent or close to insolvency, there is a trend in case law that directors are obliged to consider creditor interests, which will replace shareholder interests as the primary focus of fiduciary duties.[66] In the US decision, *Crédit Lyonnais Bank Nederland NV v. Pathe Communications Corp.*,[67] this trend was presented within the framework of the corporation as an autonomous collective entity, representing a 'community of interests'. According to the judge, '[a]t least where a corpora-

---

[58] Pope and Puxty, *supra* n.57.

[59] This represents a significant challenge to taxation law. See generally Warren, *supra* n.57. A key tenet in Australia's tax reform programme is the concept of 'neutrality', or taxation by reference to economic equivalence: see T Edgar, 'Australia Releases Issues Paper on Taxation of Financial Arrangements' (1997) 14 *Tax Notes International* 327, at 328. *Cf* M Cashmere, "Equity as Debt" (1996) 31(8) *Australian Lawyer* 34, who describes the concept of neutrality as an 'alarming trend'. On particular problems in the context of close corporations, see M A Gibson, 'The Intractable Debt/Equity Problem: A New Structure for Analyzing Shareholder Advances' (1987) 81 *Northwestern University Law Review* 452.

[60] See Macey, *supra* n.38; Dallas, *supra* n.44, at 47.

[61] Warren, *supra* n.57.

[62] *Ibid.*, at 489–91.

[63] Irrespective of these developments in financial engineering, some commentators challenge the characterisation of shareholders as residual risk bearers. See, e.g., Blair, *supra* n.36, at 229, who argues that in fact shareholders bear little residual risk in the modern corporation, due to the existence of limited liability, portfolio diversification and exit rights.

[64] L M LoPucki, 'The Death of Liability' (1996) 106 *Yale Law Journal* 1.

[65] See, e.g., Easterbrook and Fischel, *supra* n.24, at 404.

[66] See, e.g., *Walker v. Wimborne* (1976) 137 CLR 1; *Kinsela v. Russell Kinsela Pty Ltd (in liq.)* (1986) 4 NSWLR 722; *Nicholson v. Permakraft (NZ) Ltd (in liq.)* [1985] 1 NZLR 242; *Sycotex Pty. Ltd v. Baseler* (1994) 122 ALR 531.

[67] 1991 Del Ch LEXIS 215, 108–9.

tion is operating in the vicinity of insolvency, a board of directors is not merely the agent of the residue [*sic*] risk bearers, but owes its duty to the corporate enterprise'. However, the interests of the 'corporate enterprise' will not necessarily coincide with the interests of any particular group of stakeholders.[68]

Finally, the familiar connection under corporate law principles between the concept of 'control' and share ownership[69] has been weakened. A major issue in modern social science has been to determine whether it is shareholders, managers or banks that truly control the large corporation.[70] As was recognised in the Australian decision, *CanWest Global Communications Corporation* v. *ABA*,[71] although the meaning of 'control' can vary with context,[72] in some circumstances 'control' can be established through a combination of debt and equity positions.[73] This approach to control focuses on commercial and economic reality rather than traditional legal tests in, for example, revenue cases, which focus on control of a majority of votes in general meeting.[74]

Where a company's gearing is high, exposing debt-holders to higher risk, negotiated covenants may increase the participation rights of major creditors in corporate operations, enabling them to exercise a high level of supervision and control over strategic decision-making.[75] When this occurs, creditors act far more like 'insiders' or owners of the corporation[76] than under a standard adversarial conception of the debtor–creditor relationship, where creditors are viewed as 'outsiders'.[77] Project financing is a clear example of this commercial scenario.[78] While the stereotypical debtor/creditor relationship is short-term and finite, project financing arrangements can continue for decades. Whereas, like traditional lenders, project debt providers rarely have voting rights, they

---

[68] See, e.g., Allen J in *Crédit Lyonnais Bank Nederland NV* v. *Pathe Communications Corp*. 1991 Del Ch LEXIS 215, 108, who states that in certain circumstances directors recognise that 'the right (both the efficient and the fair) course to follow for the corporation may diverge from the choice that the stockholders (or the creditors, or the employees, or any single group interested in the corporation) would make if given the opportunity to act'. See also L Lin, 'Shift of Fiduciary Duty Upon Corporate Insolvency: Proper Scope of Directors' Duty to Creditors' (1993) 46 *Vanderbilt Law Review* 1485; R K S Rao, D S Sokolow and D White, 'Fiduciary Duty A La Lyonnais: An Economic Perspective on Corporate Governance in a Financially-Distressed Firm' (1996) 22 *Journal of Corporate Law* 53.

[69] See W W Bratton, 'Corporate Debt Relationships: Legal Theory in a Time of Restructuring' [1989] *Duke Law Journal* 92, at 103.

[70] See N Fligstein and P Brantley, 'Bank Control, Owner Control, or Organizational Dynamics: Who Controls the Large Modern Corporation?' (1992) 98 *American Journal of Sociology* 280.

[71] (1997) 147 ALR 539.

[72] *Ibid.*, at 555.

[73] *Ibid.*, at 541 and 562.

[74] *Ibid.*, 555.

[75] See Williamson, *supra* n.45, at 1212; P Cellupica, 'The Insecure Place of Secured Debt in Corporate Finance Theory' (1988) 11 *Harvard Journal of Law and Public Policy* 487, at 491–2.

[76] See J J Hass, 'Insights into Lender Liability: An Argument for Treating Controlling Creditors as Controlling Shareholders' (1987) 135 *University of Pennsylvania Law Review* 1321; Williamson, *supra* n.45, at 1209.

[77] For a discussion of the range of different conceptions of the debtor/creditor relationship in corporate law, see Bratton, *supra* n.69, at 98*ff*.

[78] See Scheinkestel, *supra* n.53.

may have far more influence regarding control of operations.[79] There are, to be sure, legal considerations which may constrain a project debt provider from seeking, via protective covenants, too high a level of control.[80] However, these legal considerations are precisely the same as apply to a majority shareholder in a parent/subsidiary context. With the potential expansion of liability imposed upon a 'shadow' director of a company, with whose directions or instructions the board is accustomed to act,[81] neither a parent company, nor a bank, will wish to exercise this degree of control.

Traditional corporate law remedies with respect to managerial conduct have assumed a clear distinction between debt and equity. While individual shareholders had access to remedies such winding up on the just and equitable ground, the oppression remedy and derivative suits for certain breaches of fiduciary duty, corporate law's self-help policy for creditors tended to restrict them to enforcement of express contractual provisions.[82] Nonetheless, particularly in the case of long-term financing arrangements, it is often thought to be impossible, or at least inefficient, for a creditor to attempt complete protection by covenants.[83] Since the alleged ability of creditors to protect themselves has been used as a major justification for denying them access to the oppression remedy, [84] this may need to be reassessed in the future. Greater doctrinal convergence might come, however, not from shared remedies by creditors and shareholders, but through greater reliance by courts on principles of good faith, including the parties' reasonable expectations, in construing contractual provisions between creditor and corporate borrower.[85]

---

[79] See Scheinkestel, *supra* n.53 at 105–8.

[80] See S C Gilson and M R Vetsuypens, 'Creditor Control in Financially Distressed Firms: Empirical Evidence' (1994) 72 *Washington University Law Quarterly* 1005, at 1014, suggesting that at least part of the reason banks are reluctant to acquire board seats results from the increased risk of legal liability.

[81] Corporations Law s 60(1)(b). On the issue of third party liability for corporate actions generally, see R Carroll, "Shadow Director and Other Third Party Liability for Corporate Activity" in I Ramsay (ed.), *Corporate Governance and the Duties of Company Directors* (Melbourne, University of Melbourne Centre for Corporate Law and Securities Regulation, 1997), 162; P M C Koh, 'Shadow Director, Shadow Director, Who Art Thou?' (1996) 14 *Company and Securities Law Journal* 340.

[82] This is a widely-accepted view of the corporate debt relationship. See generally W W Bratton, 'The Interpretation of Contracts Governing Corporate Debt Relationships' (1984) 5 *Cardozo Law Review* 371.

[83] See generally, M W McDaniel, 'Bondholders and Corporate Governance' (1986) 41 *The Business Lawyer* 413; M W McDaniel, 'Bondholders and Stockholders' [1988] *Journal of Corporate Law* 205; Scheinkestel, *supra* n.53, at 111–12; L E Mitchell, 'The Fairness Rights of Corporate Bondholders' (1990) 65 *New York University Law Review* 1165.

[84] *Cf* D D Prentice, 'The Theory of the Firm: Minority Shareholder Oppression: Sections 459–461 of the Companies Act 1985' (1988) 8 *Oxford Journal of Legal Studies* 55, at 64; J Ziegel, 'Creditors as Corporate Stakeholders: The Quiet Revolution—An Anglo-Canadian Perspective' (1993) 43 *University of Toronto Law Journal* 511, at 530.

[85] See Scheinkestel, *supra* n.53, at 115–16; W W Bratton, 'The Interpretation of Contracts Governing Corporate Debt Relationships' (1984) 5 *Cardozo Law Review* 371. See also *Crédit Lyonnais Bank Nederland NV* v. *Pathe Communications Corp.*, 1991 Del Ch LEXIS 215 and J Beatson and D Friedmann (eds.), *Good Faith and Fault in Contract Law* (1995).

THE CORPORATION AS EMPLOYER—THE BLURRING OF
THE BOUNDARY BETWEEN EMPLOYEES AND SHAREHOLDERS

Just as creditors are treated as 'outsiders' to the corporation under shareholder-centred aggregate models of the corporation,[86] so too are employees.[87] This image is consistent with labour law principles, which continue (in the face of its patent inaccuracy in the modern world) to envisage both employer and employee as natural persons.[88] Each group must rely predominantly on contract to protect its interests. This model renders the corporate status of the employer invisible and irrelevant. Employer and employee are seen as distinct parties with separate, and indeed conflicting,[89] interests, which are accommodated through compromise in the process of adversarial contractual bargaining.[90] This contractual model underpins Australia's new enterprise bargaining regime, which focuses on individual workplace bargains and assumes that the parties themselves can best judge what is in their own interests, thereby promoting greater flexibility and efficiency.[91]

A number of communitarian scholars, adopting a more expansive aggregate model of the corporation, have focused on employee vulnerability.[92] Law and economics scholars, such as Professor Macey, do not deny however that the interests of employees can be seriously harmed by corporate transactions. Rather, they claim that employees, like creditors, are capable of protecting their position *ex ante* via contracting, which includes collective bargaining.[93] Others, however, regard this faith in the bargaining process as misplaced and unrealistic.[94] A recurring theme in work challenging a law and economics vision of the

---

[86] See Bratton, *supra* n.69, at 103.

[87] See, e.g., K Greenfield, 'The Place of Workers in Corporate Law' (1998) 39 *Boston College Law Review* 283, who states that '[w]orkers have no role, or almost no role, in the dominant contemporary narrative of corporate law'.

[88] The recent Waterfront Dispute in Australia was a forceful reminder of just how relevant the corporate status of an employer can be. See *Patrick Stevedores Operations No 2 Pty. Ltd* v. *Maritime Union of Australia* (1998) 153 ALR 643.

[89] K W Wedderburn, 'Trust, Corporation and the Worker' (1985) 23 *Osgoode Hall Law Journal* 203, at 236.

[90] See K V W Stone, 'The Post-War Paradigm in American Labor Law' (1981) 90 *Yale Law Journal* 1509, at 1511 and 1545.

[91] See generally J Hill, 'At the Frontiers of Labour Law and Corporate Law: Enterprise Bargaining, Corporations and Employees' (1995) 23 *Federal Law Review* 204.

[92] See, e.g., M A O'Connor, 'Restructuring the Corporation's Nexus of Contracts: Recognizing a Fiduciary Duty to Protect Displaced Workers' (1991) 69 *North Carolina Law Review* 1189; M A O'Connor, 'Promoting Economic Justice in Plant Closings: Exploring the Fiduciary/Contract Law Distinction to Enforce Implicit Employment Agreements' in Mitchell, *supra*, n.6, 219.

[93] See Macey, *supra* n.38, at 26; J R Macey, 'Externalities, Firm-Specific Capital Investments, and the Legal Treatment of Fundamental Corporate Changes' [1989] *Duke Law Journal* 173.

[94] See, e.g., K V W Stone, 'Policing Employment Contracts Within the Nexus-of-Contracts Firm' (1993) 43 *University of Toronto Law Journal* 353, at 375–7; K V W Stone, 'Employees as Stakeholders Under State Nonshareholder Constituency Statutes' (1991) 21 *Stetson Law Review* 45, at 54*ff*.

corporation is the invisibility of 'power' under the model,[95] through its reliance on classical contract theory, which assumes that parties are bargaining at arm's length.[96] Critics reject the attempted privatisation and legitimation[97] of arrangements through the symbol of 'voluntary exchange'. The financial necessity for most citizens to find work limits the degree to which industrial law contracts can be truly regarded as voluntary.[98]

As in the case of creditors, shareholder-centred models of the corporation assume employee interests are distinct from those of other constituencies, and that employees are outsiders to corporate law.[99] Familiar as we now are with the shareholder-centred contractual model of the corporation, it has been a puzzling picture to 'European eyes',[100] where issues of industrial democracy became more closely integrated in company law, via either fiduciary duties or participatory rights in governance of the corporation.[101] According to Wedderburn, this is simply an aspect of the question, 'what are the modern conditions . . . on which private capital in a mixed economy can be allowed the privilege of incorporation with limited liability?'[102]

The point has sometimes been made that traditionally directors and managers themselves have seemed to view their duties as owed to a broader range of constituencies than merely shareholders,[103] however it is possible that this is changing with the current dominance of the contractual model of the corporation and the rise of institutional shareholders. At a practical level, too, some commentators have argued that it is incongruous to restrict corporate membership to shareholders (particularly in an age of portfolio diversification), when 'employees may have made a much greater investment in the enterprise by their years of

---

[95] See, e.g., Dallas, *supra* n.39, at 26; G Teubner, 'Unitas Multiplex: Corporate Governance in Group Enterprises' in D Sugarman and G Teubner (eds.), *Regulating Corporate Groups in Europe* (Baden-Baden, Nomos, 1990), 67, at 74.

[96] See P S Atiyah, *The Rise and Fall of Freedom of Contract* (Oxford, Clarendon Press, 1979), at 402–4.

[97] See, e.g., Bratton, *supra*, n.18 at 438–9; Millon, *supra* n.6; R M Buxbaum, 'Corporate Legitimacy, Economic Theory, and Legal Doctrine' (1984) 45 *Ohio State Law Journal* 515: Teubner, *supra* n.7, at 131; Stone, *supra* n.90.

[98] See Selznick, *supra* n.5, at 39–40; P I Blumberg, 'Limited Liability and Corporate Groups' (1986) 11 *Journal of Corporation Law* 573, at 618; W Streeck, 'Status and Contract: Basic Categories of a Sociological Theory of Industrial Relations' in Sugarman and Teubner, *supra* n.95, 105.

[99] *Cf* P L Davies and K W Wedderburn, 'The Land of Industrial Democracy' (1977) 6 *Industrial Law Journal* 197.

[100] Wedderburn, *supra* n.89, at 250. See also C Schmitthoff, 'Employee Participation and the Theory of Enterprise' [1975] *Journal of Business Law* 265.

[101] See, e.g., K J Hopt, 'Directors' Duties to Shareholders, Employees, and Other Creditors: A View From the Continent' in E McKendrick (ed.), *Commercial Aspects of Trusts and Fiduciary Obligations* (Oxford, Clarendon Press, 1992), 115; G Teubner, 'Corporate Fiduciary Duties and Their Beneficiaries: A Functional Approach to the Legal Institutionalization of Corporate Responsibility' in Hopt and Teubner, *supra* n.26, 149; F K Kübler, 'Dual Loyalty of Labor Representatives' in Hopt and Teubner, *supra* n.26, 429, at 438*ff*.

[102] Wedderburn, *supra* n.89, at 250.

[103] *Ibid.*, at 230; L Sealy, 'Directors' "Wider" Responsibilities—Problems Conceptual, Practical and Procedural' (1987) 13 *Monash University Law Review* 164, at 174.

service, may have much less ability to withdraw, and may have a greater stake in the future of the enterprise than many of the stockholders'.[104]

At a judicial level, there is a tension between principles of strict contract and fairness of outcome, again paralleling the use of good faith in interpretation of debt contracts.[105] In the UK case, *Malik* v. *Bank of Credit and Commerce International SA (in liq.)*,[106] for example, the House of Lords endorsed the principle that there is to be implied by law in contracts of employment a term of mutual trust and confidence. This implied term was hardly interesting *vis-à-vis* employees, who have long been under a duty of loyalty and good faith to the employer. The radical aspect of the decision lay in its mutuality—in the expansion of the principle to the obligations of employer in contracts of employment. [107] It is an aspect of modern society that almost all employers are corporations.[108] Thus, a duty of trust and good faith in the employer will generally, in the case of a corporation, reside with the board of directors. Such a duty of trust and confidence in a corporate employer could arguably operate as the functional equivalent of a fiduciary duty to employees.[109] Nicholls LJ gave some hint of the policy reasons for the emergence of the implied obligation in stating:

> Employment, and job prospects, are matters of vital concern to most people. Jobs of all descriptions are less secure than formerly, people change jobs more frequently, and the job market is not always buoyant. . . . An employment contract creates a close personal relationship, where there is often a disparity of power between the parties. Frequently the employee is vulnerable.[110]

There are also commercial developments which have the potential to blur the boundaries between the labour and investment functions, putting pressure on the simple picture of employee as 'outsider' to the corporate enterprise.[111] Employees today may have an investment stake in the corporation via a number of possible routes. The most direct is through the increased popularity of employee share plans. In some companies, as well as providing financial participation for employees, the share plans have been structured in such a way as to promote actual participation in governance by employees, through, for example, pass-through voting of shares or representation at the level of the trustee.[112]

---

[104] C W Summers, 'Codetermination in the United States: A Projection of Problems and Potentials' (1982) 4 *Journal of Comparative Corporate Law and Securities Regulation* 155, at 170. See also Blair, *supra* n.36, at 239.

[105] See Bratton, *supra* n.82.

[106] [1997] 3 All ER 1.

[107] *Ibid.*, at 15–16, citing with approval an article by D Brodie, 'The Heart of the Matter: Mutual Trust and Confidence' (1996) 25 *Industrial Law Journal* 121.

[108] See Mason, *supra* n.36, 1.

[109] See generally, O'Connor, *supra* n.92.

[110] [1997] 3 All ER 1, at 8.

[111] See generally K V W Stone, 'Labor and the Corporate Structure: Changing Conceptions and Emerging Possibilities' (1988) 55 *University of Chicago Law Review* 73.

[112] See, e.g., P I Blumberg, 'Employee Participation in Corporate Decision Making' in A F Westin and S Salisbury (eds.), *Individual Rights in the Corporation* (New York, Pantheon Books, 1980) 335, at 345ff.

Schemes such as these have the potential to provide employees with a stake in the company's success and to create 'corporate goals', in place of conflicting goals between groups.[113] Strategies such as these are deliberately designed to undermine the image of employees as 'outsiders' to the enterprise.

Also significant is the impact of indirect investment in Australian corporations by workers through the medium of institutional investment. Since the introduction of the Superannuation Guarantee Charge (SCG) in 1992, superannuation in Australia has been transformed from 'a voluntary collective investment used by a minority of the workforce to an almost universal, compulsory retirement savings policy'.[114] Alterations to governance structures in the institutions themselves to allow greater participation by beneficiaries potentially have radical implications for governance at the corporate level. The investment of funds compulsorily acquired from the workforce[115] presents a potential challenge to a 'private' and 'voluntary' image of the corporation.

NORMATIVE ASPECTS—COLLECTIVISATION OF SHAREHOLDER/MANAGEMENT
INTERESTS AND 'THE SUPERMODEL SYNDROME' IN EXECUTIVE
REMUNERATION

Many of the commercial developments discussed above point to a blurring of the boundaries between corporate constituencies, and a tendency to treat groups such as creditors and employees as more closely integrated within the corporate enterprise. Nonetheless, there are other developments, both in theory and commercial practice, which point in the opposite direction, and clearly treat shareholder interests as privileged and preeminent.

First, at a theoretical level, most versions of a contractual model of the corporation elevate shareholder interests, but deflate shareholder rights of participation in the corporation, by stressing the shareholder's role as investor rather than owner.[116] Some recent theories of relational investing go further, however, by advocating protection of shareholder interests through increased participation in corporate governance. The model proposed by John Pound, for example, reasserts owner control through shared management of the corporation by institutional shareholders and the board.[117] According to Pound, his model of

---

[113] See G Fitton and G Price, *Employee Share Planning in Australia* (Melbourne, Information Australia, 1990), ch 2; Parkinson, *supra* n.15, at 423–6; Department of Industrial Relations, *Financial Participation by Employees: A Review of Theoretical and Practical Issues*, DIR Research Paper No 8 (Canberra, Department of Industrial Relations, 1988), at 6–7.

[114] Australian Law Reform Commission and Company and Securities Advisory Committee, *Report No 59, Collective Investments: Superannuation*, Mar. 1992, lix.

[115] In accordance with Clark's fourth stage of capitalism: R C Clark, 'The Four Stages of Capitalism: Reflections on Investment Management Treatises' (1981) 94 *Harvard Law Review* 561, at 565–6.

[116] See Hill, *supra* n. 20.

[117] See Pound, 'The Rise of the Political Model of Corporate Governance and Corporate Control', *supra* n.25; Pound, 'The Promise of the Governed Corporation', *supra* n.25. See also

shareholders as managerial partners has descriptive power as a result of the increasing collectivisation and influence of institutional investors.[118] It is estimated, for example, that international and Australian institutional investors hold approximately 65 per cent of available capital of companies listed in Australia.[119] Pound's normative claim is that such a model of shared power provides greater legitimacy for the exercise of managerial power, by ensuring that management will maximise corporate performance for the benefit of shareholders.

At a commercial level, one development, which more than any other has the potential to guarantee the pre-eminence of shareholder interests over those of other groups, is the rise of pay for performance remuneration for executives and directors. Pay for performance remuneration comes in many guises, essentially tying a substantial portion of remuneration to corporate performance. The goal of pay for performance in linking managerial reward to profit maximisation is to create a self-executing governance technique, which can ensure managerial accountability by creating a novel 'collectivisation' of shareholder and management interests. The rise of pay for performance remuneration reflects a recent shift in paradigm whereby remuneration, traditionally treated as a fiduciary problem, was recharacterised as a problem of misalignment between the interests of principal and agent.[120] The shift in paradigm was largely brought about by Jensen and Murphy's influential article, 'CEO Incentives—It's Not How Much You Pay, But How'.[121] This revision directly reflects a private, contractual model of the corporation, which restricts corporate law to the internal relationship between shareholders and managers.[122] It is no accident that the rise of pay for performance has coincided with the rise of powerful institutional investors.

For many commentators, this shift towards treating the shareholder as managerial partner and 'collectivising' the interests of management and institutional shareholders is the ultimate solution to the division between ownership and control. Nonetheless, there are a number of dangers and undesirable policy effects which may flow from such a model. First, the model privileges shareholder interests at the expense of other groups within the company. It is, for example, a matter of concern that the collectivisation of management and

---

D G Smith, 'Corporate Governance and Managerial Incompetence: Lessons from Kmart' (1996) 74 *North Carolina Law Review* 1037.

[118] Some commentators are sceptical, however, about the likelihood that this form of governance will occur in practice: see J E Fisch, 'Relationship Investing: Will It Happen? Will It Work?' (1994) 55 *Ohio St Law Journal* 1009; T A Smith, 'Institutions and Entrepreneurs in American Corporate Finance' (1997) 85 *California Law Review* 1.

[119] Australian Investment Managers' Association, *Corporate Governance: A Guide for Investment Managers and Corporations* (2nd edn., 1997), at 5 and 13.

[120] See C M Yablon, 'Bonus Questions: An Essay on Executive Compensation and Income Inequality' (Continuing Legal Education Conference Paper, University of Sydney Law School, 1997), at 4*ff*. This echoes Berle's model of corporate governance: see Smith, *supra* n.117, at 1058.

[121] [1990] *Harvard Business Review* 138.

[122] See Millon, *supra* n.6, at 202.

shareholder interests should have occurred in Australia at a time when there has been a major shift towards 'decollectivisation' of labour interests through enterprise bargaining systems.[123] Evidence in the USA, where the vast majority of workers are not unionised,[124] suggests that these developments have produced a skewed distribution of wealth—specifically, 'circumstances in which shareholders are gaining and workers are not'.[125] There are a range of issues where the strengthening of shareholder interests may directly increase employee vulnerability. Reports in the financial press about the announced closure of a major steel factory in Newcastle, Australia, for example, suggested that the decision had been prompted by institutional shareholder influence and pressure, reflecting Pound's model.[126] A model, however, treating employees as themselves insiders to the enterprise, would suggest that employee participation in decisions specifically affecting their interests, such as plant closures, is desirable and important in conferring legitimacy.[127] Corporate restructuring can also radically affect employee interests, and recent legislative changes in Australia under the Company Law Review Act 1998 will provide management with far greater flexibility and discretion in this regard.

Secondly, the rise of pay for performance remuneration, though favoured by institutional shareholders, may nonetheless present dangers to the interests of employees and indeed to the long-term interests of the corporate enterprise itself. This is a result of what may be termed 'the supermodel syndrome' in executive remuneration. In an era of takeovers and institutional investor pressure, corporate executives, like supermodels, have a potentially short shelf-life. Pay for performance provides them with strong incentives to increase corporate profitability during their tenure.[128] The ways in which profitability can be increased are limited, but a common contemporary technique is downsizing of the workforce. Long-term research and development can also suffer as a result of the supermodel syndrome. There is a growing concern that pay for perfor-

---

[123] See R C McCallum, 'Crafting a New Collective Labour Law for Australia' (1997) 39 *Journal of Industrial Relations* 405.

[124] See, e.g., H Hansmann, 'Worker Participation and Corporate Governance' (1993) 43 *University of Toronto Law Journal* 589; Leung, *supra* n.36, at 594–5.

[125] J N Gordon, 'Employees, Pensions, and the New Economic Order' (1997) 97 *Columbia Law Review* 1519, at 1534, who notes that, while corporate profits increased by 250% from 1980–95 in the USA, wages of average workers actually declined in real terms during that period.

[126] Contrast the shareholder-centred approach in 'BHP's rescue operation: investors welcome radical surgery for ailing division', *Australian Financial Review*, 30 Apr. 1997, with the pro-worker report, 'BHP's real target: 8,000 jobs', *Sydney Morning Herald*, 30 Apr. 1997.

[127] See, e.g., Parkinson, *supra* n.15, at 402*ff*; P L Davies, 'Employee Representation on Company Boards and Participation in Corporate Planning' (1975) 38 *Modern Law Review* 254, at 256; Wedderburn, *supra* n.89, at 248–9.

[128] This is mirrored by strong competitive pressures on institutions and their fund managers, who may also be driven to maximise short-term profits: see M Lipton, 'Corporate Governance in the Age of Finance Corporatism' (1987) 136 *University of Pennsylvania Law Review* 1, at 7–8; M Lipton, T N Mirvis and S A Rosenblum, 'Book Review: Corporate Governance in the Era of Institutional Ownership' (1995) 70 *New York University Law Review* 1144, at 1147–8; E B Rock, 'The Logic and (Uncertain) Significance of Institutional Shareholder Activism' (1991) 79 *Georgetown Law Journal* 445.

mance schemes, coupled with the problem of the supermodel syndrome, may provide perverse incentives for corporate managers to focus almost exclusively on short-term profits.[129] Some US executives, such as Michael Eisner, have become 'bone-chillingly rich',[130] largely on the basis of pay for performance.[131] Statistics show that, in 1997, the average American CEO earned 326 times the pay of an average factory worker[132] and 728 times more than a minimum wage earner.[133] Under the Jensen and Murphy alignment of interests model of remuneration, size of remuneration under pay for performance packages is unproblematical. Nonetheless, there is growing criticism of the theoretical underpinnings to pay for performance. Critics reject the idea of remuneration as a private contractual matter between shareholders and managers, pointing to the fact that excessive remuneration can be particularly damaging to worker morale [134] and indeed to the economy as a whole.[135] Increasingly, these critics point to executive remuneration and income inequality as a social issue.

Thirdly, the interests of institutional investors may diverge from the interests of their beneficiaries, who have in the past had little opportunity to exercise a voice in institutional investment policies.[136]

These matters suggest that, from a normative perspective, an exclusive focus on shareholder interests through shareholder/management collectivisation may be undesirable (particularly when coupled with decollectivisation of labour interests). This is not to deny however that shareholder participation in corporate governance can be valuable. Focus by some communitarian scholars on conflicts between shareholders and other stakeholders might suggest that controlling shareholders will always use participatory rights to benefit themselves at the expense of other groups. Nonetheless, where what is at stake is conflict of interest or self-dealing by managers,[137] monitoring by shareholders may benefit all other groups in the corporate enterprise, and form a network of monitoring by interested groups.[138]

---

[129] See, e.g., J A Kreinberg, 'Reaching Beyond Performance Compensation in Attempts to Own the Corporate Executive' [1995] *Duke Law Journal* 138.

[130] Yablon, *supra* n.120.

[131] Pay for performance in the USA is reinforced by tax law. See generally J Hill, ' "What Reward Have Ye?" Disclosure of Director and Executive Remuneration in Australia' (1996) 14 *Company and Securities Law Journal* 232, at 236.

[132] 'Executive Pay', Special Report, *Business Week*, 20 Apr. 1998.

[133] Executive PayWatch, 'Runaway CEO Pay', <http://www.aflcio.org/paywatch/problem/index.htm>.

[134] C M Yablon, 'Overcompensating: The Corporate Lawyer and Executive Pay' (1992) 92 *Columbia Law Review* 1867, at 1877.

[135] Kreinberg, *supra* n.129, at 144–6; Parkinson, *supra* n.15, at 201–2.

[136] See R M Buxbaum, 'Institutional Owners and Corporate Managers: A Comparative Perspective' (1991) 57 *Brooklyn Law Review* 1, at 45ff.

[137] See L E Mitchell, 'A Theoretical and Practical Framework for Enforcing Corporate Constituency Statutes' (1992) 70 *Texas Law Review* 579, at 591 and 632.

[138] See G G Triantis and R J Daniels, 'The Role of Debt in Interactive Corporate Governance' (1995) 83 *California Law Review* 1073.

CONCLUSION—IMPLICATIONS FOR CORPORATE THEORY

A basic contention of this chapter is that these diverse commercial developments, blurring the boundaries between debt/equity and labour/capital represent a fundamental challenge to traditional corporate theory, and to shareholder-centred models of the corporation in particular. In the field of financial and accounting theory, for example, Pope and Puxty argue that an enterprise theory—under which the corporation is viewed as a social institution operating for the benefit of a range of interested groups in society—provides a more coherent underlying philosophy for financial statements than accounting orthodoxy, which is represented by a shareholder-centred proprietary model.[139]

In the realm of corporate law itself, there is also much support for such a view of the public corporation, stressing its connection with society as a whole.[140] This approach treats the corporation as an autonomous legal entity, unifying the interests of a range of different groups. It is consistent with Dodd's treatment of managerial duties,[141] which adopted a broad-based entity model of the corporation, in contrast to Berles' aggregate shareholder-centred model.[142] Dodd's model imbued the corporation with long-term interests transcending those of any single group within in its boundaries.

In recent times, some scholars have also attacked the assumption, which underlies pay for performance structures, that the alignment of shareholder and management interests is all that counts. They argue that the fundamental objectives of corporate governance systems must be the long-term health of the corporate enterprise as a whole, and that, to achieve this, corporate law needs to seek to align not just the interests of managers and shareholders, but also the interests of a range of other groups associated with the corporation, such as employees, suppliers and creditors.[143]

Almost 40 years ago, Abram Chayes rejected a shareholder-centred conception of the corporation as outmoded. According to Chayes:

> [a] concept of the corporation which draws the boundary of 'membership' thus narrowly is seriously inadequate. It perpetuates . . . the superficial analogy of the seventeenth century between contributors to a joint stock and members of a guild or citizens of a borough. The error has more than theoretical importance because the line between those who are 'inside' and those who are 'outside' the corporation is the line

[139] See, e.g., Pope and Puxty, *supra* n.57, at 896–7; E C Lashbrooke, 'The Divergence of Corporate Finance and Law in Corporate Governance' (1995) 46 *South Carolina Law Review* 449. See also Scheinkestel, *supra* n.53, at 107, suggesting that it may be more useful to treat debt and equity as different points on a spectrum, than as dichotomous.

[140] See, e.g., Buxbaum, *supra* n.15; Teubner, *supra* n.7, at 131; Blumberg, *supra* n.15; P Selznick, *The Moral Commonwealth: Social Theory and the Promise of Community* (Berkeley, University of California Press, 1992), ch 9; Steinmann, *supra* n.26; M Stokes, 'Company Law and Legal Theory' in W Twining (ed.), *Legal Theory and Common Law* (Oxford, Blackwell, 1986), 155, at 176–80.

[141] Dodd, *supra* n.29.

[142] Berle, *supra* n.22; Berle, *supra* n.29.

[143] See Lipton, Mirvis and Rosenblum, *supra* n.128, reviewing Blair, *supra* n.36.

between those whom we recognize as entitled to a regularized share in its processes of decision and those who are not. A more spacious conception of 'membership', and one closer to the facts of corporate life, would include all those having a relation of sufficient intimacy with the corporation or subject to its power in a sufficiently specialised way.[144]

A number of the developments discussed in this chapter only increase the disjunction, of which Chayes spoke, between commercial reality and corporate theory in its application to large public companies.[145]

---

[144] A Chayes, 'The Modern Corporation and the Rule of Law' in Mason, *supra* n.26, 25, at 41; Selznick, *supra* n.140, at 346–7.

[145] See also Mason, *supra* n.36; Wolfe, *supra* n.19, at 1696.

3

Scenes From a Wharf: Containing the Morality of Corporate Law

PETA SPENDER[1]

> The deeper question that haunted this dispute is . . . how can justice bloom in the face of corporate subversion?[2]

INTRODUCTION

The dramatic events of April and May 1998 involving the Maritime Union of Australia (MUA) and Patrick Stevedores swept corporate law out of the boardrooms and business pages and onto the streets and prime time television. Rarely has a case received as much attention; the media scrutiny it received has probably only been surpassed by the *Azaria Chamberlain* case. The events could have featured in a Hollywood plot: a secret corporate group restructure followed by a secret paramilitary operation followed by an insolvency leading to the lock out of 1,400 waterside workers; the workers challenge the restructure, the lock out and the insolvency, arguing a conspiracy to cast off companies and their unionised workforces; the courts adjudicate the dispute and deliver judgments live to air.

For corporate lawyers, the Patrick dispute predominantly concerns the extent to which ethical systems in corporate law are insulated from or are qualified by the ethical constraints of labour law. Corporate law presents a closed system of norms, and after recounting the dispute in the first part of this chapter, I will map out the norms of corporate law which are relevant to the dispute. It will be argued that corporate law is a system which is normatively closed and has a logic and objectives designed to fulfil certain transactions and stakeholders. Employees are not one of these stakeholders. Generally speaking, the Patrick arrangements were in harmony with the norms and doctrine of corporate law because principles such as limited liability and separate legal personality

---

[1] Unless otherwise stated all references to legislation are to the Corporations Law 1989. The author wishes to thank Robyn Carroll and Steve Bottomley for reading an earlier draft.

[2] G Orr, 'Conspiracy on the Waterfront' (1998) 11 *Australian Journal of Labour Law* 159, at 185.

contemplate these arrangements. The Patrick corporate restructure was there-fore 'legal'. However, this 'legal' arrangement gave rise to considerable ethical difficulties.

The outcry which ensued from the lock out of the employees and the public scrutiny of the litigation exerted considerable pressure upon the norms of cor-porate law. A portion of the outcry is glimpsed in the third part of this chapter. A question which arose for the judges hearing the litigation was whether cor-porate doctrine should respond to the 'external reality'. The Federal Court answered this question affirmatively and used the remedy of the interlocutory injunction and an implied term of the employment contract to displace corpo-rate law doctrine. These devices will be examined in the fourth part of the chapter.

However, by adopting a formalist interpretation of the voluntary administra-tion provisions, the majority in the High Court opted for an analysis which favoured the insularity or closure of corporate law. The High Court appre-hended the dispute as a corporate dispute, which led to a misconception of the insolvency and the reinvention of industrial law rights as corporate rights. The decision of the High Court of Australia will be explored in the fifth part of the chapter.

THE PATRICK DISPUTE

The Participants

In March 1996 the Liberal—National Party Coalition won the Australian fed-eral election having promised during the election campaign to substantially restructure industrial relations and to 'reform the waterfront'. The Government considered that a significant impediment to reform was the waterfront enter-prise union—the Maritime Union of Australia (MUA). The MUA has repre-sented workers in a closed shop on the waterfront for many years.[3] In 1997 there were approximately 3,000 waterside workers who worked in container port operations, all of whom were eligible to become members of the MUA. Primarily two port operators control Australian container traffic—P&O Ports and Patrick Stevedoring. Between them the two operators control about 95 per cent of national container lifts.[4] The Patrick group of companies has the larger market share[5] and operates stevedoring businesses in various ports around

---

[3] The MUA was established in 1993 with the merger of the Waterside Workers Federation and the Seamans' Union. The Waterside Workers Federation had been operating since the 1870s.

[4] S O'Neill, 'Outline of the Waterfront Dispute', Current Issues Brief, No 15 (Department of the Parliamentary Library, 1998), at 5.

[5] At least according to its press releases: see Patrick Stevedores—News Releases of 28 Jan. 1998, 4 Feb. 1998, 13 Feb. 1998 and 18 Feb. 1998; http://www.patrick.com.au/nrel.

Australia. The group is controlled by Lang Corporation Ltd, a company listed on the Australian Stock Exchange.

Immediately after the election, the Government set up task forces to deal with the wider issue of workplace relations. Shortly afterwards, the Workplace Relations Act 1996 (Cth) was passed which enshrined the use of workplace agreements, and its freedom of association provisions gave employees the right to decide whether or not to join a union, thereby targeting closed shops. However, section 298K of the Workplace Relations Act also prohibited an employer from dismissing an employee or otherwise damaging the employment relationship because the employee was a member of a union.[6]

The Events

The event which captured national and international attention occurred at 11 pm on 7 April 1998 at the change of shift at Patrick docks throughout Australia. Teams of security guards accompanied by guard dogs, and in many cases masked and armed with automatic weapons, refused entry to the employees who had turned up to work. The lock-out affected approximately 2,000 employees.[7] The companies which employed the workers had been placed into voluntary administration. Although the employees had not been dismissed, their dismissal was imminent because the employing companies within the Patrick group were said to be insolvent—they were said to have no assets and no way of continuing in business. A secret corporate restructuring which had been effected in September 1997 had left the workers employed by companies whose only asset was a contract to supply labour. This contract had been terminated by an upstream company in the group, triggering an insolvency of the employer companies. The next day, the Minister for Workplace Relations and Small Business, Mr Reith, presented a bill designed to establish a government-run redundancy scheme for retrenched waterfront employees based on a government guaranteed loan of 250 million Australian dollars.[8]

The Corporate Restructure

Prior to September 1997, each of the employer companies owned and ran its own stevedoring operation, employing MUA workers for this purpose. The profits derived from these businesses were substantial.[9] According to Lang Corporation, the restructuring was necessary 'to avoid customer confusion, confusion as to which entity owned which assets, to allow better performance

---

[6] Workplace Relations Act 1996 (Cth), s 298K.

[7] Consisting of 1,400 full-time workers and 600 part-time or casual workers.

[8] *The Age*, 9 Apr. 1998. See also N Seddon and S Bottomley, 'Commonwealth Companies and the Constitution' (1998) 26 *Federal Law Review* 271, at 303.

[9] *Patrick Stevedores Operations No 2 Pty. Ltd* v. *Maritime Union of Australia* (1998) 153 ALR 643, at 648, *per* Brennan CJ, McHugh, Gummow, Kirby and Hayne JJ.

monitoring and to allow borrowing at better rates'.[10] However, there was no express denial that a reason for undertaking the restructure was to facilitate the termination of the employees' employment.[11] Each of the employer companies sold its property, plant, equipment and all its contractual interests (other than an agreement to supply its employees' labour) to another company in the group, Patrick Stevedores Operations No 2 Pty. Ltd (PSO), under the terms of a business purchase agreement.[12] The total purchase price was approximately 315 million Australian dollars. The employer companies retained only their employees. The four employer companies used the proceeds from this sale to repay debts and to buy back a large proportion of their own shares. The share buyback involved the expenditure of between 60 and 70 million Australian dollars, paid to other companies in the Patrick group. After the restructuring the employer companies were still owed between 16 and 17 million Australian dollars by other Patrick companies. Although the employer companies did not owe any moneys other than wages and associated on-costs, their assets were at some stage charged to secure the indebtedness of other companies in the Patrick group.[13] The chargees were a syndicate of banks whose total debt amounted to between 236 and 270 million Australian dollars.

PSO now owned the stevedoring businesses which had previously been conducted by each of the four employer companies. To run the businesses it needed labour, and so PSO entered into a labour supply agreement with each of the four employer companies. This agreement was now the only significant asset held by each of the employer companies. Each labour supply agreement had a term which stated that it could be terminated by PSO if there was any interference with, delay in or hindering of the supply of labour.[14] The restructure also resulted in the reduction of the boards of the employer companies to the statutory minimum[15] so that Mr Bill Clayton became the sole director of each employer company.

---

[10] *Maritime Union of Australia v. Patrick Stevedores Operations No 1 Pty. Ltd* (1998) 153 ALR 602, at 612, *per* North J.

[11] *Ibid.*

[12] The description of the restructuring is substantially taken from the judgment of North J in *Maritime Union of Australia v. Patrick Stevedores Operations No 1 Pty. Ltd* (1998) 153 ALR 602 and S. Bottomley, *The Patrick Stevedores—MUA Dispute: The Facts*, Seminar Paper, Australian National University, 13 May 1998.

[13] *Patrick Stevedores Operations No 2 Pty. Ltd v. Maritime Union of Australia, supra* n.9, at 673, *per* Gaudron J.

[14] Each Labour Supply Agreement contained the following clauses:
Clause 2.3: 'In the performance of the Services the Contractor will: . . . (h) ensure that the performance of the Services are not interfered with or delayed or hindered for any reason.'
Clause 13.1(b): 'In the event of a breach of clause 2.3(h) of this Agreement [PSO] may terminate this Agreement immediately.'
Clause 13.3: 'If an application is made to wind up either party, voluntarily or otherwise, or a receiver, receiver and manager, liquidator, administrator or controller (as defined in the Corporations Law) is appointed over any assets of either party, this Agreement will terminate immediately.'

[15] Corporations Law, s 221 states that one director is sufficient. Each of the employer companies had six to seven directors prior to the restructure but the other directors resigned between Sept. 1997 and Mar. 1998: G Thornton, *Report to Creditors—Patrick Companies under Administration*, 16 May 1998, at 9.

The restructuring took place without the workforce's knowledge. A more traditional method of contracting out labour would have required the creation of new employment companies and the transfer of existing contracts of employment to them. Such an arrangement would have required the agreement of each employee.[16] Although the legal entities who contracted with the employees did not change, the nature of the business and viability of those companies had changed fundamentally.

The Termination of the Labour Supply Agreement

Other extraordinary events paralleled the corporate restructure and the termination of the labour supply agreement. First was the so-called 'Dubai operation', a mission led by two SAS officers to train a group of non-unionised military personnel in waterfront work, using the docks of the United Arab Emirates' port. The mission foundered when information about the mission was made public and the International Transport Federation pressured the UAE government into cancelling the men's visas. The Australian government and Patrick Stevedores denied involvement in the operation but those denials have been disputed in the Australian media.[17] The second was the establishment by the National Farmers Federation[18] of a group of companies (PCS) to hire and train non-union stevedoring labour upon facilities which were owned by Patrick at Webb Dock in Melbourne. When the MUA became aware of this, it responded by a series of rolling stoppages.[19] As stated above, the labour supply agreement provided that PSO could terminate the labour supply agreement without notice in the event of any delay or hindrance in the supply of 'services', that is, labour. These MUA stoppages hindered the supply of labour and the employer companies were consequently in breach of the labour supply agreement.

A meeting took place on 27 March 1998 between Mr Corrigan (Chief Executive Officer of PSO) and representatives of the banking syndicate, where Mr Corrigan revealed the plan to terminate the labour supply agreements and to place the employer companies in administration.[20] Early in the evening of 7 April a further meeting was convened at the Patrick offices. At this meeting certain manœuvres occurred in the following sequence: PSO invoked the clause to terminate the labour supply agreements; PSO signed contracts with PCS for the

---

[16] Orr, *supra* n.2, at 161.

[17] See, e.g., D Elias, 'War and Peace', *The Age*, 17 June 1998; K Murphy, 'Government knew of Dubai "from start" ', *Australian Financial Review*, 6 May 1998, at 5.

[18] The National Farmers Federation (NFF) is a national interest group, which represents farm enterprises and commodity councils in economic issues relating to rural industry, trade and industrial relations.

[19] Most of these stoppages were legal because they occurred during a bargaining period and were therefore 'protected action' under the Workplace Relations Act.

[20] Elias, *supra* n.17. This meeting was established by documents produced on subpoena issued by the MUA: see *Maritime Union of Australia* v. *Patrick Stevedores No 1 Pty. Ltd (under administration) and Ors (No. 3)* (1998) 695 FCA (16 June 1998), http://www.austlii.edu.au.

supply of labour to its stevedoring operations; the security trustee of the syndicate of banks gave notice of the crystallisation of its charge over the Patrick group and the director of the employer company resolved that liabilities of the employer companies exceeded whatever was owing to them and an administrator should therefore be appointed.[21]

As stated by the *Australian Financial Review*:

> Within three hours, the final blueprint drawn up on that table would be used to ignite a firestorm. Patrick would restructure its operations with breathtaking audacity by withdrawing financial support from four subsidiary labour hire companies. An administrator would be appointed and the labour hire contract severed. The workforce would be marched off the docks by security guards and . . . nine new companies . . . would be contracted to replace the dockers. As a finale, Workplace Relations Minister Peter Reith would announce a $250 million scheme to fund waterfront redundancies.
>
> So neat, so clean and all before midnight.[22]

The Litigation

The MUA commenced proceedings in the Federal Court of Australia seeking urgent orders restraining the employer companies from replacing MUA employees with non-union labour. The MUA pleaded several breaches but its primary argument was that various parties—the Patrick companies, the PCS companies, the Minister and others—had conspired to effect a breach of section 298K of the Workplace Relations Act. Although a dismissal had not been effected it was alleged that the final stage of the conspiracy involved the dismissal of the entire work force by the administrators due to the alleged insolvency of the employer companies. The illegal act would thereby be executed by a party whose motives could not be challenged. As stated by counsel for the MUA, Julian Burnside QC:

> the appointment of an administrator at the very last stages of the conspiracy, involve[s] bringing in an innocent who will have no rational choice but to dismiss the employees: . . . that further step involves the company directly in a contravention of section 298K by a dismissal for a prohibited reason, and the reason is the reason which impelled all of the prior steps.[23]

Justice North found there were serious questions to be tried that the employers had breached the Workplace Relations Act:

> The cancellation of the labour supply contract and the appointment of administrators on 7 April 1998 were made possible by a complex inter-company transaction which occurred in September 1997. By dividing the functions of employing workers and own-

---

[21] *Patrick Stevedores Operations No 2 Pty. Ltd* v. *Maritime Union of Australia, supra* n.9, at 650.

[22] P Williams, 'Unchained. How these men broke open the docks', *Australian Financial Review*, 11–12 Apr. 1998, at 23.

[23] Transcript of proceedings, High Court of Australia, 28 Apr. 1998.

ing the business between two companies, the Patrick group put in place a structure which made it easier to dismiss the whole workforce. It is arguable, on the evidence, that this was done because the employees were members of the Union. So there is an arguable case that the Patrick employers acted in breach of s 298K(1) of the Act.[24]

His Honour made interlocutory orders returning the situation to the pre-7 April position. This included orders restraining PSO from terminating the labour supply agreements and requiring the employer companies (now run by administrators) to give effect to those agreements. PSO was also required to acquire its labour only from the employer companies.

Patrick appealed to the Full Court of the Federal Court, which upheld North J's orders unanimously, with one change intended to protect the administrators from personal liability for employees' wages. Patrick appealed to the High Court. The majority of the High Court (Brennan CJ, McHugh, Gummow, Kirby and Hayne JJ) varied the orders given by North J. Gaudron J dismissed the appeal. Callinan J dissented.

Although further litigation ensued[25] the focus of the dispute returned to bargaining. Some of the bargaining took place within the context of the deed of arrangement which was proposed by the administrators; otherwise the parties bargained via industrial procedures. Ultimately the matter settled. The terms of the settlement were that 620 workers were offered redundancy and a further 200 jobs in security, cleaning and maintenance were contracted out to companies employing union labour; thus the MUA maintained its closed shop. Most importantly, the corporate restructure was unravelled, and the employees of the employer companies were transferred in employment to Patrick Stevedores Holdings Pty. Ltd. The companies in administration were wound up and the labour supply agreements terminated immediately upon the transfer of the employees to the holding company. The final term of the settlement agreement stated that all parties to future employment arrangements will respect the provisions of the Workplace Relations Act, including the right of union members to be represented by their union and the freedom of association provisions.

CORPORATE LAW MORALITY EXPLORED

An Autopoietic Framework

In this chapter, autopoietic theory will be used to explain the interaction between corporate law norms and external ethical pressures in the Patrick

---

[24] *Supra* n.10, at 605.

[25] On 22 May 1998 Patrick issued a cross-claim in the conspiracy action alleging that the MUA had been 'interfering with Patrick's customer relationships by inducing people to interfere with their award obligations'. On the same day the Australian Competition and Consumer Commission commenced proceedings in the Federal Court alleging that the MUA had breached the secondary boycott provisions of the Trade Practices Act by organising international black bans on ships and local blockades of Patrick's cargo-handling terminals.

dispute. One external pressure was labour law, but another was the public disapproval of the corporate arrangements manifested during the dispute.

Autopoiesis is a biological term which describes a system in which the elements of the system generate the network of operations producing the elements of the system. An autopoietic system can be contrasted with an allopoietic—'other produced'—system in which the elements are either fixed or generated by forces or elements from the system's environment. Although the elements of an autopoietic system almost certainly change, they change according to operations (criteria) of the system, not in direct response to outside pressure; so the system is 'closed'.[26] Even where the elements of the system change in response to outside pressure (here the system is 'open'), the system responds to pressures on its own terms, according to its own criteria and not upon terms established by the environment.

In biology, the autopoietic paradigm accounts for the power of organisms to control or affect the environments in which they collectively evolve and to maintain their identity in the face of pressures from these environments. Luhmann used the paradigm to explain the operation of the legal system in society. He argued that social systems are autopoietic and the legal system as a subsystem of the social system is also autopoietic. The value of autopoiesis for legal theory is that it accounts for two characteristics of the legal system: self-motivation (the dynamism of legal systems) and self-maintenance (the resistance of legal systems to outside forces). As stated by Jacobson, 'legal systems give rise to legal norms in ways that cannot be mechanically traced to forces from the environment, such as politics or religion'.[27] Luhmann preserves the autonomy of autopoietic legal systems by insisting that they are closed to legal norms (normatively closed) but open to information from the system's social environment (cognitively open).[28]

In this chapter I will apply autopoietic theory to corporate law. The value of the theory lies in explaining the normative closure of corporate law: the reproduction of particular norms in corporate law and the exclusion of certain interests from its operation. Everything that enters the sphere of corporate law is assessed according to its operations or criteria, and everything that does not fit into the code is excluded. This is clearly demonstrated by the exclusion of certain stakeholders from the corporate law, such as employees. Further, corporate law produces information internally, using its own codes and programmes. This is demonstrated by the transformation of subjects by corporations law, so that employees, wives or brothers become creditors, shareholders and directors.

---

[26] H Maturana, 'Autopoiesis' in M Zeleny (ed.), *Autopoiesis, A Theory of Living Organisation* (New York, North Holland, 1981) 21.

[27] A Jacobson, 'Autopoietic Law: The New Science of Niklas Luhmann' (1989) 87 *Michigan Law Review* 1647, at 1667.

[28] N Luhmann *The Differentiation of Society* (New York, Columbia University, 1982), at 122.

At certain times the system is cognitively open when it receives information from the external environment. This process has been described as follows:

> the environment acts on the system not by directing information to it . . . but by means of the perturbations that it inflicts on the system's means of closure.[29]

Teubner elaborates by arguing that the system (corporate law) is 'forced by the uproar outside, by the "noise" of the economic actors, to vary its internal "order" until relative quiet returns'.[30] Once the relative quiet returns reflexive reasoning resumes, as does normative closure.

Corporate Law Norms in the Patrick Case

This section will relate the norms of corporate law which were operative in the Patrick dispute. The first limb involves a consideration of fundamental principles underpinning the corporate law, such as limited liability and separate legal personality. The application of these principles within corporate groups gives rise to difficulties because the separate legal personality of individual companies within the group is preserved. This atomisation insulates companies in the group from the responsibilities of other companies and enables companies with substantial liabilities to be dispensed with. Limited liability also shields individual companies in so far as they are shareholders of other companies in the group except in limited circumstances where insolvent trading has occurred. The analysis treats the corporation as a nexus of contracts.[31] This paradigm currently dominates Australian corporate law.[32]

The second limb considers the exclusion of employee interests from corporate law doctrine. Overall, corporate law and practice have ignored the interests of employees, though this omission has been under attack for decades. Within the realm of corporate law, the legal model of the company and the interpretation of corporate interests as synonymous with shareholder interests externalises the interests of employees.

---

[29] J-P Dupuy, 'On the Supposed Closure of Normative Systems' in G Teubner (ed.), *Autopoietic Law: A New Approach to Law and Society* (Berlin, W. de Gruyter, 1988) 51, at 55.

[30] G Teubner, 'Social Order from Legislative Noise' in G Teubner (ed.), *State, Law and Economy as Autopoietic Systems* (Milan, Giuferb, 1988) 62.

[31] This analysis regards the corporation as a utilitarian invention designed to reduce the costs of administering a web of ongoing contracts between people. Thus corporate law is a set of standard instructions for contractual governance. The concept has its origins in R Coase, 'The Nature of the Firm' (1937) 4 *Economica* 386, and was elaborated by M Jensen and W Meckling, 'Theory of the Firm: Managerial Behaviour, Agency Costs and Ownership Structure' (1976) 3 *Journal of Financial Economics* 305.

[32] The main body currently responsible for legislative reform of Australian corporate law is the Corporate Law Economic Reform Program and this body bases its platform upon the nexus of contract model of the corporation. However, many commentators object to the model: see, e.g., L Mitchell (ed.), *Progressive Corporate Law* (Boulder, Westview Press, 1995).

Corporate Groups

All this pretence seems unusual and probably highly unethical to most ordinary Australians. But it is par for the course in commercial manoeuvrings.[33]

The limited liability of shareholders is at the heart of corporate law and the development of the modern corporation. Although the corporation ostensibly developed to facilitate fundraising in large-scale ventures, it was clear by the time of *Salomon's case* that individual trading with limited liability was legitimate.[34] Once separate legal personality was recognised for the private company,[35] this personality and its companion—limited liability—became the *raison d'être* of corporate law. Moreover very soon after the passage of the Companies Act (UK) and its antipodean successors it became apparent that the primary motive for incorporation was not the raising of capital but the 'desire for emancipation from the "tyranny of unlimited liability" '.[36] Although tax planning now vies with limited liability as the primary motive for incorporation, it is clear that limited liability remains a fundamental characteristic of the corporation. As stated by Freiberg:

> Increasingly, companies are not created to facilitate the accumulation of capital for the purposes of private, productive enterprises, but for the purpose of protecting accumulated wealth by placing it out of the reach of creditors.[37]

The creation of a corporation in order to shift assets away from creditors is now an acceptable form of corporate planning, and the doctrine of limited liability insulates investors in companies from the claims of creditors. This clearly places creditors at risk, but creditors can protect themselves by determining how much risk they will bear in dealing with the firm and adjusting their contractual terms to compensate for any risks that limited liability will impose upon them.[38] Different considerations apply to involuntary creditors such as tort creditors because terms cannot be negotiated prior to the event and the creditworthiness of the tortfeasor cannot be assessed.[39]

---

[33] H Glasbeek and R Mitchell, 'Breaking Custom on Labour Law', *Australian Financial Review*, 27 Apr. 1998, at 18.

[34] P Ireland, 'The Rise of the Limited Liability Company' (1984) 12 *International Journal of the Sociology of Law* 239, at 255.

[35] A proposition which was decided in *Salomon* v. *Salomon & Co. Ltd* [1897] AC 22.

[36] A Freiberg, 'Abuse of the Corporate Form: Reflections from the Bottom of the Harbour' (1987) 10 *University of New South Wales Law Journal* 67, at 69, quoting F Palmer, *Private Companies* 11th edn., (London, Stevens & Sons, 1901), at 6.

[37] *Ibid.*

[38] H Hansmann and R Kraakman, 'Towards Unlimited Shareholder Liability for Corporate Torts' (1991) 100 *Yale Law Journal* 1879, at 1919.

[39] Some commentators have argued that shareholders should be liable in particular circumstances for tort claims: see, e.g., Hansmann and Kraakman, *supra* n.38; R Carroll, 'Corporate Parents and Tort Liability' in M Gillooly (ed.), *The Law Relating to Corporate Groups* (Sydney, Federation Press, 1993) 91. Note also the statements of Rogers AJA in *Briggs* v. *James Hardie & Co. Ltd* (1989) 7 ACLC 841, at 863–4.

Employees have traditionally been classified as voluntary creditors, and many writers place employees upon an equal footing with financial creditors, arguing that the vulnerability of employees to limited liability is balanced by the priority they are accorded upon liquidation.[40] Others argue that employees suffer the most severe informational disabilities of all consensual creditors and have the least capacity to absorb losses.[41] These qualities mean that employees will be unable to assess the risks in dealing with the firm and will also be unable to decline to deal with the firm if the risks seem excessive in comparison to the net advantage which they will otherwise derive from the transaction.[42] Despite these arguments, employees have not received additional protection and the needs of creditors have not substantially displaced limited liability, except in particular contexts involving insolvency.

Limited liability also promotes the expendability of particular corporations. The absence of minimum share capital requirements allow easy access to the entity at low cost. Such a low cost vehicle is readily expended. Corporate expendability may have reached its zenith in Australia during the 1970s when companies with substantial tax liabilities were expended by being liquidated or 'sent to the bottom of the harbour'.[43] The bottom of the harbour schemes pushed the commercial morality of limited liability beyond acceptable limits but their proliferation demonstrates clearly the observation of Hadden that there is a continuum between legitimate and illegitimate conduct.[44]

A particular application of Hadden's observation concerns the operation of limited liability and expendability in corporate groups. The reasons for creation of a corporate group are manifold. The formation of subsidiaries allows an enterprise to grow, for example, where a subsidiary is incorporated to conduct a new line of business or a partly owned subsidiary is set up pursuant to a partnership or joint venture.[45] Operating an enterprise by way of a group can also lower taxation through loss transfers and incorporation of subsidiaries in tax havens.[46] However, a primary reason why corporations grow into corporate groups is that this structure allows some companies in the group to be insulated from the liability incurred by other legal units within the enterprise.[47] This insulation will promote expendability, as described by Templeman LJ:

[40] Pursuant to Corporations Law, s 556 and its equivalent provisions. See R Posner, 'The Rights of Creditors of Affiliated Corporations' (1976) 43 *University of Chicago Law Review* 505; Companies and Securities Advisory Committee (CASAC), *Corporate Groups Discussion Paper* (1998).

[41] A Muscat, *The Liability of the Holding Company for the Debts of its Insolvent Subsidiary* (Aldershot, Dartmouth, 1996), at 184.

[42] Hansmann and Kraakman, *supra* n.38, at 1921.

[43] P McCabe and D Lafranchi, *Report of Inspectors Appointed to Investigate the Particular Affairs of Navillus Pty. Ltd and 922 Other Companies* (1982).

[44] T Hadden, 'Fraud in the City: The Role of the Criminal Law' [1983] *Criminal Law Review* 500, at 500–1.

[45] *Ibid.*, at 14–5.

[46] I Ramsay and G Stapledon, *Corporate Groups in Australia* (Melbourne, Centre for Corporate Law and Securities Regulation, University of Melbourne, 1998), at 14.

[47] Muscat, *supra* n.41, at 47.

A parent company may spawn a number of subsidiary companies. . . . If one of the subsidiary companies . . . turns out to be the runt of the litter and declines into insolvency to the dismay of its creditors, the parent company and other subsidiary companies may prosper to the joy of shareholders without any liability for the debts of the insolvent company.[48]

How is expendability promoted in the group context? Apart from some accounting requirements, the law does not recognise unity of enterprise and therefore does not vest responsibility in the corporate group itself.[49] Liability is imposed upon the individual components rather than the group itself. Thus the legal personality of single entities within the group is preserved.[50] Limited liability operates to ensure that the assets of one group member may not be used to satisfy judgment against another company in the group. The only coherent principle which displaces this rule is insolvent trading.[51] The rule may also be displaced by judicial decision to lift the corporate veil, although the body of case law in which this occurs is motley and indeterminate.[52]

Farrar argues that many of the problems in this area emanate from the confusion of separate legal personality with limited liability. He states that the rise of corporate groups coupled with a strict application of the *Salomon* principle has led to 'the possibility of limited liability within limited liability' which arguably goes beyond the intention of the legislature.[53]

Applying the above observations to the Patrick dispute, it is clear that the restructure occurred to enable the group to expend the employer companies and consequentially their employees. These companies were only connected to the remainder of the group by the tenuous labour supply agreements with their peremptory severance clauses. It is clear from the discussion above that these arrangements do not breach corporate law.

---

[48] *Re Southard and Co. Ltd* [1979] 1 WLR 1198, at 1208, *per* Templeman LJ.

[49] CASAC, *supra* n.40, at 13 ff.

[50] *Walker* v. *Wimborne* (1976) 137 CLR 1, at 6–7; *Industrial Equity* v. *Blackburn* (1977) 137 CLR 567.

[51] Where insolvent trading has occurred, a holding company will be liable for the debts of its subsidiary: Corporations Law, s 588V. Recent case law also establishes that a holding company may be liable for insolvent trading due to its status as shadow director of a subsidiary due to the combined operation of ss 60 and 588G of the Corporations Law: *Standard Chartered Bank* v. *Antico* (1995) 13 ACLC 1378. For discussion of these developments, see P Koh, 'Shadow Director, Shadow Director, Who Art Thou?' (1996) 14 *Company and Securities Law Journal* 340; R Carroll, 'Shadow Director and Other Third Party Liability for Corporate Activity' in I Ramsay (ed.), *Corporate Governance and the Duties of Company Directors* (Melbourne, Centre for Corporate Law and Securities, Regulation, 1997).

[52] Farrar argues that the cases can be grouped according to 'facade' and 'single economic entity': J Farrar, 'Legal Issues Involving Corporate Groups' (1998) 16 *Company and Securities Law Journal* 184, at 185. Compare the following comments of Landers about the US case law on piercing the corporate veil: '[a]lthough the literature of veil piercing is gargantuan, most of it simply describes the various factual patterns that support piercing. Devoid of any consistent doctrinal basis, the cases themselves defy any attempt at rational explanation': J Landers, 'A Unified Approach to Parent, Subsidiary, and Affiliate Questions in Bankruptcy' (1975) 42 *University of Chicago Law Review* 589, at 620.

[53] Farrar, *supra* n.52, at 189.

Employees in Corporate Law

Traditionally, neither commercial practice nor corporate law has protected the interests of employees. Management conduct of large corporations still unquestionably reflects the overriding objective of improving earnings per share and raising the market value of shares.[54] The increasing participation of institutional shareholders in corporate governance has intensified this process.[55] The ethos of profit maximisation for the benefit of shareholders was recently demonstrated by the fall of BHP from its iconic status as the friendly 'big Australian' with the closure of its Newcastle plant under pressure from shareholders.[56] Another Australian *cause célèbre* was the closure of the Cobar copper mine in February 1998.[57]

The traditional model of the corporation in law recognises only two internal organs—the board and the general meeting of shareholders. The directorial duty of care is owed to the company but, except in situations of insolvency, the interests of that body are co-terminous with the interests of shareholders. Employees do not fall within the corporate body to which directors owe fiduciary duties. This approach has been under attack for a sustained period as a part of the social responsibility debate, that is, are directors bound by their fiduciary duties to promote the interests of shareholders exclusively or can they pay regard to a broader constituency in acting in the best interests of the company?[58] Hill has documented the progression in the debate from its inception in the contest between Berle and Dodd in the early 1930s.[59] Berle considered that shareholders should be the sole focus of directors' fiduciary duties and the primary

---

[54] P Blumberg, 'Corporate Responsibility and the Social Crisis' (1970) 50 *Boston University Law Review* 157, at 204.

[55] It is estimated that international and Australian institutional investors hold approximately 65% of the available capital of listed companies in Australia, Australian Investment Managers' Association, *Corporate Governance: A Guide for Investment Managers and Corporations* (1997), at 5 and 13.

[56] 'BHP's rescue operation: investors welcome radical surgery for ailing division', *Australian Financial Review*, 30 Apr. 1997, at 1; 'BHP's real target: 8000 jobs', *Sydney Morning Herald*, 30 Apr., 1997, at 1.

[57] The Cobar mine was run by Cobar Mines Pty. Ltd whose parent company was Ashanti Goldfields Ltd. The only asset held by Cobar Mines was a contract to supply labour, whereas the holding company retained assets such as the land, buildings and equipment. The insolvency of Cobar Mines was precipitated by the revocation of a promise made by an upstream company to fund Cobar Mines. Due to the division of assets within the group, there were no other assets to satisfy the claims of workers or the townspeople of Cobar: *Sydney Morning Herald*, 21 Feb. 1998, at 35. Although Ashanti originally refused to pay the $9.6 million owing for leave and superannuation entitlements, it came under pressure from the Australian Securities and Investments Commission (ASIC), the Australian corporate regulator, and eventually agreed to pay $6.5 million towards the entitlement: ASIC Media Release, 7 Dec. 1998.

[58] J Hill, 'At the Frontiers of Labour Law and Corporate Law: Enterprise Bargaining, Corporations and Employees' (1995) 23 *Federal Law Review* 204, at 210.

[59] A A Berle, 'Corporate Powers as Powers in Trust' (1931) 44 *Harvard Law Review* 1049; E Dodd, 'For Whom Are Corporate Managers Trustees?' (1932) 45 *Harvard Law Review* 1145; A A Berle, 'For Whom Corporate Managers *Are* Trustees: A Note' (1932) 45 *Harvard Law Review* 1365.

goal of directors in exercising their fiduciary duties should be the maximisation of shareholder profit. Dodd argued that directors may exercise their fiduciary powers to benefit a wider constituency, notably employees, creditors and consumers.[60] Hill argues that since the Berle/Dodd debate corporate doctrine has shifted in diverse ways from the narrow Berle approach to one that is more consonant with Dodd's vision.[61]

In relation to employees, this claim is, with respect, overly optimistic. Certain legislative changes have protected employee interests: the most important examples are the priority accorded to certain employee entitlements upon winding up[62] and the recognition of employee share schemes.[63] However the main body currently responsible for legislative reform is the Corporate Law Economic Reform Program and this body bases its platform upon the nexus of contract model of the corporation, accompanied by the fiduciary principle where shareholders are the primary beneficiaries. The reported cases feature very few disputes where there has been a direct contest between shareholder and employee interests.[64] The famous examples are cases involving gifts to employees such as *Hutton* v. *West Cork Railway*[65] where Bowen LJ sagely reminded us that there should be 'no cakes and ale' for employees 'except as required for the benefit of the company' and *Parke* v. *Daily News Ltd* where the court held that use of the proceeds of sale of a company to make an *ex gratia* payment to redundant employees rather than being returned to shareholders was *ultra vires*. Plowman J summed up the philosophy of the law in this area when he stated:

> the defendants were prompted by motives which, however laudable, and however enlightened from the point of view of industrial relations, were such as the law does not recognise as sufficient justification.[66]

There have been other obiter comments made about the value of taking into account the interests of the wider community and how those interests can be reconciled with those of the shareholders,[67] but overwhelmingly the standard of shareholder primacy remains. In fact Blumberg considered that the Berle view had ultimately been vindicated.[68]

Employee interests may sometimes be promoted indirectly because the particular

---

[60] Hill, *supra*, n.58, at 210.

[61] *Ibid.*, at 212.

[62] Corporations Law, s 556.

[63] E.g., restrictions on providing financial assistance to acquire shares do not apply to an employee, provided legislative requirements are satisfied (ss 113(1), 260C(4)) and employees employed by a proprietary company or any of its subsidiaries are excluded for the purposes of the maximum proprietary company membership rule (s 113(1)).

[64] S Fisher, 'Corporate Gifts—Some Organising Principles', Conference Paper, Corporate Law Teachers' Association Conference, University of Technology Sydney, 1994.

[65] (1883) 23 Ch D 654, at 673.

[66] [1962] Ch 927, at 963.

[67] E.g., *Teck Corp. Ltd* v. *Millar* (1973) 33 DLR (3d) 288, at 313 (Berger J).

[68] Blumberg, *supra* n.54, at 174, states: 'In areas other than charitable contributions the fundamental question of the primacy of profit-orientation as the test of validity of corporate action has not yet been resolved in favour of recognition of interests other than those of the shareholder'.

employees fall within the description of another stakeholder (for example, creditor) or because their interests are aligned with another body (for example, the corporate entity) during the defence of a takeover bid.[69] In the Patrick dispute the MUA pleaded breach of section 1324 Corporations Law and that employees as creditors have standing under that section.[70] A potential breach of section 232(2) Corporations Law also may have arisen because the employer companies were technically insolvent and therefore the extension of the directorial fiduciary duty to creditors operates.[71] However, there is a problem about the timing. Section 232(2) could not be used to unravel the corporate restructure because the restructure occurred prior to the point at which the employer companies either approached insolvency or became insolvent, therefore no duty would be owed at that time.

The operation of corporate law in the Patrick restructure revealed its qualities as a system which is self-referential and normatively closed. It is built upon the norms of limited liability and separate legal personality. Although employees *per se* are disregarded, they are frequently transformed into the category of voluntary creditors who must adjust their terms to compensate for the risks that limited liability places upon them, including the risk of corporate expendability. Even though the production and reproduction of these norms in corporate groups gives rise to potential injustice, the closure of the system protects these norms and renders transactions based on these norms legal.[72]

'THE UPROAR OUTSIDE'

There is always a danger of romanticising one's youth, but in my days—if I can use that expression—people were not inclined to ask if something was legal in the way

---

[69] The courts have held that the directors of a target board may be acting *bona fide* in the interests of the company as a whole if they defend a takeover bid, even if shareholders will receive a substantial premium. Upon this reasoning the beneficiary of the duty is the corporate entity, not the shareholders as a body: see *Pine Vale Investments Ltd* v. *McDonnell & East* (1983) 8 ACLR 199; *Darvall* v. *North Sydney Brick and Tile* (1989) 15 ACLR 230.

[70] *Broken Hill Proprietary Co. Ltd* v. *Bell Resources Ltd* (1984) 2 ACLC 157; *Allen* v. *Atalay* (1994) 12 ACLC 7; *Airpeak Pty. Ltd* v. *Jetstream Aircraft Ltd* (1997) 23 ACSR 715. Section 1324 Corporations Law gives the Court power to grant an injunction restraining a contravention or attempted contravention of the Corporations Law upon the application of a person "whose interests have been, are or would be affected by the conduct."

[71] *Walker* v. *Wimborne, supra* n.50; *Kinsela* v. *Russell Kinsela Pty. Ltd (in liq.)* (1986) 10 ACLR 395. Section 232(2) Corporations Law states that "an officer of a Corporation shall at all times act honestly in the exercise of his or her powers and in the discharge of the duties of his or her office."

[72] This statement may be qualified by the secrecy surrounding the restructure. Secrecy negates the 'voluntary creditor' arguments and, given that the restructure was effected during a pre-existing relationship, it adds an element of misrepresentation. Consider the following comments of Posner: '[t]he other and more important case in which piercing the corporate veil may be warranted is where separate incorporation is misleading to creditors. . . . If corporations are permitted to represent that they have greater assets to pay creditors than they actually have, the result will be to increase the costs that creditors must incur to ascertain the true creditworthiness of the corporations with which they deal. Misrepresentation is a way of increasing a creditor's information costs, and the added costs are wasted from a social standpoint to the extent that the misrepresentation could be prevented at a lower cost by an appropriate sanction against it'. Posner regards such misrepresentation as fraud justifying piercing the corporate veil: Posner, *supra* n.40, at 520–1.

that the people advising Patrick may have asked, but the question was: did it pass the smell test? [73]

The paradox of corporate law as an autopoietic system is that it may construct its own reality by recursive operations but at the same time it is exposed to the constraints of external reality. On Teubner's view, the 'uproar outside' forces the system to vary its internal order until relative quiet returns. What was the 'uproar outside' in the Patrick dispute?

After the 7 April lock out, pickets sprang up in every Patrick port in Australia. Patrick sought injunctions against the picketers[74] and then sought further injunctions when the injunctions were breached.[75] The International Transport Workers' Union placed black bans on ships loaded by non-union labour on Patrick wharves and Patrick unsuccessfully sought injunctions against these black bans in the UK High Court. Surveys taken during the dispute indicated that the dismissal attracted significant public disopprobrium which increased over the duration of the dispute.[76] Frank Costigan QC, who was instrumental in exposing the bottom of the harbour frauds, stated:

> The events surrounding the late-night sacking of the workers, enforced by security guards and dogs, coupled with asset stripping of the employing companies, constitute an example of financial, corporate and industrial misbehaviour which is unacceptable in this country.
>
> It is for the courts to determine its legality. For my part, I am bound to declare that it is offensive to ordinary concepts of decent behaviour.[77]

Evidence presented during the hearings pointed to 'corporate and industrial misbehaviour' and, in particular, a scheme to legally dismiss the workforce then to rehire non-union labour.[78] Although—as Glasbeek and Mitchell remind us—such corporate manœuvrings are commonplace, in this case the manœurvrings were used to sanction what would otherwise have been an immoral exercise under labour law. The critical question was whether corporate law would be cognitively open to the ethics of labour law or would remain normatively closed. Callinan J in the High Court preferred the latter course:

---

[73] Commonwealth of Australia, *Parliamentary Debates*, Senate, 29 May 1998, 3197 (Senator Cooney).

[74] *Patrick Stevedores Operations Pty. Ltd* v. *MUA & Ors*, Supreme Court of Victoria, *per* Beach J, 20 Apr. 1998, http://scaleplus.law.gov.au.

[75] *MUA & Ors* v. *Patrick Stevedores Operations Pty. Ltd*, Court of Appeal, Supreme Court of Victoria, *per* Winneke P, Brooking and Charles JJA, 28 Apr. 1998, http://scaleplus.law.gov.au.

[76] E.g., surveys taken by the Morgan Poll and published in *The Bulletin*, 5 May 1998, showed that the number of respondents who approved of the dismissal of the workers had dropped from 50% to 46% in the period from 15/16 Apr. to 21/22 Apr. In the same period, the number of respondents who disapproved rose from 39% to 46%: Morgan Poll, http://www.roymorgan.com/polls/1998, Finding No 3079.

[77] F Costigan, 'Asset-shifting rings a bell', *Sydney Morning Herald*, 23 Apr. 1998, at 17.

[78] E.g., see the briefing paper of the meeting between representatives of the Patrick group and Mr Reith, dated 12 Mar. 1997, extracted in the judgment of North J, *supra* n.10, at 610–1.

Business people and corporations must be entitled to set a rate of return at a level that they need to achieve to justify the effort and capital employed in a business, in default of which they are entitled to discontinue that business and use their capital and effort elsewhere.[79]

Orr rejoined:

Patrick did not simply discontinue its business but was seeking to cast off a unionised workforce in a manner designed to avoid some of the protections of the *Workplace Relations Act*.[80]

Jacobson has argued that cognitive openness and therefore change occurs in common law jurisdictions by the communication of individuals.[81] The process is demonstrated by the communications of the Federal Court, using the devices of the interlocutory injunction and the implied term of trust and confidence in the employment contract. The next section will question the effect of these devices upon corporate law norms and doctrine.

THE FEDERAL COURT

At first instance and in the Full Court, the Federal Court was receptive to labour law doctrine and adopted an interpretation of the dispute which allowed labour law discourses to flourish. However, in doing so, the judges used the remedy of the interlocutory injunction and substantive labour law to displace corporate law doctrine. These two devices will be analysed in turn.

Interlocutory Injunctions and the Corporate Veil

The great irony of the waterfront dispute is that the key tactical breakthrough came when the MUA turned back against Patrick the legal remedy normally used by employers against unions in industrial disputes—the interlocutory injunction.[82]

It is important that the MUA sought interlocutory injunctions in these proceedings.[83] Its importance for corporate law lies in the fact that the doctrine of separate legal personality is frequently ignored by the courts when interlocutory relief is sought. Interlocutory injunctions have been described by Leubsdorf as 'the most striking remedy wielded by contemporary courts'[84] and they may be used creatively by courts to lift the corporate veil.

---

[79] *Patrick Stevedores Operations No 2 Pty. Ltd* v. *Maritime Union of Australia* (1998) 153 ALR 643, 648, at 709, *per* Callinan J.

[80] Orr, *supra* n.2, at 172.

[81] Jacobson, *supra* n.27, at 1681.

[82] *Australian Financial Review*, 26 June 1998, at 24.

[83] An interlocutory injunction is an injunction that is limited so as to apply only until the final hearing or final determination by the court of the rights of the parties: I Spry, *Equitable Remedies*, 5th edn., Sydney, Law Book Company, 1997), at 446.

[84] J Leubsdorf, 'The Standard for Preliminary Injunctions' (1978) 91 *Harvard Law Review* 525.

The object of an interlocutory injunction is to preserve the *status quo* pending the final hearing of the action or determination of the dispute.[85] An injunction may be issued at a time when the evidence is incomplete and without the benefit of a full hearing. The standard which is adopted aims to balance the damage caused by errors incidental to hasty decision-making with the irreparable harm which may occur if urgent relief is not granted. The test for the grant of an interlocutory injunction is whether there is a serious question to be tried and whether the balance of convenience favours the grant. However, the grant or refusal of the interlocutory injunction will often irrevocably determine the issue between the parties, either due to the nature of the dispute itself or because the parties settle the dispute outside the courts.[86] Moreover, an appellate court will only in exceptional circumstances interfere with the discretion exercised by a court in granting or refusing an interlocutory injunction. It is not enough that the appellate court would have exercised its discretion differently.[87]

As a general proposition the courts increasingly ignore the strict mandates of the corporate veil when they are dealing with interlocutory matters.[88] McHugh J expressed the philosophy as follows:

> Why should the court be bound by all this formalism at this late stage of the 20th century? They were not bound by it in the *MUA Case*.[89]

It might be that the judicial perception is that the balance of convenience favours substantive rights over formal rights. North J expressed this view when considering the balance of convenience in the *Patrick* case:

> Section 298K(1) of the *Workplace Relations Act* gives an important protection of the individual rights of employees to belong to a union if they choose. The Court should perhaps be more ready to protect such rights than merely financial interests.[90]

---

[85] *American Cyanamid Co.* v. *Ethicon Ltd* [1975] AC 396, at 406.

[86] *Kolback Securities Ltd* v. *Epoch Mining NL* (1987) 8 NSWLR 533, at 536, *per* McLelland J.

[87] Spry, *supra* n 83, at 447; *Hadmore Productions Ltd* v. *Hamilton* [1983] 1 AC 191, at 220; *Garden Cottage Foods Ltd* v. *Milk Marketing Board* [1984] AC 130.

[88] In *Cardile* v. *LED Builders Pty Ltd* (1999) 162 ALR 294 the High Court held that a Mareva injunction could be granted against the shareholders of the defendant and a related company (neither of whom was a defendant in the action). For another example of this development, compare the House of Lords decision in *Lonrho Ltd* v. *Shell* [1980] 1 WLR 627 with *Sabre Corporation P/L* v. *Russ Kalvin's Hair Co.* (1993) 124 ALR 400. In *Lonrho* a party to litigation was seeking discovery of documents which were held by a subsidiary 100% owned by the defendant. The applicant argued that the documents were in the 'power' of the parent company because, as sole shareholder, it could procure the board to produce the documents or amend the articles to entitle the shareholders to inspect and take copies of the documents. It was held that the documents were not within the 'power' of the parent company and they were not required by the Supreme Court Rules to procure production any more than a natural person is obliged to ask a close relative or anyone else who is a stranger to the suit to provide him with copies of documents in the ownership or possession of that other person. In *Sabre* it was held that if a document is owned by a company but the party has control of the company then the party can require the company to produce it.

[89] Transcript of proceedings before the High Court of Australia in *Cardile* v. *LED Builders Pty. Ltd*, 7 Oct. 1998.

[90] *Supra* n.10, at 605.

His Honour found a serious issue to be tried in that, by dividing the functions of employing workers and owning the business between two companies, the Patrick group put in place a structure which made it easier to dismiss the whole workforce. It was also arguable that this was done because the employees were members of the Union. So there was an arguable case that the Patrick had acted in breach of section 298K(1) of the Workplace Relations Act.

The injunctions granted by North J compelled the operating companies to treat the employer companies as their sole supplier of labour under the labour supply agreements which he regarded as necessary to maintain the employment of the employees to prevent the fulfilment of the alleged conspiracy. Another injunction was directed to the employer companies requiring them treat the labour supply agreements as remaining on foot. A further order restrained each Patrick respondent from dealing with or divesting its assets other than in the ordinary course of business. So framed, the orders took effect as mandatory injunctions. Traditionally courts are reluctant to issue mandatory injunctions and Dal Pont and Chalmers state that the 'bulk of English and Australian authority suggests that . . . the court must feel a "high degree of assurance" that at the trial it will appear that the injunction was rightly granted'.[91] Several judges have questioned this approach, notably Gummow J who has commented that, although 'there has been a natural reluctance to decree burdensome relief without a full hearing, prohibitory injunctions may have that tendency just as much as mandatory relief'.[92] However, both schools of thought were accommodated by North J in his *Patrick* judgment, when he stated that although he favoured the Gummow J view, he had reached the 'high degree of assurance' required by the stricter view.

The power of the Federal Court to make these orders was challenged on appeal to the Full Federal Court, where the issue of the separate legal personality of the corporate respondents, particularly the operators, was dealt with squarely. The Full Court stated:

> Although these companies were closely associated with the Patrick employers, being all members of the group of companies ultimately owned by Lang Corporation Ltd, and Patrick Stevedores Operations Pty Ltd being the owner of all the shares in the four employer companies, the two companies that North J called 'Patrick operators' are different legal entities to the four companies he called 'Patrick employers'.[93]

Patrick argued that because the Workplace Relations Act contained no accessorial provisions,[94] it does not extend to orders that affect the rights of or impose

---

[91] G Dal Pont and D Chalmers, *Equity and Trusts in Australia and New Zealand* (North Ryde, LBC Information Services, 1996), at 585.

[92] *Businessworld Computers Pty. Ltd* v. *Australian Telecommunications Commission* (1988) 82 ALR 499, at 502–4.

[93] *Patrick Stevedores Operations No 2 Pty. Ltd* v. *Maritime Union of Australia* (1998) 153 ALR 626, at 631.

[94] E.g., 'aiding and abetting' or 'knowingly concerned' such as in the Trade Practices Act 1974 (Cth), s 75B.

duties on persons other than the employer.[95] The Full Court agreed, stating that it was 'extremely doubtful' that the Workplace Relations Act authorised the orders made by North J. But—and here's the rub—it did not follow that those orders were beyond power. The Federal Court has power, pursuant to section 23 of the Federal Court Act 1976 (Cth), to make orders, including interlocutory orders, as the Court thinks appropriate. Here North J had found a serious question for trial that a conspiracy to breach the Workplace Relations Act had occurred and it was necessary for the court to grant injunctive relief to prevent or mitigate irreparable damage. So the combination of the cause of action in conspiracy (which necessarily involves additional parties who need not be sued under the Workplace Relations Act) and the nature of the remedy sought (an interlocutory injunction) allowed for a departure from strict adherence to the principle of separate legal personality.

In the High Court Callinan J disagreed with this reasoning, stating that the courts should be

> cautious in making orders based on special legislation relating to parties of a particular status or in a particular relationship, binding upon persons or corporations not having the requisite status or not being in the relevant relationship.[96]

However, the majority and Gaudron J generally concurred with the orders made by North J, the majority judgment stating that the width of the interlocutory orders was justified to prevent frustration of the process of the Federal Court. Gaudron J referred to this type of order as a 'jurisdiction protection order'. The majority judgment stated:

> If the power of the Federal Court to prevent the frustration of its process was to be effective, extraordinary orders were needed to ensure that, if the employees were successful in the final hearing, the employer companies, from which the employees derived such security of employment as they had, could be maintained in existence as stevedores or as the continuing suppliers of labour in the stevedoring business. If that could not be done, the conduct of the Group which had altered the position of the employees to their prejudice would lead inevitably to the dismissal of the employees.[97]

The extract focuses upon the true locus of the impugned conduct—the corporate group. However, in the High Court an analytical shift occurred which placed much greater emphasis upon the insolvency and the placement of the employer companies into voluntary administration. This issue will be dealt with in the fifth part of this chapter.

---

[95] Relying on *Ascot Investments Pty. Ltd* v. *Harper* (1981) 148 CLR 337.
[96] *Supra* n.9, at 701.
[97] *Ibid.*, at 659, *per* Brennan CJ, McHugh, Gummow, Kirby and Hayne JJ.

The Implied Term of Trust and Confidence

The Federal Court also relied upon substantive doctrines of labour law to miti-gate the effect of the corporate restructure, in particular the implied term of trust and confidence. The term is well established in contracts of employment in England and states that the employer will not act in a manner likely to destroy or seriously damage the relationship of trust and confidence between employer and employee.[98] In the case of *Malik* v. *Bank of Credit and Commerce Inter-national SA (in liqn)*[99] the House of Lords found that the term was breached by an employer bank which had operated a dishonest and corrupt business. The two employee plaintiffs lost their jobs when the bank collapsed in 1991. They claimed that their association with the bank had 'stigmatised' them and placed them at a serious disadvantage in finding new jobs. The House of Lords allowed them to pursue their claim for damages for the stigma against the liquidator of the bank.

The term is implied into employment contracts as a matter of law. In order for Australian courts to follow *Malik* and imply the term into Australian employment contracts, the test of necessity established in *Byrne* v. *Australian Airlines*[100] would need to be satisfied. This means that it will be necessary to imply the term only if, without the term, the contract would be, from the view-point of the employee, 'rendered nugatory', 'deprived of its substance, seriously undermined or drastically devalued in an important respect'.[101] At least one commentator has stated that there should be little difficulty for an Australian court in finding that the implied term exists here when called upon to decide the matter authoritatively.[102]

In the Patrick dispute, the MUA argued that the term should be implied into the employment contract and that it had been breached. Justice North found that there was a serious question to be tried that, first, the employer companies were in breach by entering into the business purchase agreement and the labour supply agreement and appointing the administrators; secondly, that there was an agreement between the Patrick defendants to replace the union workforce with non-union labour, and that they knew this would require the employer companies to breach the implied term.[103]

However, the implied term will constitute a 'cognitive opening' only if it effects a change to corporate law doctrine. This is tricky because the traditional model of the corporation in law does not recognise employee interests—they are

---

[98] D Brodie, 'The Heart of the Matter: Mutual Trust and Confidence' (1996) 25 *Industrial Law Journal* 121.

[99] [1997] 3 All ER 1, at 15.

[100] (1995) 185 CLR 410.

[101] G McCarry, 'Damages for Breach of the Employer's Implied Duty of Trust and Confidence' (1998) 26 *Australian Business Law Review* 141, at 144, citing the judgment of McHugh and Gummow JJ in *Byrne, supra* n.100, at 453.

[102] McCarry, *supra* n.101, at 144.

[103] *Supra* n.10, at 612–3.

outside its parameters. Technically, the nexus of contracts model of the corporation could more readily interconnect with employee interests because, unlike previous theories, the contractual analysis has no place for a reified notion of the company.[104] The position of shareholders is explained in terms of their relationship with the other parties and their rights as contractual entitlements to which all the parties would agree *ex ante*. Increasingly labour law itself has relied upon the contractual model of employee entitlement which emphasises individual workplace bargains. There is a danger, in emphasising private arrangements between autonomous individuals, because the nexus of contract theory is ideological as well as explanatory. However, the theory's promotion of liberal utilitarianism has been mitigated by scholars who emphasise relational contracting[105] and contract law itself which increasingly imposes good faith obligations.[106] If we assume that labour law can interlock with the corporation as a nexus of contracts and that relational contracting is possible, it is important to consider what effect the terms of the labour contract might have on the corporation.

In the Patrick dispute, it is significant that a term of an employment contract was able to impugn a corporate restructure. In implying the term, North J evaded the mandates of separate legal personality in the corporate group by finding an agreement or a conspiracy and rendered limited liability otiose by holding the group accountable. Thus cognitive openness resulted in corporate norms yielding to labour law morality.

THE HIGH COURT: STRATEGIC INSOLVENCY AND MURDER BY DEATH

Operational closure of law raises the suspicion of a new legal formalism, of a self-sustaining autarchy of law.[107]

By comparison with the Federal Court the majority in the High Court perceived the dispute as a corporate law dispute. In particular their Honours found that the provisions of the Workplace Relations Act operated within the context of the voluntary administration and that the discretion of the administrators should not be fettered by that Act. By recognising the insolvency, the High Court adopted formalist reasoning—that formal compliance with Part 5.3A of the Corporations Law was sufficient to allow a voluntary administration to continue. The decision gave rise to significant confusion. Its reasoning was con-

---

[104] R Grantham, 'The Doctrinal Basis of the Rights of Company Shareholders' (1998) 57 *Cambridge Law Journal* 554, at 579.

[105] E.g., M Whincop, 'A Relational and Doctrinal Critique of Shareholders' Special Contracts' (1997) 19 *Sydney Law Review* 314; M Whincop, 'Overcoming Corporate Law: Instrumentalism, Pragmatism and the Separate Legal Personality Concept' (1997) 15 *Company and Securities Law Journal* 411.

[106] J Beatson and D Friedmann (eds.), *Good Faith and Fault in Contract Law* (Melbourne, Oxford University Press, 1995), at 15.

[107] G Teubner, 'Introduction to Autopoietic Law' in Teubner, *supra* n.29, at 2.

tentious because it attributed the characteristics of a real insolvency to a strategic insolvency. In autopoietic terms, the decision amounted to normative closure; the court applied reflexive reasoning to allow corporate law norms to exclude labour law norms.

Voluntary Administration Generally

Voluntary administration is regulated by Part 5.3A of the Corporations Law. Following the recommendations of the Australian Law Reform Commission (ALRC),[108] this Part was introduced into the Corporations Law through the Corporate Law Reform Act 1992 (Cth) and came into effect in 1993. The ALRC recommended the procedure to allow companies facing liquidity problems to deal with those problems over a short period in an attempt to preserve their property and business. The investigations conducted by the ALRC indicated that the existing corporate rescue procedures were too costly and unwieldy. Accordingly, there was very little emphasis upon or encouragement of a constructive approach to corporate insolvency by, for example, 'focussing upon the possibility of saving a business . . . and preserving employment prospects'.[109]

Section 435A states the object of Part 5.3A as follows:

> The object of this Part is to provide for the business, property and affairs of an insolvent company to be administered in a way that:
> (a) maximises the chances of the company, or as much as possible of its business, continuing in existence; or
> (b) if it is not possible for the company or its business to continue in existence—results in a better return for the company's creditors and members than would result from an immediate winding up of the company.

The effect of the provisions is to impose a short 'breathing space' within which an insolvency practitioner (the administrator) can to examine the position and make an informed recommendation to the company's creditors.

The administrator is generally appointed by a resolution of the board that, in the opinion of the directors voting for the resolution, the company is insolvent or is likely to become insolvent at some future time and an administrator should be appointed.[110] The administration procedure is open to companies which are not insolvent at the time when the resolution is passed, provided that the directors are satisfied that there is a likelihood that the company will become insolvent at some future time.[111] The latitude in the timing allows directors to initiate

---

[108] Australian Law Reform Commission, *General Insolvency Inquiry* (Report No 45, 1988) (Harmer Report).

[109] *Ibid.*, at para 52.

[110] Corporations Law, s 436A. A person is solvent under s 95A(1) if he or she is able to pay all his or her debts as and when they become due and payable. Under s 95A(2) a person who is not solvent is insolvent.

[111] P Crutchfield, *Corporate Voluntary Administration Law* (North Ryde, LBC Information Service, 1997) at 63.

the procedure before the duty to prevent insolvent trading arises.[112] The main governance task of the administrator is to convene a series of creditors' meetings which decide the company's future. These meetings must be convened within a short period—generally 60 to 88 days from the date of appointment.[113] Creditor voting in these meetings operates so that resolutions may be carried or not by the vote of the creditors upon a majority of voices. However, a poll may be required by the chair (usually the administrator) or two or more creditors. Votes on the poll are calculated on the value of the total debts owed to all the creditors voting. In the event of no result, the chair can use his casting vote.[114] Section 439C of the Corporations Law states what matters the creditors may decide in the meetings: to execute a deed of arrangement (if the company can trade out of the problem), end the administration (if the company is not insolvent), or to wind up the company. In exercising their vote, creditors will often act upon the report of the administrator which makes recommendations to the creditors about which of the options it is in their interests to choose.

The independence of administrators is a significant matter since they are vested with very broad powers of control[115] although this power is counterbalanced by provisions which make the administrators personally liable for debts which they incur during the performance of their functions or powers.[116] Administrators must be qualified as registered liquidators[117] and will be disqualified if they have a conflict of interest, for example, indebtedness to a related party.[118] Of course this does not mean that they will always act independently. A recent study indicated that administrators did not always act impartially and in the interests of creditors. For example administrators in the study frequently controlled creditors meetings by canvassing for proxy votes and using their casting vote.[119]

---

[112] Pursuant to the Corporations Law, s 588G.

[113] Corporations Law, s 439B(2).

[114] Voting is generally regulated by Corporations Law, ss 600A–600E and Regs 5.6.19 and 5.6.21.

[115] Corporations Law, s 437A.

[116] In particular Corporations Law, s 443A.

[117] Corporations Law, s 448B.

[118] Corporations Law, s 448C.

[119] Australian Securities Commission, *A Study of Voluntary Administrations in New South Wales*, Research Paper 98/01 (Canberra, Australian Government Printing Service, 1998), at 20. See also *Aloridge Pty. Ltd* v. *Christianos* (1994) 12 ACLC 256 where Burchett J found that the appointment of an administrator was made in order to wrest control of the company away from a provisional liquidator in the expectation that the administrator would be more compliant. Indeed Burchett J stated that the evidence led to a clear conclusion that the administrator was biased in favour of a director and major shareholder of the company. Routledge has commented that '[t]here is evidence of a general perception in the corporate community that administration will provide a "soft landing' for the officers of insolvent companies'; J Routledge, 'Voluntary Administration and Commercial Morality: Aligning the Competing Interests' (1997) 5 *Insolvency Law Journal* 125, at 132.

The Patrick Administration and its Effects

[A] couple of accountants, bound more by the perils of insolvency law, will have more say in how many wharfies are needed to perform what work and on what terms.[120]

Bill Butterell and Peter Brock were appointed administrators of the employer companies on 7 April 1998. Butterell had had 30 years' experience as an insolvency practitioner. Brock had had 14 years' experience as a liquidator and receiver, mainly in manufacturing and motor dealerships. Nothing was particularly unusual about their appointment except that it took place at 10.50 pm. Mr Clayton (the sole director of the employer companies) resolved earlier in the evening to appoint the administrators after the labour supply agreements had been terminated. The factual basis of this resolution was subsequently challenged by the administrators who reported that the employer companies appear to have been solvent at the time of the restructure and were able to pay their debts up to the date of the administrators' appointment.[121] However, as stated above, the employer companies had guaranteed a 270 million Australian dollar facility provided by the banking syndicate to the Lang group. Pursuant to this arrangement the banks had a fixed and floating charge over the assets of the employers for which they had lodged proofs of debt claiming $236 million dollars. The assets of the employer companies were substantially less than the secured debt of the banking syndicate.

The appointment of the administrators temporarily shifted the focus of waterfront reform. As often occurs in corporate law, a change of governance structure effected a transformation in the nature of the legal relationships and reconceptualised corporate subjects. The primary strategy pursued by the MUA was to seek to end the administration[122] or postpone the creditors' meetings to enable industrial negotiations to take place between the union and the company. It considered that such negotiations—on matters such as redundancy numbers and changes to work practices—should proceed through enterprise agreements and the Industrial Relations Commission.[123] But, with the appointment of the administrators, the employees became creditors and these issues became subsumed by insolvency law and practice. Critically, the banking syndicate emerged as an adversary as the MUA attempted to secure its bargaining position; and the huge debt claimed by the syndicate potentially allowed it to outvote the employees in creditors meetings. The MUA argued that the syndicate's

---

[120] *Australian Financial Review*, 5 May 1998, at 18.

[121] Thornton, *supra* n.15, at 27–8.

[122] Pursuant to the Corporations Law, s 447A, the Court may order that the administration of a company should end because, *inter alia*, the company is solvent or the provisions of Part 5.3A are being abused. The court may also declare under Corporations Law, s 447B, that the purported appointment of an administrator was not valid or remove an administrator under s 449B. During the proceedings before North J, counsel for the MUA issued an application for termination of the administration but then told his Honour that they would not move under that application until the hearing and determination of the principal proceedings.

[123] *Australian Financial Review*, 19 May 1998, at 8.

claim was too contingent given that it secured the indebtedness of other companies in the group.[124] However, the union also argued that it held proxies from 1,400 of its members which entitled each member to votes worth one million dollars each based on unpaid employment entitlements and the claim for damages in the conspiracy action.[125] Eventually the MUA was successful in securing an adjournment of the creditors meeting to enable discussions to take place between the union and Patrick.[126]

So how and why had the appointment of an administrator so utterly changed the conduct of the dispute? We can begin to answer this question by examining the High Court's analysis of the administration.

The High Court Interpretation of the Voluntary Administration

The current High Court has assumed the position of a tightrope walker. Being above the crowd but at the centre of its attention, the court wants to preserve its traditional role as the supreme arbiter of legal rights rather than political or economic interests, yet simultaneously to reinforce its authoritative voice in a secular and politically jaded society that increasingly turns to it for definitive answers to intractable social problems or large scale contests of interests.[127]

The administrators argued at each phase of the litigation that the Court should not order the employer companies to retain the workforce. Rather, the Court should let the administrators determine what the employer should do. This approach, it was argued, recognised the role of the administrators to exercise

---

[124] In *Brashs* v. *Katile* (1994) 13 ACSR 504 the Full Court of the Supreme Court of Victoria held that 'creditors' for the purposes of Part 5.3A are the same persons as those who could prove on a winding up. It has been held that creditors with unliquidated or contingent claims are able to vote on a scheme of arrangement. This category may include unliquidated claimants in tort, notwithstanding potential difficulties of assessment of value in these cases: *Re RL Child & Co. Pty. Ltd* (1986) 10 ACLR 673, at 674; *Bond Corporation Holdings Ltd* v. *Western Australia* (1992) 10 ACLC 715, at 719. In *Re Zambena Pty. Ltd* (1995) 13 ACLC 1020 it was held that guarantors were contingent creditors of the company, were entitled to vote at a meeting of creditors convened under Part 5.3A and could be bound by a deed of company arrangement.

[125] In *Green* v. *Giljohann* (1995) 17 ACSR 518 the court held that an employee was a creditor under a deed of company arrangement. However, there has been some debate about whether employees are creditors for an administration because they are entitled to priority payment on a winding up. O'Donovan argues that no injustice flows from denying employees the status of 'creditors' and the concomitant right to vote because administration should proceed on the basis that employees must be paid what they are entitled to under the Law: J O'Donovan, 'Employees, Voluntary Administrations and Deed of Company Arrangements' (1994) 12 *Company and Securities Law Journal* 457, at 457–8. Keay concurs with this view: A Keay, 'Voluntary Administrations: The Convening and Conduct of Meetings' (1996) 4 *Insolvency Law Journal* 9, at 18–19. Note however, that the Legal Committee of the Companies and Securities Advisory Committee has recommended that employees should be permitted to vote on a deed of company arrangement even if they have priority under that deed. The Committee noted the prescribed priority provisions may be excluded under the deed: *Corporate Voluntary Administration, Final Report*, June 1998, at 62.

[126] *Australian Financial Review*, 23–24 May 1998, at 4.

[127] Orr, *supra* n.2, at 173.

their powers to fulfil the objects of Part 5.3A, that is, to maximise the chances of the employer companies continuing in existence or, if that is not possible, to provide a better return for creditors and members than would result from an immediate winding up. North J at first instance in the Federal Court regarded these arguments as being beside the point. He stated:

> But the claims raised in these proceedings allege wrongful acts by the employers. The administrators need not necessarily have any concern about these claims and they may not have powers to address the issues arising from the claims. The Court has both the concern and the powers. There is nothing in the scheme of Part 5.3A which suggests that the administrator must be left to administer the companies without the intervention of the Court in such circumstances. On the contrary, the fact that administrators may not be able to address the matters raised in the proceedings makes it necessary for the Court to do so.[128]

The High Court majority took a different view. Their Honours considered that the Workplace Relations Act regulates the relationship of employer and employees but it does not alter or purport to alter the general regime prescribed under the Corporations Law for the administration of the assets of insolvent companies. The Corporations Law in Part 5.3A prescribes a regime which defines and protects the interest of third parties—creditors—in the deployment and distribution of a company's assets. Although the Workplace Relations Act deals with companies as employers it does so 'indifferently' and does not affect the regimes prescribed by laws dealing with bankruptcy and insolvency. The problem with the orders made by North J at first instance was that they took away from the administrators the discretions conferred upon them by the Corporations Law.

> The administrator must act impartially as among all parties having or claiming to have an interest in the present or future assets of the company and must make those decisions which, in the light of contemporary circumstances, best serve those interests. It is for the administrator, in exercise of the discretionary powers conferred by s437A, to decide whether or not to carry on the company's business and the form in which it should be carried on during the administration.[129]

Justice Gaudron substantially agreed with North J, stating that the powers and discretions conferred upon the administrators are not at large and must be exercised in accordance with the general law. In particular, the operation of the Workplace Relations Act is not circumscribed by legislative provisions such as section 437A which confer powers and discretions to be exercised in accordance with the general law. Callinan J considered that all orders made by North J should be discharged, so the issue at hand was irrelevant to his reasoning.

The majority and Gaudron J diverged on the question whether corporate law is or should be insulated from external doctrine and whether the ethical parameters of corporate law are qualified by labour law. Clearly the majority

---

[128] *Supra* n.10, at 621.
[129] *Supra* n.9, at 663, *per* Brennan CJ, McHugh, Gummow, Kirby and Hayne JJ.

considered that the exigencies of the administration necessitated a minimal interference by labour law. Is this position justified?

The High Court judgment was handed down at 12 noon on 4 May 1998. The television channels had suspended their usual programming of talk shows and midday movies and were presenting live coverage of the decision.

[CHANNEL NINE NEWS THEME]

Announcer: This is a special presentation of national Nine News. The High Court is about to bring down its decision on one of the biggest and most bitter industrial disputes of this century!

Paul Lyneham: Well I think there's a bit of surprise at the fact that you've got so many judges coming out so clearly on this. They hadn't sat so long just to rubber stamp North, that's for sure, otherwise they could have all been home for morning tea on day one. But the question was, the devil is always in the detail on these things of course, and we've got this long judgment, we're just out of the court room. . . . the devil is always in the detail on these things.[130]

The overwhelming reaction to the High Court decision was confusion. This confusion lasted several days during which all parties to the dispute claimed victory. Orr argued that the High Court had misconceived the case at hand:

to give purified respect to corporations law principles giving an administrator an unfettered right to decide if and how to trade . . . in the interests of some putative third party creditors, misconceived the case at hand.[131]

So did the High Court, in particular the majority, misconceive the case at hand? Recall the argument of the MUA that the final stage of the conspiracy involved the dismissal of the workforce by the administrators because the workforce would therefore be dismissed because of insolvency and not for motives which could be impugned by the Workplace Relations Act. It was not possible for the High Court upon an interlocutory application to form a concluded view about this allegation,[132] but there was clear evidence that the Patrick group had been restructured in such a way that the insolvency of the employer companies could be rapidly triggered by upstream companies through summary termination of

---

[130] *The Media Report*, Radio National Transcripts, 7 May 1998, http://www.abc.net.au/rn.

[131] Orr, *supra* n.2, at 159.

[132] There were several critical comments made from the Bench during the High Court hearing about the paucity of evidence presented by Patrick: e.g., the exchange between Mr Gyles (Counsel for Patrick) and McHugh J when his Honour was unsuccessfully seeking information about the share capital of the employer companies, transcript, 27 Apr. 1998. Further comments were made by Mr Burnside (Counsel for the MUA) the following day:

'Mr Burnside: . . . we cannot get the 1997 accounts and we have not been favoured with the 1998 balance sheet to date, or even [a] provisional balance sheet to date. All that was put forward was some figures, which are very difficult to understand, showing revenue to February 1998 and expenses to February 1998, but because the banking is done on a group basis it is impossible to dissect them and find out which companies are trading with profit or with a loss. It is just not possible.

McHugh J: One of the reasons for the restructuring was so it would be easier to monitor the performance of the individual operations.

Mr Burnside: That was one of the stated reasons, yes.'

the labour supply agreements. This arrangement allowed the upstream companies to control the solvency of the employer companies and expend them as necessary. Was this an insolvency which justified implementation of the objects of Part 5.3A, which focus upon rescuing insolvent companies for the greater protection of creditors and members?

To answer this question it is necessary to define the wider objectives of bankruptcy law.

> Bankruptcy law prevents a costly and destructive race to the firm's assets by offering a collective proceeding that freezes the rights of all investors in the firm, values them then distributes them according to a priority scheme that the parties agreed would be used in this event.[133]

There are four essential tenets of insolvency law which are pertinent to the Patrick dispute.

1. *Collective action*—insolvency law at its core is concerned with collective action and is designed to keep individual actions against the insolvent company from interfering with the best use of assets for the investors as a group.[134] The 'agreement' referred to is the creditors' bargain and mirrors the agreement that the creditors would have made amongst themselves if they had been able to negotiate before the onset of insolvency. Under this model the rules must ensure that no one creditor (or investor) has the ability to exploit the insolvency by individual action and receive more than her entitlement.[135]

2. *Harmony with non-bankruptcy rights*—insolvency law should harmonise with the general law wherever possible.

3. *Strategic behaviour*—whenever bankruptcy law changes the relative value of non-bankruptcy rights, incentives are created for inappropriate uses of the bankruptcy process. Strategic insolvency arises where the bankruptcy is invoked due to strategic decision-making rather than being a passive response to market forces. Delaney argues that a strategic bankruptcy arises when a firm mobilises the bankruptcy process in order to transform ties with other institutions or groups of individuals.[136]

4. *Rehabilitation*—this tenet is specific to the reorganisation or rescue procedures, because rehabilitation is an independent goal of the law in this area.[137] This tenet focuses upon the value of rehabilitation for providing a fresh start

---

[133] D Baird, 'The Uneasy Case for Corporate Reorganisations' in J Bhandari and L Weiss (eds.), *Corporate Bankruptcy* (New York, Cambridge University Press, 1996), 339.

[134] D Baird and T Jackson, 'Corporate Reorganisations and the Treatment of Diverse Ownership Interests: A Comment on Adequate Protection of Secured Creditors in Bankruptcy' (1984) 51 *University of Chicago Law Review* 97, at 100.

[135] Baird, *supra* n.133, at 345.

[136] K Delaney, *Strategic Bankruptcy* (Berkeley, University of California Press, 1992), at 59.

[137] Notably the Harmer Report, *supra* n.108, and the Insolvency Law Review Committee, *Insolvency Law and Practice* (Cmnd 8558, 1982) (Cork Report).

and the valid perception that corporate insolvency produces disastrous consequences for creditors, employees and the economy.[138]

So did the High Court misconceive the insolvency in the *Patrick* case?

Applying tenets 1 to 4 above, there was ample evidence presented during the hearings that the insolvency had been deliberately triggered and therefore constituted a strategic insolvency. Jackson has argued that bankruptcy law should not be used to enhance the value of non-bankruptcy rights.[139] For example, in the United States, collective bargaining agreements cannot be unilaterally avoided, instead the employer must bargain with the union for changes in the terms and conditions of employment. In bankruptcy, however, it has been held that collective bargaining agreements are executory contracts that can be rejected.[140] Jackson argues that petitions which are filed in order to have access to this 'rule change' should be rejected because there is no common pool or collective action problem. These are 'one-creditor' cases which represent a misuse of bankruptcy due to tenet 1.[141] This analysis is compelling when applied to the Patrick case, although it does involve consideration of the role of the banking syndicate and whether Orr is correct in asserting that they were 'putative third party creditors'.

The decision was also out of step with tenet 2 because the 'right' to the unimpeded exercise of the administrator's discretion was not in harmony with other rights protected by the law, that is the rights protected by the Workplace Relations Act. In the absence of a strategic insolvency, the group would have no entitlement to dismiss a unionised workforce en masse.

In applying tenet 4 one must consider whether the rescue procedures of Part 5.3A should continue to operate. As Brown has commented, 'throwing someone a lifebelt is not rescuing them if they are not drowning, but waving'.[142] The imperatives of the situation did not fit at all with the objectives of Part 5.3A. Given the commercial blueprint, this was not an administration which could achieve rehabilitation or a fresh start without court intervention. There was no chance of a better return to creditors. In fact, due to the reconceptualisation of employee entitlements, there was a chance that some creditors would receive considerably less.

In conclusion and applying tenet 3, the High Court majority judgment did misconceive the insolvency. It was open to the majority to uphold the reasoning of North J and interpret Part 5.3A purposively having regard to the ALRC Report and the objects set out in section 435A.[143] It is not surprising that every-

---

[138] K Lightman, 'Voluntary Administration: The New Wave or the New Waif in Insolvency Law? (1994) 2 *Insolvency Law Journal* 70; Cork Report, *supra* n.137, at para 204.

[139] T Jackson, *The Logic and Limits of Bankruptcy Law* (Cambridge, Harvard University Press, 1986), at 193–4.

[140] Bankruptcy Act, s 1113.

[141] Jackson, *supra* n.139, at 194.

[142] D Brown, *Corporate Rescue* (Chichester, Chancery Law Publishing, 1996), at 1.

[143] Corporations Law, s 109J permits courts to have access to extrinsic material, including Law Reform Commission Reports, in interpreting the Corporations Law.

one claimed victory because a fearless exercise of discretion by the administrator might nevertheless fulfil the conspiracy and lead to a breach of the Workplace Relations Act. The confusion caused by the judgment was partially attributable to the incongruity of applying the logic of real insolvency to a strategic insolvency.

> In June 1983, Continental Airlines' senior vice president . . . jotted down some notes during a meeting . . . .: 'I don't believe we can get these [labour] concessions on a voluntary, persuasive basis. We must get [an] awfully big stick. . . . Most effective stick might be Chapter 11. . . .'
> Three months later, Continental declared bankruptcy and abrogated its labour contracts with its unions. Continental's CEO, Frank Lorenzo, began referring to the company as 'the new Continental' and to any employee working for the firm after its bankruptcy as a 'founding employee'. One of the 'founding employees' at 'the new Continental' found his salary immediately reduced from $45,000 to $30,000.[144]

CONCLUSION

The Patrick dispute predominantly concerns the extent to which norms or ethical systems in corporate law are subject to the ethical constraints of labour law. The question of insulation of corporate law norms and doctrine was resolved in different ways at various points in the litigation. In the Federal Court proceedings, there was significant interference with corporate law doctrine under the influence of the discretionary award of the interlocutory injunction and the implied terms of employment contracts. However, by insisting upon the unfettered operation of the voluntary administration, the High Court opted for an interpretation of corporate law which permitted insularity.

The wider issue for corporate law is that of its dynamism. Should the morality of corporate law be contained? To what extent does protection of its norms require its autonomy and the corresponding exclusion of certain stakeholders from its ambit? Teubner suggests that the compartmentalisation of the law by unified normative principles cannot be sustained, rather the law must provide differentiated solutions for specific interests and social fields. He states:

> it appears as if the practice of the courts is organising 'Law's Empire' anew. The courts destroy the unity of law and replace it by a multiplicity of fragmented legal territories.[145]

---

[144] Delaney, *supra* n.136, at 1–2.
[145] G Teubner, *Law as an Autopoietic System* (Oxford, Blackwell, 1993), at 106.

4

Directors' Liabilities to Third Parties

MITSUMASA TANABE

INTRODUCTION

It goes without saying that a contractual relationship arises between a company and a person, when a director on the company's behalf makes a contract with that person. Therefore, generally the director has no liability to pay the debt owed by the company to that person. Where a company is both a going concern and solvent, no problem of a director's liability to the third party emerges, but in a case where the company is insolvent or doubtfully solvent, there may be a problem in relation to the director's liability to the third party.

Directors' liabilities to third parties as well as to the company have become one of the major issues in Japan. The purpose of this chapter is to introduce the views of the courts and academics in Japan on the issue of the directors' liabilities to third parties, after first taking a glance at how this issue has been treated in major European countries.

OVERVIEW OF SOME EUROPEAN LAWS

English Law

The orthodox view of the directors' duties to third parties under English law may be summarised as follows. Directors owe no fiduciary or contractual duties nor any duty of care to persons who deal with their company, as long as they make it clear to those persons that they are contracting on the company's behalf. They are, therefore, not liable to pay debts incurred by the company at a time when they know the company to be insolvent. If directors mismanage the company's affairs deliberately or negligently, so that the company becomes unable to pay its debts, or so that the security of debenture-holders becomes insufficient, they are not personally liable to the creditors or debenture-holders. The only circumstance in which creditors can sue directors personally at common law is where they have been guilty of a tort toward the creditors in addition to a breach of duties owed to the company. Consequently, directors are personally liable to persons who lend money to the company if they obtain the loan by fraudulent misrepresentation.[1]

There has also been a contrary view that the principle that the directors must act in the best interests of the company is not confined exclusively to considering the interests of its shareholders, but may include the interests of creditors. According to this view where the directors deal with assets in a way prejudicial to creditors at a time when the company is insolvent then this constitutes a breach of fiduciary duty to the company. In such circumstances there may also be a duty owed direct to the creditors.[2]

Finally, it should be noted that when the company is wound up the directors may be made personally liable by order of the court to contribute toward payment of the company's debts if they have been guilty of fraudulent trading within the meaning of section 213(1) of the Insolvency Act of 1986 or wrongful trading within the meaning of section 214 of the same Act. The duties of the directors created by sections 213 and 214 are owed strictly to the company not to the creditors.[3] There are no provisions on the issues of directors' duties to observe or supervise the other directors.

German Law

German stock companies are usually huge and limited in number. The issue of the directors' liability to third parties, which we are discussing here, is not a major topic with regard to stock companies. However, in the case of limited liability companies, it is reported that third parties sometimes sue the *Geschäftsführer* of a company which has gone into bankruptcy. The *Geschäftsführer* of a company owes a duty to apply to the court for a commencement order of proceedings for bankruptcy or judicial reconciliation at least within three weeks from the time when the cause of insolvency occurs.[4] The insolvent company must not pay any debts. If it does, it is a breach of section 64 of the GmbHG Act, and the *Geschäftsführer* has to contribute the amounts of money paid to the company. The duty of the *Geschäftsführer* created by this provision is owed to the company not to the creditors. Besides this, a creditor who deals with a company, at a time when it is threatened with insolvency may sue the *Geschäftsführer*, if the dealing results in a tort.[5]

---

[1] R R Pennington, *Company Law* 7th edn., (London, Butterworths, 1995), at 814.

[2] This was the view of Lord Diplock in *Lonrho Ltd* v. *Shell Petroleum Co. Ltd* [1980] 1 WLR 627.

[3] C Ryan, *Company Directors: Liabilities, Rights and Duties* 3rd edn., (Bicester, CCH Editions, 1990), at 129.

[4] GmbHG Act, s 64.

[5] H Matui, 'Hasantekijougo ni keiyakuteiketu si ta saikensha ni taisuru yuugenkaisha gyoumusikkousha no sekinin' ('The Liability of the Geschäftsführer to a Contracting Party after Bankruptcy') in S Maruyama (ed.), *Doitu kigyouhouhanrei no tenkai-shoshuu (Development of the Courts' Decisions on Corporate Law in Germany)* (1995), at 213.

French Law

The issue of directors' liabilities to third parties has become a major topic in France, due to there being many small-sized stock companies, and due to many cases where creditors suffer damage from corporate bankruptcies. Section 244(I) of the Commercial Company Act 1966[6] provides that the directors are liable to the company or to the third parties jointly and severally or severally according to the general rules, if they act in breach of the provisions of this Act or if there is any negligence in performing their duties, especially declaring a bogus dividend or allowing it without opposition.

In France the liabilities of directors to third parties have been regarded as being a matter of the application of generally applicable law, namely the law of tort. When a director deals with a person at a time when he knows or negligently fails to apprehend that the company is insolvent, it is understandable that he is liable for any loss of the person under the general rules of tort. But, when a director is not involved in the trading, it is arguable when and why he is liable to the third party under those rules. French courts traditionally have acknowledged a director's duty to monitor the other directors. For example, a representative director Z bought lots of casks of rum from X at a time when the company was threatened with insolvency; soon after the dealing the company went into bankruptcy leaving X's price unpaid. X sued another director Y. The court held that Y was liable to X for the damage suffered as he could have prevented Z's act of negligence with foresight and prudent care. The court also stated that Y would only escape such liability if he could establish that he had a proper reason for not knowing of Z's act of negligence, or Z's act was an undetectable fraud, or Z ignored Y's directions.[7]

Thus, a director's duty to monitor the other directors has been acknowledged, but academics have not reached a consensus about what grounds give rise to the duty. Some people take note of remuneration which a director receives and consider that a director's obligation to act for the company as a consequence of this remuneration includes paying attention to the other directors' behaviour. This view establishes a director's duty of observance, but is not enough to make it clear why he owes this duty to third parties. A dominant view is that a director owes a duty to observe the other directors, because he is a member of the board of directors. As mentioned above , the Commercial Company Act indicates that directors' liabilities to the company or to third parties shall be tested according to the general rules of law, rather than under any special duty created by the Act itself.

---

[6] Loi no 66–537 du 24 juillet 1966, sur les sociétés commerciales.

[7] Cass. com., 10 mai 1948 (1949) JCP 11 4937, cited in C Nunoi, 'Furansu kabusikikaisha ni okeru torisimariyaku no sekininn' ('Directors' Liabilities in French Company Law') (1984) 91(3) *Hitotsubashi Ronshuu* 428; and see T Hakoi, 'Furansu ni okeru torisimariyaku minjisekininn— houri no keisei to tenkai' ('Historical Development of the Theory of Directors' Civil Liabilities in France') (1992) 42 *Waseda hougakkaishi* 334.

Status quo

Section 226–3 of the Japanese Commercial Code provides that directors are liable to a third party for any damage caused deliberately or by gross negligence in the course of performing their duties as directors. This has become one of the most frequently used provisions of the Commercial Code, which appears to be a consequence of there being so many (about one million) small and medium-sized stock companies in Japan. When a company goes into bankruptcy leaving its debts unpaid, its creditors usually sue the directors personally, asserting damage due to their misconduct or gross negligence in the course of the performance their duties.

The courts and academics differ in their interpretation of section 226–3 of the Commercial Code. First, there is an argument regarding its basic function. Does it aim at protection of third parties or is it intended to limit the liability of directors? Secondly, the scope of coverage comes up for discussion. Does this provision cover only damage caused directly by misconduct of directors, does it cover only indirect damage, or does it cover both types of damage? The arguments regarding these issues will be introduced more closely below.

The Scope of Application

Direct Damage and Indirect Damage

A third party may suffer damage if directors, on behalf of a company, buy goods from him knowing the company to be insolvent. The same damage can arise if the directors induce the company to obtain a loan from a bank at a time when the company is threatened with insolvency. In these circumstances, directors' behaviour directly causes damage to the third parties, so-called 'direct damage'.

A creditor of a company sometimes suffers damage indirectly from the conduct of directors, so-called 'indirect damage'. Such cases occur when directors mismanage the company's affairs deliberately or through gross negligence, so that the company becomes unable to pay its debts. If directors sell the company's goods or lend money anticipating that they will not be able to recover their money because the buyer or borrower is threatened with insolvency, this can amount to 'indirect damage'.

One point should be made. It is not clear in every case whether the damage suffered is 'direct' or 'indirect'. Nevertheless, some scholars insist that section 266–3 covers only direct damage or only indirect damage. The grounds for each view will be introduced below.

The View Limited to Direct Damage

Matsuda considers that section 266–3 of the Commercial Code is applicable only to direct damage to a third party.[8] That is to say, directors are liable to a third party in respect of damage suffered if they act for the benefit of the company or the benefit of the directors themselves to the prejudice of the third party knowing, or without knowing through gross negligence, that the third party will incur the damage. According to the general rules of tort law under the Civil Code,[9] a person who injures others is liable if he does it deliberately or negligently. The word 'negligently' in this context includes an act of slight negligence. Scholars who support the view that section 266–3 is limited to direct damage only consider that directors have to deal with lots of hazardous affairs of the company promptly and it is therefore proper for directors to be immune from liability for damage caused by their slight negligence. According to this view, they should be liable only when they have caused damage in bad faith or through gross negligence.

This view remains a minority one, and it is criticised on the basis that it makes directors' liabilities narrower than those of employees. While an employee's slight negligence constitutes a tort under the general rules of the Civil Code, according to this view directors are not liable to a third party for any damage caused by them through slight negligence, excluding the application of the general rules of tort law. It is hardly possible to find any reasonable ground for this imbalance of liabilities between directors and employees.

The View Limited to Indirect Damage

Not a few scholars believe that section 266–3 of the Commercial Code is applicable only when a third party incurs damage indirectly as a result of directors' behaviour in breach of their duties in bad faith or through gross negligence. This is based on the argument that when directors' misconduct results in a tort a third party should sue them under the general rule of tort. The academics advocating this view state that any person who deals with a company should take good care over the creditability of the company and this should keep it from suffering loss. However, the problem is that creditors are not in a position to prevent the company from incurring damage by its directors' wrongdoing or breach of their duties. As creditors have no effective legal measures to protect their interests in the company from the harmful conduct of its directors, a special provision, it is argued, has been provided for the relief of creditors. This provision allows creditors to sue directors who cause damage to the company by neglecting their duties in bad faith or through gross negligence, and who thereby eventually give

---

[8] J Matsuda, *Watakusi no shousuuiken (My Minor Opinions at the Supreme Court)* (1971), at 41.

[9] Civil Code, s 709.

rise to damage to the creditors. The proponents of this view propose that direct damage of a third party should be dealt with under the general rules of tort law and that section 266–3 of the Commercial Code should cover only indirect damage to a third party.

Although this view is logical and is supported by a number of scholars it remains a minority one because a wide range of remedies for creditors incurring loss through directors' breach of duties cannot be achieved by interpreting the provision in this way.

The View Including Direct and Indirect Damage

The Supreme Court has stated that the relationship between a company and its directors is a mandate contract,[10] so the director owes a duty to the company to manage the company's affairs with the standard of care of a good manager.[11] Since there is no contractual relationship between a director and a person who deals with the company, the director is not liable under general principles to the third party for any damage caused by the director's breach of duty to the company. However, considering the fact that the company's business depends on the performance of its directors, section 266–3 of the Commercial Code has been provided to protect the interests of the third parties. Under this provision, directors are liable to a third party for any damage caused directly or indirectly by the directors neglecting their duties in bad faith or through gross negligence.[12]

The majority of academics support this view because in a society such as Japan with so many small-sized stock companies the protection of creditors is essential. This view including direct and indirect damage to third parties is functional and makes it needless to classify a third party's damage as 'direct' or 'indirect' in ambiguous cases.

The Director's Duty to Observe Other Directors

Representative Directors

The board of directors is empowered to manage the affairs of the company, and it owes a duty to supervise the behaviour of directors.[13] It is argued that each director, as a member of the board, owes a duty to observe the performance of the other directors. If a third party incurs damage as a result of some wrongdoing of director X, the other director, Y, of the same company may be liable to the third party for the damage if Y neglects, deliberately or through gross negligence, his or her duty to observe X.

---

[10] Commercial Code, s 254(3).
[11] Civil Code, s 644.
[12] Supreme Court decision of 26 Nov. 1969, minshuu 23.11.2150.
[13] Commercial Code, s 260.

Is being a nominal director a defence in a lawsuit? There was a case in which this argument was made: a company's director and owner, B, entreated Y, a man of credit in the community, to be the representative director of the company. Y gave his consent unwillingly on the condition that he would not be involved in the company's affairs and would leave all business to B. Y was registered on the company register as the representative director of the company, but he was not involved in the business at all. B bought steel materials from X on behalf of the company and issued a promissory note in payment knowing the company to be insolvent so that it could not pay the note at its maturity. X brought an action against Y asserting that Y had been in breach of a duty to observe B. The Supreme Court held that Y was liable to X for the damage and stated that a representative director owed a duty to observe all the affairs of the company with the care of a good manager. If he did not engage in the business of the company, leaving all affairs to the other director, and overlooked the other director's behaviour or the other director's neglect of duty, he should be regarded as liable as he himself neglected his duty in bad faith or through gross negligence.[14]

Does the mere fact that a representative director does not engage in business of the company make him liable for any damage to a third party? The Supreme Court has also considered and answered this question: a company's representative director, Y, was not involved in the management of it at all, leaving everything up to other director, A. The company went into bankruptcy due to the economic depression. One creditor, X, instituted an action against Y asserting that he suffered loss owing to Y's neglect of his duty to supervise A. The Supreme Court turned down this claim, reasoning that the liability of a director to a third party under section 266–3 of the Commercial Code arose only when a reasonable relationship of cause and effect could be seen between the damage suffered by the third party and the representative director's neglect of duty to supervise other directors. Further, if a director (A), being involved in the affairs of the company, was not liable to the third party because of his performance of his duty in compliance with the laws and articles of association, then the representative director, Y, was not liable because there was no reasonable relationship of cause and effect between the damage of the third party and the neglect of his duty.[15]

Nominal Directors

Every stock company is required to have at least three directors.[16] It is not always easy for small-sized company to find suitable directors. Therefore it sometimes happens that the owner's wife, his acquaintances, his relatives or the eldest employee is asked to become a nominal director to fulfil the requirement

[14] *Supra* n.12.
[15] Supreme Court decision of 16 July 1970, minshuu 24.7.1061.
[16] Commercial Code, s 255.

to have three directors. It is by no means rare in small-sized stock companies in Japan that a director is not involved in the management of the company. In these cases, is a person who becomes such a nominal director liable to a third party for any damage caused by some wrongdoing of an executive director on the ground of neglecting the duty to observe?

Theoretically, every director, irrespective of whether he or she is a representative director or not, owes a duty to act as a director and to observe other directors. No excuse that one is a mere nominal director is permitted in theory. In the case of a representative director, the courts do not make any allowance for his being a nominal director, but in the case of a plain director who is not a representative, there has been some hesitation in applying the abovementioned provision strictly to a nominally appointed director who neglects a duty to observe other directors.

Although many actions of this kind have been brought to the courts, in a number of cases the defendant directors who did not engage in the business at all, neglecting the duty to observe other executive directors, have not been held liable to third parties. Of course, there have been some cases where such directors have been held to be liable for neglecting their duties of observance. One case is worth picking out. The representative director, A, and another director, B, were responsible for the financial affairs of the company, the balance sheet of which was in the red. They drew up false accounts showing the business to be running well. They obtained a loan from a bank, X, on the company's behalf using the false accounts, but the company went into bankruptcy soon after the loan. X sued Y, one of the directors of the company, asserting that Y was liable for X's damage, because he had neglected his duty to observe A and B. Although Y had not continued beyond compulsory education and had no comprehension of accounting, he had been nominated a director because he was the eldest employee at the company. He had never been involved in the management of it, and only worked in the company's factory. The Osaka High Court stated, presumably commiserating with Y, that X could win the suit if it could establish two facts: that Y had known the wrongdoing by A and B or had carelessly overlooked their behaviour, and that Y could have effectively prevented the wrongdoing if he had performed his duty to observe. The Court found in this case that Y could not have effectively prevented the wrongdoing, even if he had tried to, because two of the three directors in collaboration with each other had been involved in the dealing with the bank. Y was held not to be liable to X for its damage.[17]

CONCLUSION

If a director does something wrong in the course of performing his duty as the director resulting in a tort, it goes without saying that he has to compensate a

[17] Osaka High Court Decision of 27 Apr. 1978, hanreijihou 897, 97.

victim for loss under the general rules of tort law. The same thing can be said in the case of an employee. However, while it is proper to discuss the liability of a director to a third party from the standpoint of tort law, it should also be acknowledged that the law of tort is not enough to tackle a director's liability to a third party, especially the liability of a director who does not engage in the business and neglects the duty to observe the other directors.

It would be desirable for the Companies Act or the Commercial Code to have some special provision dealing with the directors' liabilities to third parties and making it clear in what circumstances such liabilities would arise. This is an issue for the very reason that a company is an artificial person and its management is confided to its directors. Usually current creditors have no effective means of controlling the directors' conduct. They must, therefore, rely on the facts that the affairs of the company are properly administered by its directors and that a director acting on the company's behalf is engaging in transactions *bona fide*.

It is not satisfactory that creditors should be protected only through the directors' duty to the company. Rather, directors should assume a duty to act *bona fide* in the interests of the whole company including the interests of creditors. They should be liable to the third parties for any damage caused directly or indirectly by their conduct in bad faith or through gross negligence, so long as there is a reasonable relationship of cause and effect between the damage and directors' neglect of their duties. As is often the case in a shareholders' representative suit, the business judgement rule developed in US case law should be recognised in cases where a third party who suffers indirect damage brings an action against the directors.

5

Protecting Minority and Public Interests in Nigerian Company Law: The Corporate Affairs Commission as a Corporations Ombudsman

AMEZE GUOBADIA

INTRODUCTION

In 1960 at the time the Jenkins Committee on Company Law Amendment was set to undertake the task of reforming UK company law, Clive Schmithoff reduced to three what he considered the priorities of that Committee. They were:

(a) to make such alterations in the structure of company organisation as modern life demands;
(b) to make shareholding as safe for the small investor as possible; and
(c) to create a simple historically unencumbered companies code.[1]

Of the three, he considered that the second, making 'shareholding safe for the small shareholder as investor and minority shareholder'[2] was the most vital. In furtherance of this object, he recommended the creation of a new division of the Board of Trade with special powers. According to him, 'the future protection of the small investor is a matter of public interest . . . The new Division should become the watchdog of the small investor and the investing public in general'.[3]

At about the same time as Schmithoff wrote the aforementioned article, K W Wedderburn had laid a foundation for his argument on the need for a Corporations Ombudsman in the United Kingdom. There was at the time, in his view:

a growing awareness that the future control of companies and their management will need a much more active administrative agency than the Companies Division of the

---

[1] C Schmithoff, 'Implications of Company Law Reform' [1960] *Journal of Business Law* 151.
[2] *Ibid.*, at 152.
[3] *Ibid.*, at 160.

Board of Trade can at present be . . . the need for some extra and agile supervisor is felt more as the Power of Shareholders to control is demonstrated to be ineffectual.[4]

In a later article, the same writer reiterated the need for such an agency in the United Kingdom when, commenting on company law developments there, he observed as follows:

the reason why the British observer recoils from major extensions of jurisdiction to protect investors and others from serious mismanagement is not the substance of the matter. It is the forum. . . . But British Courts are singularly ill fitted to investigate and provide redress. An administrative agency or Commission would more readily—and more acceptably—establish remedies for such 'unfair mismanagement'. Such a body might yet 'become a Corporations Ombudsman, ready to investigate, probe, or adjudicate in the interest of shareholders'.[5]

This introductory reference to the company law of the United Kingdom is an outgrowth of the linkage between Nigerian company law and the former, upon which it is largely modelled. It will be recalled that quite apart from the ambiguities in drafting, defects of conceptualisation and loopholes for exploitation which had been found in the now repealed Companies Act 1968,[6] there was the fundamental and nagging problem of the inefficiency of the Companies Registry in its monitoring role as well as the inadequacy of the law with regard to the protection of the 'small investor' or 'minority shareholder'. All these pointed to a vital need for reform. The reform movement came some 30 years after the Jenkins Committee was set up, that is towards the end of the 1980s with the Law Reform Commission at the helm of affairs. Drawing significantly from the experiences of other jurisdictions, especially those of the Commonwealth and Britain in particular, the Law Reform Commission directed attention to, among other matters, the need for:

(a)   a more effective mechanism for investor protection generally and in particular, for minority protection;
(b)   monitoring companies; as well as
(c)   effectively investigating and giving redress or remedies in cases of maladministration and mismanagement in companies.[7]

To facilitate these ends, the Companies and Allied Matters Act 1990 (CAMA),[8] the final product of the reform movement, established the Corporate Affairs Commission (CAC). In addition, the already existing Securities and Exchange Commission (SEC) had its regulatory powers over the activities of companies in the securities market enlarged by vesting it directly with the power

---

[4] K W Wedderburn, 'A Corporations Ombudsman' (1960) 23 *Modern Law Review* 663, at 668.
[5] K W Wedderburn, 'Companies, Courts and Management' (1983) 46 *Modern Law Review* 643, at 644–5, quoting Wedderburn, *supra* n.4, at 670.
[6] Which was a replica of the UK Companies Act 1948.
[7] The emphasis being on remedies or solutions that are more easily available than recourse to courts.
[8] Cap 59, Laws of the Federation of Nigeria (LFN) 1990.

to administer Part XVII of CAMA, governing 'dealings in Companies Securities'.[9] The dynamics of a relatively active securities market in recent times underscore the relevance of the SEC in the corporate sector.[10] In the view of one writer:

> with the replacement of the Companies registry with the Corporate Affairs Commission, an independent agency with wide powers of control and supervision of companies, I believe the stage is set for a more effective administration of company law.[11]

Seven years after its establishment, the effectiveness of the CAC is yet to be authoritatively and empirically established. Taking the following as key indices of effectiveness,(a) establishing remedies for 'unfair management', (b) investigating, probing or adjudicating in the interest of shareholders, and (c) effective supervision of companies in the general matters left to it, this essay examines the effectiveness of the CAC in the achievement of these goals which, in the main, attach to its role as a Corporations Ombudsman.[12]

It must be observed from the outset that the role of the CAC in the corporate system is very much circumscribed by the aforementioned role assigned to SEC. Thus, all those issues that arise in relation to dealings in companies securities which often elicit so much suspicion and controversy and which could otherwise fall within the purview of the functions, investigative or adjudicatory, of a corporations ombudsman (such as insider dealing, the control of public invitations in the public offer and sale of securities, unit trusts, reconstructions, mergers and takeovers of companies) are, under the enabling provision of CAMA,[13] not within the competence of the CAC. In the light of this observation, therefore, some consideration will be given to the issues of whether (a) the aforementioned powers of SEC operate as a hindrance to the effective performance of the CAC as an ombudsman, (b) there is room for a multiplicity of bodies to perform the role of a corporations ombudsman, and (c) the viability of expanding the functions and powers of the CAC.

---

[9] See CAMA, s 541. Specifically the following are covered by Part XVII: public offer and sale of securities; unit trusts; reconstructions, mergers and takeovers of companies; insider trading.

[10] The SEC Act, Cap 406, LFN 1990, had vested the management of these matters in the SEC, an agency with the requisite expertise to administer matters relating to company securities.

[11] E O Akanki, 'Preface' in E O Akanki (ed.), *Essays on Company Law* (Lagos, University of Lagos Press, 1992).

[12] An 'ombudsman' is defined by *Webster's Encyclopedic Unabridged Dictionary of English Language* as '[a] commissioner appointed by a legislature in some Scandinavian countries, New Zealand and elsewhere to hear and investigate complaints by private citizens against government officials or agencies'. To situate this definition in context in the case of companies, such complaints would be against company officials, organs and related agencies.

[13] CAMA, s 541.

THE CAC: ESTABLISHMENT, FUNCTIONS AND POWERS

The CAC was established by 'Section 1(1) of CAMA as a body corporate with perpetual succession and a common seal'.[14] Its functions span the spectrum of company activities ranging from formation to winding up of companies. While details of all these activities are not necessary here,[15] it will be sufficient to mention a few of them. With regard to the formation of companies, the CAC registers a company on submission to it of the required incorporation documents.[16] It has the power to refuse to register a company for reasons set out in the Act.[17]

The CAC keeps registers of certain charges requiring registration under CAMA with respect to each company.[18] Its other functions of a routine administrative nature include calling or directing the holding of a general meeting and giving such ancillary or consequential directions as it thinks fit where default is made in holding a meeting of the company required by section 213 of CAMA.[19] Of particular relevance to the subject of this chapter are those functions of the CAC which relate to the prevention of mismanagement of companies[20]; and arranging or conducting investigations into the affairs of any company where the interests of the shareholders and the public so demand.[21] These responsibilities of the CAC are designed to prevent what has been described by one writer as 'corporate irregularity, mismanagement, fraud and oppression of minorities'.[22]

The CAC and Minority Protection

Although it is long established that companies are to be run democratically, that is with due deference to majority rule,[23] the strict application of this principle has been known to work hardship on the minority in certain circumstances.

---

[14] CAMA, s 2(a).

[15] See further, C O Okonkwo, 'The Corporate Affairs Commission' in Akanki, *supra* n.11, 14 at 18.

[16] See CAMA, ss 35 and 36.

[17] CAMA, s 36(1)(a)–(e). The reasons set out include: non-compliance with the provisions of CAMA or any other applicable law, illegality of the proposed objects of the company; incompetence or disqualification of the subscribers; conflict between the proposed name of the company and an existing trade mark or business name registered in Nigeria.

[18] See CAMA, s 198.

[19] The powers of the CAC in this regard are set out in CAMA, s 213(2). For a discussion of the issue of calling a corporate meeting in situations of deadlock and default, see A Guobadia, 'Going Beyond the Articles in the Conduct and Regulation of Corporate Meetings: *Okeowo* v. *Migliore* Revisited' (1984–7) 12 *Nigerian Journal of Contemporary Law* 17–27. It is interesting to note that now, apart from the court, the CAC is another body that may direct the calling of such a meeting. This was not previously the case.

[20] See CAMA, s 7(1)(a).

[21] CAMA, s 7(1)(c).

[22] See Okonkwo, *supra* n.15.

[23] The rule in *Foss* v. *Harbottle* (1843) 2 Hare 461; and see also *Burland* v. *Earle* [1902] AC 83.

Often, majority rule seems to overlook the fact that what Schmithoff has described as the 'small investor' and the minority in companies should be entitled to protection, particularly in situations where the actions of the majority are manifestly unfair. Consequently, common law principles, have, over time, recognised exceptions to the basic principle of majority rule. According to common law principles, the minority may sue in the following situations:

(a)   where the Act proposed or done by the majority was *ultra vires*[24];
(b)   where the act in question, though not *ultra vires*, required a special procedure or majority which was not complied with;[25]
(c)   where there was an actual or threatened breach of the plaintiffs' personal rights;[26] and
(d)   where the persons in control of the company were in fraud on the minority or the company.[27]

There was also the general omnibus ground for an action to be brought in the interest of justice. The shareholder could proceed by way of a personal action to defend a straight personal right; and could also sue by way of a derivative action in cases of wrongs done to the company. Although the action is brought by the shareholder, it would really be suing on behalf of the company on the basis of rights derived from the company. The shareholder could also bring a representative action on behalf of itself and all other shareholders in the same class.

Under section 201 of the repealed Companies Act 1968 any member of a company who complained that the affairs of the company were being conducted in a manner oppressive to some part of the members (including the member in question), could petition the court for an order. The facts of such a petition had to justify the granting of a winding up order. This remedy was meant to be used where a winding up order, though justifiable, would unfairly prejudice that part of the members including the petitioner. In that case the Court would make any alternative order it deemed fit in the circumstances.

CAMA has made some fundamental changes to the principles governing minority protection; and this is where the role of the CAC comes in. Under section 310 of CAMA, a petition may be brought to court for an order under CAMA in relation to a company for relief on the grounds of what is termed 'unfairly prejudicial and oppressive conduct'. Apart from the following persons who may bring such a petition:

(a)   a member of the company,
(b)   a director or officer or former director or officer of the company,
(c)   a creditor,
(d)   any other person who, in the description of the court is the proper person to make an application under section 311 of CAMA,

[24]   *Hutton v. West Cork Railway* (1883) 23 Ch D 645.
[25]   *Edwards v. Halliwell* [1950] 2 All ER 1064.
[26]   *Wood v. Odessa Water Works Co.* (1889) 42 Ch D 636.
[27]   *Menier v. Hooper's Telegraph Works* (1874) Ch App 350.

the CAC is empowered to bring such a petition *suo moto*. Section 311 of CAMA sets out the grounds upon which such an application may be brought. It should be noted here that the mandate of the CAC in this regard is wider than that of the other potential petitioners. These others may only petition to protect their own interest either as members, creditors or officers under CAMA. The CAC, on the other hand, is empowered to petition both for the protection of members and in the public interest. Accordingly, the CAC may bring a petition:

> where it appears to it in the exercise of its powers under the provisions of [CAMA] or any other enactment[28] that—
> (i) the affairs of the company are being conducted in a manner that is oppressive or unfairly prejudicial to, or unfairly discriminatory against a member or members or in a manner which is in disregard of the public interest; or
> (ii) any actual or proposed act or omission of the company (including an act or omission on its behalf) which was or would be oppressive, or unfairly prejudicial to, or unfairly discriminatory against a member or members in a manner which is in disregard of the public interests.[29]

The relief afforded members of the company on the grounds of oppressive and unfairly prejudicial conduct here is made all the more effective by the inclusion of the CAC as a potential petitioner. This is so because in situations in which a member or members are hamstrung from commencing such proceedings by technical rules of procedure, or where the wrongdoers are themselves in control of the company such that the member cannot obtain some of the material information it may require for its petition, the CAC may proceed instead.

As a closer study of CAMA will reveal later in this chapter, the CAC stands a better chance of success with obtaining such information because of its power to initiate and order investigations into companies. Indeed, as has been pointed out elsewhere, such investigations may lead to judicial proceedings.[30] Faced with the possibility of having the CAC order such investigations and the prospects of the potential consequences thereof, the officers and members of the company may be more co-operative.

Another construction is also possible. The expression 'where it appears to it in the exercise *of its powers under the provisions of [CAMA]*[31] or any other enactment' in the aforementioned section 311, which enables the CAC to bring a petition, can in fact be interpreted to mean that the CAC can so act pursuant to a report of investigations conducted or ordered into the company under sections 314 and 315 of CAMA, about which more will be said later.

In order for the provisions to be able to achieve their aim, it is better to allow some flexibility in interpretation. The power of the CAC to petition here should

---

[28] Note that the reference to 'any other enactment' further widens the scope of the powers of the CAC.

[29] CAMA, s 311(2)(c). There is an omission in sub-paragraph (ii). The provision would make sense if it were to end in the following or similar words: 'has been done or is proposed to be done'.

[30] See *Re Pergamon Press Ltd* [1971] Ch 388, at 399, *per* Denning MR.

[31] Emphasis added.

not be read as having to follow upon an investigation specifically. Investigations are only an aspect of its functions. Indeed, its other functions that appear rather general include 'the regulation and supervision of the . . . management . . . of companies under or pursuant to [CAMA]'.[32] The power to bring a petition can thus be founded upon the role of the CAC under this 'omnibus' provision.

'Oppressive', Unfairly Prejudicial and Unfairly Discriminatory Conduct

CAMA does not give any definition of the terms 'oppressive', 'unfairly prejudicial' and 'unfairly discriminatory' in section 311. In cases arising under the antecedent of the present formulation, that is section 210 of the UK Companies Act 1948, which was identical to section 201 of the repealed Companies Act 1968,[33] the courts had interpreted 'oppressive' conduct to mean conduct that is 'burdensome, harsh and wrongful'[34]; and '[a] lack of probity and fair dealing in the affairs of a company to the prejudice of some portion of its members'.[35]

Sections 310 and 311 of CAMA do not suggest that the act or conduct complained of, if against a member or members, must affect him or them '*qua* member'. This can be regarded as a logical consequence of the enlarged scope of the contract in the memorandum and articles of association now recognised by Nigerian law[36] to include officers of the company. Section 41 of CAMA provides as follows:

> Subject to the provisions of this Act, the memorandum and articles, when registered, shall have the effect of a contract under seal between the company and its members and officers and between the members and officers themselves whereby they agree to observe and perform the provisions of the memorandum and articles, as altered from time to time in so far as they relate to the company, members, or officers as such.

Accordingly, the old line of cases in which a member of a company could not sue to protect his interests in the company in a capacity other than 'member', as in *Hickman* v. *Kent or Romney Marshes Sheepbreeders' Association*[37] or *Rayfield* v. *Hands*,[38] or where a non-member, simply an officer or solicitor to the company, could not sue to protect his rights as such, as in *Eley* v. *Positive*

---

[32] CAMA, s 7(1)(a).

[33] The conduct complained of could be continuous, it could be an isolated act, or one already done; future conduct could also be anticipated because of the reference to 'proposed act or omission': see CAMA, s 311(2)(c)(ii).

[34] See *Scottish Cooperative Wholesale Society Ltd* v. *Meyer* [1959] AC 324, at 342, *per* Lord Simonds; see also *Re Harmer Ltd* [1958] 3 All ER 689. Similarly, see *Ogunade* v. *Mobil Films (WA) Ltd* (1976) 2 FRCR 101, *per* Karibi Whyte J.

[35] See *Scottish Cooperative Wholesale Society Ltd* v. *Meyer*, *supra* n.34, at 364, *per* Lord Keith of Avonholm.

[36] See A Guobadia, 'The Enlarged Scope of the Contract in the Memorandum and Articles of Association' (1991) 1 *University of Benin Law Journal* 97.

[37] [1915] 1 Ch 881.

[38] [1960] Ch 1.

Government Security Life Association Co Ltd,[39] because of the restricted scope of the contract in the memorandum and articles of association under the repealed 1968 Act is no longer authoritative.

THE CAC AND THE POWER OF INVESTIGATION

Perhaps the most striking example of the role of the CAC as a corporations' ombudsman is to be found in its power of investigation of companies. This relates to what Wedderburn has termed the 'power to go inside the company and ferret out the facts'.[40] The power of investigation here goes beyond what is immediately conjured up by the general power granted in sections 314 and 315 of CAMA. These two sections empower the CAC to arrange an investigation into the affairs of a company on the application of the company or its members. [41] Other investigations shall be arranged upon the order of a competent court.[42] In addition, the CAC may, *suo moto*, appoint inspectors or cause an investigation to be conducted into the company in one or other of the following situations:

(a) where there are circumstances suggesting that the company's affairs are being or have been conducted with intent to defraud its creditors or the creditors of any other person, or in a manner which is unfairly prejudicial to some part of its members; or

(b) any actual or proposed act or omission of the company (including an act or omission on its behalf) is or would be so prejudicial, or that the company was formed for any fraudulent or unlawful purpose; or

(c) persons concerned with the company's formation or the management of its affairs have in connection therewith been guilty of fraud, misfeasance or other misconduct towards it or towards its members; or

(d) the company's members have not been given all the information with respect to its affairs which they might reasonably expect.[43]

Section 326 also empowers the CAC to appoint inspectors to investigate the ownership of a company 'for the purpose of determining the true persons who are or have been financially interested in the success or failure (real or apparent) of the company or able to control or materially to influence the policy of the company'. Under the repealed Companies Act 1968 there were provisions designed for the conduct of investigations into companies—their affairs as well

---

[39] (1876) 1 Ex D 88 (CA).

[40] Wedderburn, *supra* n.4, at 668.

[41] CAMA, s 314(2)(a), (b) and (c).

[42] CAMA, s 315; 'court' here refers to the Federal High Court, the Court of Appeal and the Supreme Court.

[43] CAMA, s 315(2).

as their ownership.[44] Unfortunately, however, throughout the life of that statute, no investigation or inspection was conducted into any company.

Some of what these investigations entail, their aims, nature, scope, consequences as well as problems associated with them have been discussed in some detail elsewhere.[45] A brief summary of these issues is none the less necessary here as a basis for evaluating the extent, if any, to which the CAC can impact upon companies in specific aspects of their business given (a) its general power to conduct or bring about investigations under the aforementioned provisions, and (b) those other situations covered by CAMA which call for some form of investigation, inquiry or related activity by the CAC.

In *Norwest Holst* v. *Department of Trade* Lord Denning gave the following rationale for the conduct of investigations into companies:

> It is important to know the background of the legislation. It *sometimes happens that public companies are conducted in a way which is beyond the control of the ordinary shareholders*. The majority of the shares are in the hands of two or three individuals. These have control of the company's affairs. The *other shareholders know little and are told little*. They receive the glossy annual reports. Most of them throw them into the waste paper basket. There is an Annual General Meeting but few of the shareholders attend. The *whole management and control is in the hands of the directors. They are a self-perpetuating oligarchy and are virtually unaccountable* . . . Seeing that the directors are the guardians of the company, the question is asked: quis custodiet ipsos custodes? *Who will guard the guards themselves?*[46]

The emphasised portions of this statement point at the following as aims of investigations: (a) the protection of shareholders (particularly the minority) interests; and (b) the provision of additional checks on directors in order to reduce the tendency towards excessive and unbridled power.

The CAC may appoint inspectors to investigate the affairs of the company at the instance of members holding no fewer than one quarter of the class of shares issued (in the case of a company having a share capital); and where it is a company without a share capital, on the application of no fewer than one quarter in number of the persons registered as members.[47] Ordering an investigation into the affected company pursuant to this provision is a discretionary matter as the operative word used is 'may'. Upon what factors, then, will the CAC base its decision whether or not to accede to such a request from the shareholders? The provision is silent on the specific issues or factors that should be contained in the application. It would seem that, in the absence of specific guidelines on the matter, the CAC would have to take each application on its own merits and determine whether in the circumstances, an investigation is reasonable or expedient. Section 314(3) provides that an application by the members must be supported

---

[44] Companies Act 1968, ss 157–167.
[45] See A Guobadia, 'Guarding the Guards: CAMA and Investigation of Companies in Nigeria' (1996) 10 *International Company & Commercial Law Review* 364.
[46] [1978] 3 All ER 280, 291–2, emphasis added.
[47] CAMA, s 314(3).

by evidence which the CAC may require to show that there is good reason for the investigation.[48] As Gower points out, commenting on similar powers granted to the Secretary of State under UK law, there is, impliedly, room for an aggrieved shareholder in such a situation to apply to the court for a review of the CAC's refusal to order an investigation. This is because, the CAC has no discretion where there is a court declaration that the affairs of a company ought to be investigated.[49]

The circumstances under which the CAC may '*suo moto*' appoint inspectors to investigate the affairs or ownership of a company have already been extensively set out above,[50] and they are specifically stated to be in the interests of the shareholders and the public. The question is, how far do these processes protect such interests? A cursory review of the essential features shows that in the process of these investigations, the inspector is empowered to look into all books and documents of the company or other related companies.[51] He can summon officers and agents of the company[52] and examine them under oath.[53] These persons are in turn required to give every assistance to the inspectors, and their answers can be used as evidence against them subsequently.[54] The costs of an investigation are to be charged on the Consolidated Revenue Fund of the federation.[55] Under CAMA there is no payment of security for costs of an investigation. To that extent too, there is an added incentive in that security for costs does not deter the shareholder from applying for investigations to be conducted into a company.

In consequence of an investigation, the shareholder does find some protection for its interests and investment as the report of an investigator may in fact lead to judicial proceedings[56] and is admissible in any legal proceedings as evidence of the opinion of the inspector in relation to any matter contained in the report.[57] As has been pointed out elsewhere by the present writer, in spite of the

[48]   Perhaps here it should be observed that the power of the CAC to investigate the ownership of a company in CAMA, s 326 is specifically said to be exercisable by the CAC where there is 'good reason' for such an investigation.

[49]   See CAMA, s 315(1). The operative word used in this section is 'shall'.

[50]   See again CAMA, ss 315(2) and 326.

[51]   CAMA, s 316. An inspector, under CAMA, s 314 or 315 may, if he considers it necessary for the purpose of investigating the company, investigate the affairs of its holding company or the holding company of its holding company and report on the affairs of the same as far as he thinks they are relevant to his primary investigation.

[52]   CAMA, s 317(1)(b).

[53]   CAMA, s 317(3).

[54]   CAMA, ss 317(5), 319(3) and (4). Note also that the failure by any person to comply with these provisions wil be treated as contempt upon certification by the inspector in writing.

[55]   CAMA, s 324(1); although other persons (e.g., those convicted upon a prosecution instituted pursuant to the result of the investigation, or a person ordered to pay damages or restore any property in proceedings brought thereupon, or any body corporate in whose name proceedings are brought) are liable to defray payments made from the Consolidated Revenue Fund to the extent provided by CAMA.

[56]   See *Re Pergamon Press* [1971] Ch 388, *per* Denning MR. CAMA, s 322(2) refers to criminal proceedings, and s 322(4) refers to civil proceedings.

[57]   CAMA, s 325. Such a report may also found a basis for winding up by the court on the just and equitable ground: CAMA, s 323.

obvious merits in these provisions, they do not hold out enough benefit for the shareholder, as the minority in a company may not be able to muster the required strength in numbers to be able to bring an application under section 314(2), that is one quarter of the registered members of the company. It would be different if the application could be brought by the holders of a small percentage of the company's capital.[58]

More striking is the fact that, although available, some of the provisions have not proved to be efficacious in Nigeria as they have not been utilised. It is easy to recall the controversy that surrounded the shareholding of one of the 'big four' banks following upon government divestment of its interests in these banks. According to newspaper reports, it was alleged that the majority shares in this bank were cornered by one single individual or interest. This caused quite an uproar and, at a point, there were suggestions that government might in fact buy back the divested shares. There were other suggestions that government would settle for the golden share option in order to maintain some form of control or vital interest in this public company. These were mere speculations because to date nothing has happened along these lines and it would seem that the controversy has been sufficiently doused. However, what is important in the context of this chapter is that the issues in this controversy were such as could have called for investigation by the CAC into the ownership of the bank at that time in the public interest. This approach was not even suggested, let alone tried, and, within a short time of public attention being drawn to the matter of the majority shareholding getting into the hands of one individual, the controversy died down. The CAC could have initiated such investigations on its own as the enabling provision specifically empowers it to do so 'where it appears to the Commission that there is good reason so to do'.[59] While members of the company may apply under section 326(3) for such an investigation to be undertaken, the CAC is not estopped from acting on its own without such an application. In the particular case of the bank discussed above, section 326(2) would have operated to allow the inspector to 'define the scope of his investigation' with regard to such matters as a specific time frame and particular shares.[60] Thus, where the ownership of the majority shares as acquired within a particular period was in issue, an investigation could have been directed specifically at that matter.

The provisions of section 328 which empower the CAC to call for information as to persons with interests in the shares or debentures of a company can be said to have been similarly unutilised. The section provides that:

Where it appears to the Commission. that there is good reason to investigate the ownership of any shares in or debentures of a company and that it is unnecessary to

---

[58] For a fuller discussion, see Guobadia, *supra* n.45.
[59] CAMA, s 326(1).
[60] CAMA, s 326(2).

appoint any inspector for the purpose,[61] the Commission may require any person who it has reasonable cause to believe

(a) to be or to have been interested in those shares or debentures; or
(b) to act or to have acted in relation to those shares or debentures as a legal practitioner or an agent of some one interested therein;

to give the Commission any information which the person has or might reasonably be expected to obtain as to the present and past interest in those shares or debentures and the names and addresses of the person interested, and of any persons who act or have acted on their behalf in relation to the shares or debentures.[62]

Together with the aforementioned power to investigate the ownership of a company in section 326, these activities aggregate into one of the powers earlier recommended for the corporations ombudsman in the UK, that is 'to discover and declare the beneficial ownership of any other holdings or of any holdings not properly disclosed'.

There is the additional power vested in the CAC to impose restrictions on shares where in connection with such investigations it appears to it that there is difficulty in finding out information about any share arising out of the unwillingness of the persons concerned to assist in the investigation as required in CAMA.[63] The CAC does have a discretion whether or not to impose such restrictions, as the word used in the enabling provision is 'may'. The consequences of such restrictions which may be imposed upon the shares of the company continue while the restrictions subsist. They are as follows:

(a) no voting rights will be exercisable in respect of such shares;
(b) except in a liquidation, no payment shall be made of any sums due from the company on those shares, whether in respect of capital or otherwise;
(c) any transfer of those shares, or in case of unissued shares any transfer of the right to be issued therewith and any issue thereof shall be void.

These restrictions on shares have been described as 'draconian',[64] particularly as they may work injustice on innocent third parties.[65] This may account for the provisions of section 329(3) and (4) of CAMA. The former entitles *any* person aggrieved by such restrictions to appeal to the Federal High Court which 'may, if it sees fit, direct that the shares shall cease to be subject to the said restrictions'

---

[61] Emphasis added. Note that this is an alternative to full investigation.

[62] CAMA, s 328(1). Note that s 328(2) sets out the circumstances under which a person shall be deemed to have an interest in a share or debenture as follows: where that person has a right to acquire or dispose of any interest therein or to vote in respect thereof, or if his consent is necessary for the exercise of any rights, or other persons interested therein can be required or are accustomed to exercise their rights in accordance with his instructions. S 328(3) provides a penalty of a fine or a term of imprisonment for failure to give required information or for giving false information.

[63] CAMA, s 329.

[64] See L C B Gower, *Principles of Modern Company Law* 5th edn., (London, Stevens, 1992), at 622.

[65] E.g., *bona fide* purchasers of such shares and lenders on the security of such shares: see *ibid.*, at 622–3.

while the latter provides that such an order by the Court made with a view to 'permitting a transfer of those shares', may continue the restrictions relating to the issue of further shares in right of those shares or in pursuance of any offer made to the holder of the shares; and payment of sums due from the company on those shares in respect of capital or otherwise.[66]

In spite of these mitigating factors, the power granted to the CAC in sections 328 and 329 of CAMA is far-reaching. Directed at effective monitoring of companies—in this case, their ownership—the idea is to forestall some of the serious instances of fraud and irregularity in the matter of shareholding and consequential issues in the conduct of the affairs of public companies. The genesis of the controversy in the well known case of *Wallersteiner* v. *Moir*[67] illustrates the magnitude of some of these problems. It should be observed that the issues in that case could, at some point, have been handled or the case preceded by investigation into both the ownership of the company as well as the conduct of its affairs. The power to call for information into share ownership in section 328 of CAMA is particularly helpful because it is used in place of investigations in section 326. It helps to save costs incurred in a regular investigation, that is costs in terms of time and money. This is not to suggest that the provision renders investigations unnecessary. As Gower points out, '[a] full-fledged investigation may afford the best chance of getting at the truth but it is expensive and time consuming'.[68]

WINDING UP OF COMPANIES IN LIQUIDATION: THE ROLE OF THE CAC

Section 422(1) of CAMA empowers the Federal High Court to appoint a liquidator or liquidators for conducting the winding up proceedings for a company and also to perform whatever duties in relation to such a winding up the Court may impose.[69] Section 422(3)(d) further provides that where any other person

---

[66] CAMA. s 329(2)(c) and (d).

[67] [1974] 3 All ER 217.

[68] Gower, *supra* n.64, at 621. The problem of costs and other rigours in investigations is discussed elsewhere more fully: see Guobadia, *supra* n.45.

[69] Note that 'the official receiver', who for this purpose is the deputy Chief Registrar of the Federal High Court or any officer so designated for the purpose by the Chief Judge of the Court (CAMA, s 419), may be appointed liquidator. Subject to the provisions of CAMA, the liquidator is compelled to use his discretion in the management of the estate and distribution amongst creditors (see CAMA, s 427(4)). It should be noted that the liquidator is a fiduciary of sorts as established in a long line of cases from different jurisdictions. Thus Marks J in *Commissioner for Corporate Affairs* v. *Harvey* [1980] VR 669, (discussed in H R Hahlo and J H Farrar, *Hahlo's Cases and Materials on Company Law* 3rd edn., (London, Sweet and Maxwell, 1987), at 661), quoting Davidson J in *Thomas Franklin & Sons Ltd* v. *Cameron* (1936) 36 SR (NSW) 286, at 296, held: 'it appears to me then on the whole from these authorities that the liquidator is principally really an agent for the company but occupies a position which is fiduciary in some respects and is bound by the statutory duties imposed on him by the Act'. Accordingly, the liquidator is not to act in bad faith (*Knowles* v. *Scott* [1891] Ch 717); or for an improper purpose (*Silkstone and Haigh Moor Coal Co.* v. *Edey* [1900] 1 Ch 167); or allow a conflict of interest and duty (*Re Gertzenstein Ltd* [1937] Ch 115). For more, see also Lawrence J in *Re Windsor Steam Coal Co.* [1929] 1 Ch 151, at 167.

apart from the official receiver is appointed liquidator, he cannot so act until he has notified the CAC of his appointment and given appropriate security to the satisfaction of the Court.

The powers vested in a liquidator in a winding up are far-reaching. The liquidator takes over the functions/powers of the directors in the running of the company. Apart from the power (with the sanction of the court or the committee of inspection) to bring or defend any action or other legal proceeding in the name and on behalf of the company, carry on the business of the company as far as necessary for its beneficial winding up, pay any classes of creditors in full,[70] the liquidator has other powers. Among them are the power to do the following:

(a) sell the property of the company by public auction or private contract, with power to transfer the whole thereof to any person or company or sell the same in parcels;

(b) do all acts and execute, in the name and on behalf of the company, all deeds, receipts and other documents, and for that purpose to use, when necessary, the company seal;

(c) raise on the security of the assets of the company any money requisite;

(d) take out in his official name letters of administration to any deceased contributory, and to do in his official name any other act necessary for obtaining payment of any money due from a contributory or his estate which cannot be conveniently done in the name of the company, and in all such cases, the money due shall, for the purpose of enabling the liquidator to take out the letters of administration or recover the money, be deemed to be due to the liquidator himself;

(e) to do all such other things as may be necessary for winding up the affairs of the company and distributing its assets.[71]

Recognising the extent of these powers, CAMA further provides that the exercise of the powers conferred in section 425 shall be subject to the control of the court. It also empowers any creditor or contributory to apply to the court with respect to any exercise or proposed exercise of any of these powers.[72] Beyond this, however, is the measure of control exercised by the CAC over liquidators. First, at the direction of the CAC, the liquidator of a company being wound up shall pay moneys received by him into the Companies Liquidation Account of the Public Funds of the Federation kept by the CAC for that purpose.[73] Further checks on the liquidator's dealings with moneys include the penalty of paying

---

[70] CAMA, s 425(1).

[71] CAMA, s 425. There are also other powers set out in this section.

[72] CAMA, s 423. It is safe to presume here that the s refers to an aggrieved creditor or contributory.

[73] CAMA, s 428(1). This must refer to CAMA, s 12, which directs the CAC to establish a fund which shall consist of such sums as may be allocated to it by the Federal Government and such other funds as may accrue to it in the discharge of its functions.

interest[74] on such sums of money in excess of N500 (Five hundred Naira), or such other amount as the CAC approves, which the liquidator retains in his possession without justifying the same to the CAC. Other penalties for the liquidator in such a situation include denying him the whole or part of his remuneration as the CAC may think fit; removal from office; and being liable to pay any expenses occasioned by the retention of such sums.[75] Under section 429, the liquidator must, at least twice a year, send to the CAC an account of his receipts and payments as liquidator. The CAC shall cause the same to be audited, for which purpose it may inspect any books or accounts kept by the liquidator and may also demand any vouchers and other information from the liquidator.[76]

There is, however, a more potent power of control exercised by the CAC over liquidators and their conduct of the winding up of the company. This is to be found in section 432 of CAMA which directs the CAC to take cognisance of the conduct of liquidators of such companies in the following circumstances:

> where the liquidator does not perform his duties faithfully and observe all the statutory and other requirements for his duties or any complaint is made to the CAC by any creditor or contributory with regard to the performance of the liquidator.

The CAC has power and is in fact directed[77] to 'inquire into the matter and may take such action thereon as it thinks fit, including the direction of a local investigation of the books and vouchers of the liquidation'.[78] The CAC is further empowered to require the liquidator to 'answer any inquiry in relation to any winding up in which he is engaged and if the CAC deems it fit, may apply to the Court to examine the liquidator or any other person on oath concerning the winding up'.[79] In other jurisdictions where similar principles have been tested, the reaction of the Court upon such an inquiry further emphasises the fundamental and sensitive nature of the role of the liquidator. For example, in *Commissioner for Corporate Affairs* v. *Harvey*,[80] upon an inquiry into the activities of a liquidator, Marks J held that the liquidator should be removed and his remuneration disallowed for his failings.

Section 431 deals with the release of the liquidator following upon the conclusion of the liquidation, and resignation or removal from office as liquidator. In any of these circumstances, the CAC, on the application of the liquidator, causes a report on the accounts of the liquidation to be prepared. The CAC is empowered to consider such a report along with any objections raised by a creditor, contributory or other interested persons against the release of the liquidator, and to grant or withhold the release subject to the right of appeal to the

---

[74] At the rate of 20% *per annum*.
[75] See CAMA, s 428(2)(a) and (b).
[76] CAMA, s 429(3).
[77] The word used is 'shall'.
[78] CAMA, s 432(1).
[79] CAMA, s 432(2).
[80] [1980] VR 669. See also *supra* n.69.

court. Where the release of the liquidator is withheld, the Court may, on the application of any creditor, contributory or interested person, make such order as it thinks fit, charging the liquidator with the consequences of any act or default which he may have done or made contrary to his duty as such.[81]

This power of control over the liquidator granted to the CAC is certainly not out of accord with its general powers of investigation into the affairs of companies in its supervisory capacity and is certainly consistent with its role as an ombudsman. For, as Gower points out, in relation to the power of investigation into the affairs of a company, 'affairs' has been held to mean the company's 'business including its control over its subsidiaries, whether that is being managed by the board of directors, or an administrator, administrative receiver or a liquidator in a voluntary liquidation'.[82]

POWER OVER MORIBUND COMPANIES

An often overlooked matter which must be addressed effectively is the issue of moribund or defunct companies. These are largely a drain on the system. What records exist about them (usually only those dealing with their incorporation), take up valuable space in the Companies Registry at the CAC and clog up the place. These are companies that do not file returns to the CAC and/or are, as a matter of fact, not carrying on business. Often, they may have run into bad times or their promoters merely incorporated them in order to fulfill a pressing need at the time. Section 525 of CAMA empowers the CAC to strike off such companies from the register of companies. The CAC may use this power where it has reasonable cause to believe that a company is not carrying on business or in operation. The section sets out the procedure required to be followed by the CAC before finally striking off a company. This procedure, which boils down to giving notice to the affected company and giving it the opportunity effectively to contradict the allegation of being moribund, imports notions of principles of fairness in the determination of the matter by an administrative body.

The threat of striking off is one way of ensuring that companies file the annual returns, accounts and other information required by the CAC. Where a company fails to file such returns, it is a justifiable ground for treating it as defunct. Companies that have fallen back on such returns may be encouraged thereby to file the necessary returns. It should also be observed that CAMA also provides the possibility of redress for a company, member or creditor aggrieved by such striking off. Section 525(b) allows for a period of up to 20 years from the publication of the notice of striking off in the Gazette[83] to apply to the court for an order restoring the company to the register and for such other directions as the

---

[81] CAMA, s 431(3).

[82] Gower, *supra* n.64, at 677. See R. v. *Board of Trade, ex parte St Martins Preserving Co.* [1965] 1 QB 603.

[83] Note that on publication of this notice the company shall be dissolved: CAMA, s 525(5).

court may think fit in the circumstances for restoring the company and persons affected as nearly as possible to the *status quo ante* the striking off.

This power to strike off moribund companies could help to unclog the companies registry of documents which take up space unnecessarily and, in a larger context too, rid the system of those companies that are a drain on it and do not contribute anything by way of returns or services. The power of striking off is also useful in a winding up. Section 525 further provides that:

> if in any case where a company is being wound up, the Commission has reasonable cause to believe either that no liquidator is acting, or that the affairs of the company are fully wound up, and the returns required to be made by the liquidator have not been made for a period of six consecutive months, the Commission shall publish in the Gazette and send to the company or the liquidator, if any, a like notice[84]

and

> that at the expiration of three months from the date of that notice the name of the company mentioned therein shall, unless cause is shown to the contrary, be struck off the register and the company shall be dissolved.[85]

EXPANDING THE FUNCTIONS OF THE CAC?

Suppose the CAC could play a more active role in some other matters in which. as the law now stands, it has only a very limited role or none at all, would this enhance its role as a corporations' ombudsman? Would it also afford more protection for the investor? Taking a cue from the suggestion of Wedderburn that the role of 'inquiring and adjudicating' in a reduction of capital could be that of the ombudsman,[86] the possibility is examined accordingly.

Reduction of Capital

Some of the fundamental principles of company law revolve around the capital maintenance doctrine, the rationale for which was aptly summed up by Jessel MR in the well-known case of *Re Exchange Banking Co. Flitcroft's case*.[88]

---

[84] CAMA, s 525(4).

[85] CAMA, s 525(3).

[86] Wedderburn, *supra* n.4, at 669.

[87] E.g., the rules that: a company may not purchase its own shares (*Trevor* v. *Whitworth* (1887) 12 App Cas 409); finance the purchase of its own shares (see Denning MR in *Wallersteiner* v. *Moir* (1974) 3 All ER 217, and *Steen* v. *Law* [1964] AC 287); issue shares at a discount (*Ooregum Gold Mining Co. of India Ltd* v. *Roper* [1892] AC 125, and *Welton* v. *Safferay* [1897] AC 299); or pay dividends out of capital (*Re Oxford Benefit Building and Investment Society* (1886) 35 Ch D 502).

[88] (1882) 21 Ch D 519. According to Jessel MR, 'the creditor has no debtor but that impalpable thing the Corporation, which has no property except the assets of the business. The creditor, therefore, I may say, gives credit to that capital, gives credit to the company on the faith of the representation that the capital shall be applied only for the purposes of the business, and he has therefore a right to say that the corporation shall keep its capital and no return it to the shareholders.'

Arising from this, the company is not expected, in the normal run of things, to reduce its capital as the wording of section 105 of CAMA, which expresses a restriction on the reduction of issued share capital, shows.[89] Implied in this restriction though is the possibility of reduction taking place by certain defined methods which are set out in section 106 of CAMA.[90]

Accordingly, the law allows for reduction of share capital by a special resolution where the company's articles permit. This is made subject to confirmation by the court.[91] The court is empowered by section 108(1) of CAMA to 'make an order confirming the reduction on such terms and conditions as it thinks fit'. Before the court can make such an order however, it is expected to inquire into and adjudicate on certain issues. Depending on whether the proposed reduction of capital involves (a) diminution of liability in respect of unpaid share capital, or (b) the payment to a shareholder of any paid up share capital, the court shall settle a list of creditors entitled to object to such reduction.[92] Prior to this, the court is expected to 'ascertain, as far as possible without requiring an application from any creditor, the names of those creditors and the nature and amount of their debts or claims'. The court is also empowered to:

> if it thinks fit, dispense with the consent of a listed creditor whose debt or claim is not discharged or has not been determined and who does not consent to the reduction, where the company secures payment of his debt or claim by appropriating the full amount of the claim or debt;
>
> where the company admits the full amount of the debt or claim, or though not admitting it, is willing to provide for it;
>
> fix an amount where the company does not admit and is not willing to provide for the full amount of the debt or claim, or if the amount in question is contingent or not ascertained.

(This amount is fixed by the court after an inquiry and adjudication as would be done in a case of winding up of the company by the court.[93])

Details of these provisions have been spelt out here to give a picture of the extent of the court's role in these matters. It would seem that the inquiries into and determination of certain questions prior to a confirmation of a proposed

---

[89] The wording of CAMA, s 105, is as follows: '[e]xcept as authorised by this Act, a company having a share capital shall not reduce its issued share capital'.

[90] CAMA, s 106(2) provides as follows:

'(2) In particular, and without any prejudice to sub-section (1) of this section, the company may—

   (a)   extinguish or reduce the liability on any of its shares in respect of share capital not paid up; or

   (b)   either with or without extinguishing or reducing liability on any of its shares, cancel any paid up share capital which is lost or unrepresented by available assets; or

   (c)   either with or without extinguishing or reducing liability on any of its shares, pay off any paid-up share capital which is in excess of the company's wants, and the company may, if and so far as is necessary, alter its memorandum by reducing the amount of its share capital and of its shares accordingly.'

[91] CAMA, s 106(1).

[92] CAMA, s 107(4).

[93] See the full text of CAMA, s 107.

reduction of share capital, as well as the actual confirmation, could themselves properly be undertaken by the CAC. After all, the CAC is empowered to make inquiries before sanctioning the payment of interest out of capital in certain circumstances allowed under the law.[94] These functions can fit in under its general powers of supervision and management of companies.

Presently, the only function of the CAC with respect to reduction of capital is the registration of the order of the court confirming a reduction. In the aforementioned article by Wedderburn, it was suggested that the corporations ombudsman should have 'the task of inquiring and adjudicating'[95] in this matter of reduction of capital. As pointed out elsewhere by the same writer, 'British Courts are singularly ill-fitted to investigate and provide redress'[96] in such matters. This is particularly so under the adversarial system which operates in Nigeria, in which the court does not get involved in the controversy. This conditions the court to limit its activities in any issue to the discovery of relevant facts as presented by both parties to the case. What is required in the matter of reduction of capital is real investigation and inquiry which might be better suited to the court in an inquisitorial system. Given these obvious limitations of the courts in our circumstances, it does make sense for a different body to perform these functions. In its form and structure, the CAC fits the bill.

Certainly, there will be dissatisfaction from some persons affected by a decision in respect of reduction of capital, as in any decision affecting the rights and interests of persons. What should be done is that there should be a process of appeal to court from the decision of the CAC on these and other matters; a one-stop arrangement in which there is no room for redress after the CAC has taken a decision is not what is advocated here. One effect of the foregoing suggestions would be a prior streamlining of the issues by the ombudsman (that is, the CAC) which, because of the possibility of an appeal to court, may be inclined to perform these tasks fairly and properly. Since the likelihood of fairness and satisfaction exists at that level, the system may thereby limit the number of suits or petitions that may go to court therefrom and thus reduce the already heavy work-load of the courts. There will consequently be a reduction in the likelihood of vexatious and frivolous suits without by any means inhibiting the right of the prospective litigant to his 'day in court' where he insists on it.

Plausible as the argument for extending the functions and powers of the CAC may sound, it is necessary to consider the issue in the context of its performance so far. At the beginning of this chapter, it was noted that one of the problems that CAMA was promulgated to solve was the absolute inefficiency and ineffectiveness of the defunct Companies Registry in both its administrative and monitoring functions. It has already been observed that throughout the life of the repeated Companies Act 1968, no investigation was ever instituted into the

[94] CAMA, s 113(c).
[95] Wedderburn, *supra* n.4, at 669.
[96] See *supra* n.5. The same comment is applicable to Nigeria with a judicial system modelled largely on that of Britain.

affairs or ownership of any company. That may have been due, in part, to the problem of an applicant requesting an investigation having to pay security for costs,[97] as well as the fact that the defunct Companies Registry was a smaller outfit in terms of structure and composition. Being merely a department in the Ministry of Trade, it did not have the required staff as well as the necessary clout, finance[98] and corresponding independence to facilitate its duties.

The CAC on the other hand is a much larger outfit. Its membership, comprising as it does a wide variety of interests in the world of business,[99] quite apart from its own retinue of staff of the Commission who are entitled to all the rights and benefits in the Federal Public Service, means it is certainly a more formidable organisation than its predecessor. Further, the CAC generates a good income from its many activities and so it is better off financially than the defunct Companies Registry. In addition to all these advantages, it has the legal backing in the enabling provisions of CAMA to be able to carry out its duties.[100] Unlike the defunct Companies Registry, the CAC has computerised its operations and so the process of record-keeping could in fact be less cumbersome. In addition, its decentralisation into a zonal structure such that it can operate in several parts of the country means that the public can have greater access to the CAC with its services being similarly utilised.

In the light of all this, it is difficult to justify the lack of any report of the conduct of an investigation into any company—a vital aspect of its functions as a corporations ombudsman. Similarly, the CAC has yet to exercise its statutory powers over moribund companies. There is as yet no report of any company struck off the register of companies on account of being defunct. Surely, the imperatives of company law development and the public interest demand that this all-important function which combines the duties of investigation and adjudication be performed. Accordingly, it is difficult, logical as it may sound in different circumstances, to propose any further expansion of the functions and powers of the CAC beyond the matter of reduction of capital suggested earlier.[101] In the light of the obvious lapses of the CAC so far, the need now is for the efficient performance of such functions as are already ascribed to it.

[97] A plausible excuse perhaps, but only so by a long shot.

[98] See Okonkwo, *supra* n.15, at 14.

[99] E.g., representatives of the chambers of commerce, industries, nines, agriculture and labour; representatives on the various professions, i.e. law, accountancy, Manufacturers' Association, the Association of Small Scale Industrialists, the Institute of Chartered Secretaries, and the Securities and Excahnge Commission among others. See CAMA, s 2, for details.

[100] As has been shown in this chapter, it has the power to impose sanctions for breach of its directives, orders etc.

[101] Beyond the suggestion of expanding the functions of the CAC in certain respects, this chapter has not gone as far as suggesting that the dichotomy between the CAC and the SEC as to their areas of competence be reduced to allow the CAC some supervisory role in the detection and prevention of insider trading as well as abuses in the public offer and sale of securities (which are some aspects of takeovers and other matters already listed as falling under the supervision of the SEC in Chapter XVII of CAMA). Such a suggestion would not have been far-fetched (if the CAC were to take on the appropriate manpower for the performance of such functions) in the light of the earlier observation that the functions of the SEC under CAMA circumscribe the role of the CAC. In the light of the

Six years into the operation of CAMA, as has been observed earlier, there is still no record of any investigation carried out in respect of any of the several companies operating or registered in Nigeria. There is no doubt that one of the factors responsible for this is the fact that there is not enough awareness on the part of shareholders of the existence and utility of the relevant provisions of CAMA. Even if there was enough awareness, in the case of the large public companies, the individual shareholding is minimal in most cases because of the wide dispersal of shareholding in these companies. Consequently, the individual shareholder may not consider it worth his while and, what is more likely, may not be able to muster the kind of support that can set such investigations in motion. The solution to this problem may lie in the hands of the institutional investor. With sufficient awareness of the viability of the processes, the institutional investors, as trustees for the larger interests they represent, would be better placed to utilise the aforementioned provisions. The Shareholders Solidarity Association,[102] as a pressure group, can also push within individual companies to gather sufficient leverage with which to set the machinery of investigations into operation.

There is no doubt that another limiting factor is the fact that in Nigeria information about companies is usually non-existent or almost impossible to obtain beyond such mundane facts as are set out in the incorporation documents. With this dearth of vital information, on what basis does any interest group instigate proceedings? Closely related to this issue is the fact that often, in these large corporations, management is run as a closed shop. An illustration can be found in the matter of the annual general meeting, the venue for which is decided by management. Often times, it takes place too far away and in cities that may be too expensive for a lot of shareholders when compared with the expected gains from their investments in these companies. This leaves room for management to exploit. Together with the possibility of manipulating the proxy-voting machinery, this can indeed result in management running the company as a closed shop. It is time the large body of shareholders were empowered to determine the venue of these meetings.

Finally, it is logical to link this problem with the prevailing issue of a decline in or lack of standards in many areas including the corporate set up. It becomes difficult in such circumstances to initiate such action because the lone ranger who seeks to enforce some standards runs the risk of incurring the wrath and ill-feeling of those who manage the affairs of such companies. Nobody wishes to

---

failure of the CAC fully to realise its mandate so far, it can be said that the jurisdiction of the SEC over dealings in corporate securities is appropriate. Quite apart from the fact that the SEC has the specialisation to deal with such matters, the magnitude of the issues that they do generate suggest that for now the CAC seems to have enough on its plate and can hardly be saddled with any more responsibilities.

[102] As the name suggests, this is an umbrella organisation for shareholders in Nigeria. Although the number of members makes it rather unwieldy, it is possible, with proper planning, for it to operate as an effective pressure group for protecting shareholders' interests.

be in the line of fire, and this also informs the tendency to settle issues by avoiding law suits and other contentious processes into which category investigations will fall. This is particularly so because an investigation may expose all kinds of diverse interests, deals and other activities which their perpetrators may not want exposed. In most circumstances, the stakes are not that high for the individual shareholder and it is easier for him to avoid pushing for investigations. It must be emphasised that in such cases the CAC should act *suo moto* in pursuance of its role as a corporations ombudsman.

CONCLUSION

This chapter set out to assess the CAC in its role as a corporations ombudsman as well as its effectiveness in the protection of the minority shareholder and the public interest. The discussion has shown that in its proactive role it is envisaged that the CAC will go beyond being simply an ombudsman, that is it will be a 'fact finder' in order to become a defender of specific interests—the public as well as shareholders' interests.

On the issue of investor and minority shareholder protection, it has been established that the functions ascribed to the CAC give it enough scope to be able to achieve success in this. Indeed, the combined effect of the various powers given to the CAC to initiate proceedings on behalf of the oppressed or prejudiced minority in a company and the power of investigation into different facets of the company's life and dealings points the way to a lot of success in the matter of shareholder protection.

The power of the CAC over moribund companies illustrates the potential of that institution as a catalyst for necessary changes that may be brought to the economy by the power of 'striking off'. No less significant is its role in relation to winding up. The failure of the CAC to perform these functions in spite of the enabling statutory provisions, adequate finance and other facilities has been attributed to several factors—not least of which is the lack of awareness on the part of the public. With the zonal officers of the CAC in different parts of the country becoming more functional, some of these problems should be tackled. This is a reasonable expectation of the process of decentralisation.

In recent times, there has been some speculation about amendments to CAMA which are expected to address, among other things, some of the lapses of that statute with respect to the CAC. At the time of writing this piece, nothing has emerged about the precise content and extent of the proposed amendments. It is hoped that some of the problems identified in the foregoing pages will be adequately addressed by them. The combined effect of such positive amendments to CAMA and some of the suggestions made in this chapter should be a CAC with a more positive impact on the affairs of companies. Ultimately, such an organisation will be better able to fulfill its mandate as a corporations ombudsman and defender of the minority and public interests.

6

The Current US Tax Controversy over International Hybrid Entities

KEITH E ENGEL

The hybrid entity has become a recurring item of discussion within US international tax circles, finding itself regularly featured at tax conferences and in the tax press. The hybrid contains a mix of legal elements as its name suggests. In the domestic arena, the hybrid has both corporate and partnership aspects. In the international arena, the hybrid has these same mixed elements with the additional element of qualifying as a tax partnership in one country while qualifying as a tax corporation in another. It is this additional element that has made the international hybrid the latest battleground between tax practitioners and the Internal Revenue Service (the 'Service').

The discussion that follows describes the rise and use of hybrids in current US international tax planning. The first part describes the basic features of domestic hybrids, how they managed to achieve corporate limited liability while retaining partnership tax status, and how this development led to the current US system for electing tax entity classification (commonly known as the 'check-the-box' regulations). The second part describes entity classification within the international context and how US tax classification is inconsistent with foreign tax classification.

The third part examines the US international tax policy ramifications of hybrids through a series of examples involving US–Canadian structures. This examination reveals that practitioners utilise the check-the-box regulations to facilitate inconsistent classifications between domestic and foreign tax systems and that these inconsistent classifications create opportunities for tax avoidance. While, as a matter of history, the Service has largely limited its concerns to protecting US revenue, recent events suggest the Service has also become increasingly concerned about foreign tax avoidance, particularly when foreign tax avoidance leads to lower worldwide taxes overall. This latest effort to prevent foreign tax avoidance has created significant controversy. The Service contends that the use of international hybrids to avoid foreign tax creates an uneven playing field against wholly domestic US businesses operating in a fully taxed US environment. Practitioners, on the other hand, argue that the Service lacks any authority to extend its mandate beyond enforcement of US tax.

Basic Features of Domestic Hybrids

One common form of hybrid is the limited liability company ('LLC'), whose development was the catalyst for the current US tax system of elective entity classification.[1] An LLC is a non-corporate entity that contains a mix of corporate and partnership attributes, many of which can be altered by agreement.[2] The most notable corporate feature of the LLC is its limited liability protection for its owners (generally known as 'members').[3] The members can follow the corporate model of delegating their authority to LLC centralised management, or they can follow the partnership model by retaining full management authority.[4] On the partnership side, members can freely transfer their economic rights, but members cannot transfer their full management and participatory rights without consent from the remaining members unless the operating agreement provides otherwise.[5] LLCs also follow the partnership model, in that LLCs typically dissolve when a member dies, resigns, is expelled, or goes bankrupt unless the remaining members affirmatively agree to continue.[6] While many states require an LLC to have at least two members, a growing number of states now permit single-member LLCs.[7]

From a tax perspective, members may treat the LLC as a pass-through entity rather than as a corporation.[8] Pass-through treatment means that the USA imposes tax only at the member level. Owners of single-member LLCs are taxed

---

[1] Another common form of hybrid is the limited liability partnership ('LLP'). The LLP essentially operates as a general partnership with its only corporate feature being limited liability for its owners: R W Hillman, A W Vestal and D J Weidner, *General and Limited Liability Partnership under the Revised Uniform Partnership Act* (St Paul, West Pub Co, 1996), 301.

[2] E.g., A R Bromberg and L E Ribstein, *Partnership* (Boston, Little Brown, 1997), § 1.01(b)(4).

[3] J W Callison and M A Sullivan, *Limited Liability Companies: A State–by-State Guide to Law and Practice* (St Paul, West Pub Co, 1994), § 5.1. For purposes of this chapter, limited liability means protection from personal liability for the entity's debts, obligations and liabilities. Members, however, always remain liable for their own conduct in the course of the entity's business: *ibid.*, at § 5.2.

[4] E.g., Z Cavitch, *Business Organisations with Tax Planning* (New York, Matthew Bender, 1998), ii, § 33.05[2]; L E Ribstein, *Unincorporated Business Entities* (1996), 12.08.A.

[5] Cavitch, *supra* n.4, at § 33.04[4][b].

[6] E.g., J C Ale, *Partnership Law for Securities Practitioners* (New York, Clark Boardman Callaghan, 1997), xx, § 4.07[1].

[7] S D Smith, 'What are States Doing on the Check-the-box Regs?' (1997) 76 *Tax Notes* 973 at 975. See generally L E Ribstein, 'The Loneliest Number: The Unincorporated Limited Liability Sole Proprietor', *Journal of Asset Protection* (May/June 1996), 46.

[8] Treas. Reg. § 301.7701–3(a). See generally IRC § 7701(a)(2)–(3). All references to IRC refer to the US Internal Revenue Code of 1986, and all references to Treas. Reg. refer to the regs thereunder. All references to ITA refer to the Canadian Income Tax Act, RSC 1985 c.1 (5th supp.), and all references to Reg. refer to the regs thereunder.

on all LLC income as if they earned the LLC income directly,[9] and owners of LLCs with two or more members are similarly taxed on their *pro rata* share of LLC income.[10] Distributions from LLCs generally do not create tax.[11]

Unlike LLCs, corporations are separate taxable entities, thereby creating two levels of tax. The USA first taxes the corporation as the corporation earns income. The USA then taxes the corporation's shareholders when they receive a distribution of corporate income, known as a dividend.

> *Example (1) (single-member LLCs).* Facts: individual A owns all of entity X, a single-member LLC. Entity X earns $200 and distributes all after-tax earnings to A. Assume all parties are subject to the highest marginal rate of US tax (roughly 40 per cent for individuals and 35 per cent for corporations).
> Result: individual A is subject to $80 of tax with respect to entity X's income. Entity X is not subject to any tax, and no tax arises when entity X distributes its earnings to A.

> *Example (2) (two-member LLCs).* Facts: the facts are the same as Example (1), except that individuals A and B each own 50 per cent of entity X with each individual entitled to 50 per cent of entity X's proceeds.
> Result: individuals A and B are each subject to $40 of tax with respect to their 50 per cent share of entity X's income. Entity X is not subject to any tax, and no tax arises when entity X distributes its earnings to A and B.

> *Example (3) (corporations).* Facts: the facts are the same as Example (2), except that entity X qualifies as a taxable corporation.
> Result: entity X is subject to a 35 per cent rate of tax, leaving only $140. When entity X distributes its after-tax proceeds to A and B (that is, $70 each), A and B each must pay an additional $28 of tax, separately leaving them with only $42 of after-tax proceeds.[12]

Tax History of Domestic Limited Liability Classification

In the minds of practitioners today, the LLC offers the best features of a corporation and a partnership—limited liability for its owners with simultaneous pass-through tax status. How this limited liability entity achieved pass-through tax status is a function of tax history.

The issue of entity classification dates back to the earliest days of the Internal Revenue Code. This early body of law oddly enough failed to revolve around

---

[9] Treas. Reg. § 301.7701–2(a).

[10] IRC § 701.

[11] IRC § 731(a); Treas. Reg. § 301.7701–2(a).

[12] While individual taxpayers generally prefer pass-through status, corporate status provides certain alternative tax advantages, including a lower marginal rate structure. For instance, corporations have a marginal rate of 15% for the first $50,000 earned, whereas married individuals receive a 15% rate for only their first $42,350. Compare IRC § 1 with IRC § 11.

limited liability, despite its key economic significance. Instead of viewing limited liability as a decisive factor in favour of corporate status, the governing law viewed limited liability as a corporate factor that could be overcome by the presence of other partnership factors. It is this narrow role of limited liability that ultimately made the LLC regime possible and led to the Service's adoption of the current elective system for entity classification.

The distinction between corporate and non-corporate status initially focused on whether the entity had centralised management like a corporation.[13] During this early period, the Supreme Court held that an 'unincorporated joint stock association' qualified as a corporation mainly because of its corporate-like management structure. The Supreme Court was not influenced by the fact that the entity qualified as a partnership under state law with the partners being fully liable for the acts of the entity.[14] In 1935, in *Morrissey* v. *Commissioner*, the Supreme Court formulated a new multi-factored test for entity classification. This test dominated the entity-classification landscape for approximately the next 60 years.[15] Without establishing their relative weights, the Supreme Court enunciated the following four factors that ultimately became critical for distinguishing between a tax partnership and a tax corporation:

(1) whether the entity has a continuous life similar to that of a corporation, continuing without interruption for certain events that would dissolve a partnership, such as the death, withdrawal, or bankruptcy of an owner;

(2) whether the entity has centralised management similar to that of a corporation;

(3) whether the owners have limited liability similar to that of a corporation; and

(4) whether the owners can freely transfer their interests without consent of the remaining owners similar to that of a typical corporate shareholder.[16]

The authorities issued shortly thereafter continued to view limited liability as merely one factor among four. The Service issued regulations during this period that focused on the factors of continuity of life and centralised management, and further stated that an entity could qualify as a corporation despite the personal liability of its owners. The Board of Tax Appeals similarly held that a limited partnership with four general partners and nine limited partners qualified as a tax partnership.[17] By way of dicta, however, the Board indicated that, although limited liability cannot 'be taken as the sole touchstone of classification, it is nevertheless a very important means of discrimination'.[18] The Board further indicated that entities '[approach] the confines of a corporation' if all

---

[13] *Crocker* v. *Malley*, 249 US 223 (1919); and see *Hecht* v. *Malley*, 265 US 144 (1923).

[14] *Burk-Waggoner Oil Assoc.* v. *Hopkins*, 269 US 110 (1925).

[15] 296 US 344 (1935).

[16] *Ibid.*, at 359; see Treas. Reg. § 301.7701–2.

[17] *Glensder Textile Co.* v. *Commissioner*, 46 BTA 176 (1942), acq., 1942 CB 8.

[18] *Ibid.*, at 183.

their owners have limited liability, or if (i) their general partners lack substantial assets (other than an interest in the entity at issue) and (ii) act as dummies on behalf of the limited partners.[19]

By the 1950s, the Service was more concerned with partnerships masquerading as corporations than with corporations masquerading as partnerships. The Service was particularly concerned that professional groups, normally organised as partnerships, were attempting to achieve corporate status so they could deduct contributions to deferred payment plans (deductions then unavailable to partnerships). Pursuant to this aim, the Service unsuccessfully challenged the corporate status of a medical partnership in a case called *United States* v. *Kintner*[20] and then changed its regulations after this defeat so that entity classification favoured partnerships. The new regulations followed the four factor test described in *Morrisey* v. *United States* (continuity of life, centralised management, limited liability and free transferability) but weighted these tests in favour of partnership status.[21] Under this new weighting system, an entity had to have more corporate characteristics than partnership characteristics in order to qualify as a corporation rather than as a partnership.[22] In other words, corporate tax classification required that an entity have three out of the four factors favouring corporate status. On the issue of limited liability, the Service stated limited liability existed only if no member of the entity was liable for the entity's debts.[23] However, the Service also adopted part of the dicta enunciated by the Board of Tax Appeals, stating that limited liability does not exist if (i) the sole general partners lack substantial assets other than an interest in the entity at issue and (ii) are acting as dummies on behalf of the limited partners.[24]

The Service soon found itself whipsawed by its own regulations with the advent of tax shelter partnerships in the 1970s. The Service unsuccessfully challenged the partnership tax status of two entities during this period.[25] Of note were the general partners in both cases. In each case, the sole general partner was a corporation containing no substantial assets other than the entity at issue, and the corporate general partner in one of these cases was indirectly wholly owned by one of the limited partners.[26] Yet, the courts found that both general partners created unlimited liability despite their shell status because neither corporation was acting as a dummy on behalf of the limited partners. Although the Service ultimately acquiesced,[27] the Service initially responded by issuing a new set of proposed regulations that would have made it harder for entities to

[19] *Ibid.*
[20] 216 F 2d 418 (9th Cir. 1954).
[21] Treas. Reg. § 301.7701–2.
[22] Treas. Reg. § 301.7701–2(a)(3).
[23] Treas. Reg. § 301.7701–2(d)(1).
[24] Treas. Reg. § 301.7701–2(d)(2).
[25] *Zuckman* v. *United States*, 524 F 2d 729 (Ct. Cl. 1975); *Larson* v. *Commissioner*, 66 TC 159 (1976), acq., 1979–2 CB 1–2.
[26] *Zuckman*, 524 F 2d at 731.
[27] Rev. Rul. 79–106, 1979–1 CB 448.

qualify as a partnership with the Service withdrawing these regulations only one day after issue.[28] The news of the day reported that the regulations were issued without the Secretary of Treasury's signature and that the regulation came under fire from real estate interests utilising partnerships to promote investment.[29] Among other changes, the one-day regulations would have prevented taxpayers from establishing unlimited liability by relying on the personal unlimited liability of a single member. Unlimited liability would have instead existed only if all of the entity's unlimited interests outweighed all of its limited interests.[30]

Against this backdrop, the states of Wyoming and Florida respectively enacted LLC statutes in 1977 and 1982.[31] The purpose of these statutes was to attract business to both states by creating a US entity that would provide limited liability for all its members while simultaneously qualifying for partnership tax status under the four factors.[32] These efforts initially met with mixed success, with the Service issuing contradictory rulings both for and against domestic LLCs as tax partnerships.[33] Regulations addressing this issue were similarly divided. The Service under the Carter Administration initially issued regulations in 1980 that would have treated the LLC as a *per se* corporation since all LLC members lacked liability.[34] The Service under the Reagan Administration then withdrew these regulations in 1982 for further study.[35]

In 1988, the Service effectively surrendered the LLC classification question and issued a revenue ruling classifying a Wyoming LLC as a tax partnership.[36] The revenue ruling followed the regulations by applying the four factors without adding special weight to the factor of limited liability. The Service may have conceded the LLC question at this time because Congress had recently enacted statutes eliminating the most common tax abuses involving partnerships.[37] Whatever the merits of this change, the 1988 ruling initiated the widespread enactment of LLCs, with many states adopting LLC statutes just to keep pace.

---

[28] Prop. Treas. Reg. §§ 301.7701–1, 2, 3, 42 Fed. Reg. 1,038 (5 Jan. 1977), withdrawn by 42 Fed. Reg. 1,489 (7 Jan. 1977).

[29] F W Peel, 'Definition of a Partnership: New Suggestions on an Old Issue' [1979] *Wisconsin Law Review* 989, at 1000.

[30] *Ibid.*, at 1002.

[31] Cavitch, *supra* n.4, at § 33.01[2].

[32] W M Gazur and N M Goff, 'Assessing the Limited Liability Company' (1991) 41 *Case Western Law Review* 387, at 389–90.

[33] Compare Priv. Ltr. Rul. 81–06–082 (18 Nov. 1980) with Priv. Ltr. Rul. 83–04–138 (29 Oct. 1982).

[34] Prop. Treas. Reg. § 301.7701–2(a)(2)–(4), (g)(Example (1)) (17 Nov. 1980).

[35] Internal Revenue Service News Release IR–82–145 (16 Dec. 1982).

[36] Rev. Rul. 88–76, 1988–2 CB 360.

[37] In the mid-1980s, Congress had enacted passive activity loss legislation that greatly restricted the use of artificial partnership losses as well as legislation treating publicly held partnerships as *per se* corporations: see generally §§ 469 (limiting passive activity losses) and 7704 (treating most publicly held partnerships as *per se* corporations).

By April 1997, all 50 states and the District of Columbia had enacted LLC statutes.[38]

The Current Check-the-box Regime

The Service surrendered the entity classification issue once state LLC statutes became widespread. According to the Service, state law made tax corporations and partnerships virtually indistinguishable as an economic matter because both could attain limited liability status. The result meant that taxpayers acting under proper tax advice could achieve any tax classification desired without economic consequence, rendering the four-factor regime a simple waste of resources for taxpayers and the Service alike.[39]

Under the current check-the-box regulations, entity classification is largely elective. Most domestic entities with two or more members can simply choose partnership or corporate tax status.[40] If an entity fails to make an election, a default rule treats the entity as a partnership.[41] In the case of single-member entities, the member can choose either to disregard the entity as a 'tax nothing'[42] or to treat the entity as having corporate status with the default rule falling on tax nothing status. As illustrated above, the owner of a tax nothing simply disregards the entity, taking into account the income and loss of the tax nothing as if the owner generated those amounts directly.[43]

The only entities that fall outside this elective regime are those entities listed as '*per se*' corporations.[44] This list of domestic '*per se*' corporations includes entities incorporated under state or federal statute, joint-stock associations, publicly traded partnerships and other entities that were almost universally classified as corporations under the former four-factor system.[45] LLCs are not within the '*per se*' corporation list because LLCs could effectively choose either corporate or partnership tax status under the former four-factor system.

---

[38] Cavitch, *supra* n.4, at § 33.01[2]. LLC statutes initially came in two general forms: (i) bullet-proof statutes and (ii) flexible statutes. Bullet-proof statutes contain very structured LLC characteristics to ensure partnership tax status under the former four factors and accordingly have fewer drafting options under the operating LLC agreement. Conversely, flexible statutes contain more drafting options but do not provide automatic partnership tax status under the former four factors: see Smith, *supra* n.7. Today, with the demise of the four factors, most states have shifted to flexible statutes: *CCH Standard Federal Tax Reporter* (1998), xv, 43,887.027.

[39] Notice 95–14, 1995–1 CB 297.

[40] Treas. Reg. § 301.7701–3(a).

[41] Treas. Reg. §§ 301.7701–2(a), 3(b)(1).

[42] The term 'tax nothing' is a term of art commonly used to describe a single-member entity disregarded from its owner: D S Miller, 'The Tax Nothing' (1997) 74 *Tax Notes* 619.

[43] Treas. Reg. §§ 301.7701–2(a), 3(b)(1)(ii).

[44] Treas. Reg. § 301.7701–3(a).

[45] Treas. Reg. § 301.7701–2(b).

Basic Features of International Hybrids

International hybrids contain more variation than domestic hybrids. As an initial matter, taxpayers are no longer restricted to the LLC formats prescribed by US localities but can also utilise the LLC formats prescribed by foreign countries. Like domestic LLCs, foreign LLCs provide complete limited liability with a mix of partnership legal attributes. LLCs have existed in Germany, France, Brazil, Mexico and other countries long before the various US states enacted LLC legislation.[46]

More notably, the international hybrid potentially provides for inconsistent tax entity classifications in different countries. An LLC may qualify as both a US tax partnership and a foreign tax corporation, or as both a US tax corporation and a foreign tax partnership. LLCs may also qualify as a corporation in both countries or as a partnership in both, but it is inconsistent classification that has excited the tax community as of late. This desire for inconsistent classification frequently means that practitioners will elect US pass-through status for entities treated as a corporation for foreign tax purposes (known as 'classic hybrids') or US corporate status for entities qualifying as a pass-through for foreign tax purposes (known as 'reverse hybrids').

US Historic Disregard for Foreign Tax Labels

The USA has generally adhered to the position that US tax concepts apply to determine US tax classification of a foreign entity without regard to its foreign tax label.[47] In the early 1970s, the Service fully articulated this position when it declared that the former four-factor test fully applied to determine the US tax classification of a foreign entity. The impact of this four-factor test, however, depended on the non-tax 'legal relationships of the members of the organisation among themselves and with the public at large, as well as the interests of the members of the organisation in its assets'.[48] Besides the inherent logic of looking solely to US tax principles for determining US tax consequences, US disre-

---

[46] T E Geu, 'Understanding the Limited Liability Company: A Basic Comparative Primer' (1992) 37 *South Dakota Law Review* 44, at 49. For an in-depth article describing some of the salient differences between domestic and foreign LLCs, including the greater freedom of contract provided by US LLCs, see generally W J Carney, 'Limited Liability Companies: Origins and Antecedents' (1995) 66 *University of Colorado Law Review* 855.

[47] *Abbot Labs. Int'l Co.* v. *United States*, 160 F. Supp. 321, 325 (ND Ill. 1958), affirmed 267 F 2d 940 (7th Cir. 1959); *Arundel Corp.* v. *United States*, 102 F. Supp. 1019 (Ct. Cl. 1952); GCM 34,376 (13 Nov. 1970), revoked on other grounds by, GCM 39,693 (22 Jan. 1988); see Rev. Rul. 72–197, 1972–1 CB 215.

[48] Rev. Rul. 73–254, 1973–1 CB 613.

gard for foreign tax labels was justified on the basis of administrative simplicity and tax fairness for similarly situated foreign and domestic entities.[49]

US disregard for foreign tax labels fully carried over to foreign LLCs. For instance, in a 1977 revenue ruling,[50] the Service applied the four-factor test to a German GmbH (a *Gesellschaft mit beschränkter Haftung*). A GmbH is a limited liability entity with certain optional partnership provisions and generally qualifies as a partnership for German tax purposes.[51] The Service held that the entity possessed three of the four corporate factors, including limited liability, thereby creating US corporate tax classification despite the German tax label to the contrary. However, because the Service relied on the four-factor test, a limited liability GmbH could potentially qualify as a US tax partnership.[52] In a similar vein, other foreign LLCs were found to qualify as a US tax partnership or corporation depending on the circumstances.[53] The only deviation involved a strand of former Service positions indicating that certain foreign entities qualified as automatic corporations without resort to the four-factor test. Entities falling within this automatic status generally consisted of juridical entities formed under law analogous to an incorporation statute of a US state.[54] The Service eventually abandoned this juridical approach in 1988, ruling that an unlimited liability U.K. corporation qualified as a US tax partnership under the four-factor test despite its incorporated status under the U.K. Companies Act.[55] Thus, by the time the check-the-box regulations were adopted, the US tax classification system had uniformly established its disregard for foreign tax labels.

The Current Check-the-box Classification Regime

Foreign entity classification became elective when the Service made classification elective for domestic entities. The rationale for the foreign entity election

---

[49] Gen. Couns. Mem. 36,910 (4 Nov. 1976), revoked in part on other grounds by Gen. Couns. Mem. 39,693 (22 Jan. 1988).

[50] Rev. Rul. 77–214, 1977–1 CB 408, modified and superseded by, Rev. Rul. 93–4, 1993–1 CB 225.

[51] H J Gumpel, *World Tax Series: Taxation in the Federal Republic of Germany* 2nd edn., (Chicago, Commerce Clearing House, 1969), 721–2.

[52] Compare Priv. Ltr. Rul. 83–09–062 (29 Nov. 1982) (treating a GmbH as a taxable corporation) and Priv. Ltr. Rul. 79–35–019 (29 May 1979) (same) with Priv. Ltr. Rul. 96–43–023 (24 July 1996) (treating a GmbH as a tax partnership) and Priv. Ltr. Rul. 96–34–016 (23 May 1996) (same).

[53] E.g., a Brazilian LLC could qualify as either a corporation or a partnership: compare Tech. Adv. Mem. 84–01–001 (16 June 1983) (classifying a Brazilian LLC as a corporation) with Priv. Ltr. Rul. 80–19–112 (15 Feb. 1980) (classifying two Brazilian limitadas, one as a corporation and the other as a partnership). A Saudi Arabian LLC could similarly qualify as either a corporation or a partnership: compare Priv. Ltr. Rul. 80–06–086 (19 Nov. 1979) (classifying a Saudi LLC as a corporation), supplemented by Priv. Ltr. Rul. 81–13–023 (30 Dec. 1980) with Priv. Ltr. Rul. 77–37–049 (17 June 1977) (classifying a Saudi LLC as a partnership).

[54] Gen. Couns. Mem. 35,294 (6 Apr. 1973), revoked by Gen. Couns. Mem. 36,910 (4 Nov. 1976); Gen. Couns. Mem. 34,376 (13 Nov. 1970), revoked by Gen. Couns. Mem. 39,693 (22 Jan. 1988); Gen. Couns. Mem. 18,718, 1937–2 CB 476, made obsolete by Rev. Rul. 70-59, 1970–1 CB 280; Gen. Couns. Mem. 9,067, X–1 CB 337 (1931), made obsolete by Rev. Rul. 67–406, 1967–2 CB 420; Priv. Ltr. Rul. 84–26–031 (26 Mar. 1984).

[55] Rev. Rul. 88–8, 1988–1 CB 403.

was largely the same as the administrative reasons cited for domestic entities. In fact, the Service viewed the four-factor classification system as an even greater administrative burden in the foreign area because foreign entity classification required a full understanding of applicable foreign law.[56]

The elective regime for foreign entities largely comports with the elective regime for domestic entities. Single-member entities can freely choose tax nothing status or corporate status. Entities with two or more members can freely choose partnership or corporate status.[57]

One notable difference pertains to the default rules. As previously stated, taxpayer desire for pass-through status in the international context is not dominated by the largely uniform desire for pass-through tax status existing in the domestic context. Due to this lack of uniformity, the Service adopted a default rule for foreign entities that focused on general taxpayer expectations.[58] Under this approach, a foreign entity with limited liability for its owners creates corporate default status because the parties involved would normally expect limited liability entities to qualify as a corporation. Similarly, single-member foreign entities without limited liability protection for their owners obtain tax nothing default status, and foreign entities with two or more members obtain partnership default status if one or more members have unlimited liability.[59]

Again, as in the domestic entity context, certain foreign entities fall within *per se* corporate tax status. Foreign corporations on this *per se* list consist of entities that virtually always qualified as corporations under the four factor classification system. This list of *per se* foreign corporations is quite extensive, including: (1) entities described as 'corporations or companies' under Canadian law (unless all members have unlimited liability), (2) entities described as an *Aktiengesellschaft* under German law, and (3) entities described as 'public limited companies' under U.K. law.[60]

THE CURRENT INTERNATIONAL BATTLEGROUND

The General Stakes

The discussion above demonstrates that international hybrids are not a new phenomenon. Before the check-the-box regulations, the USA disregarded foreign tax labels in favour of perceived substance. Today, the USA disregards foreign tax labels in favour of taxpayer choice. This new US system in favour of taxpayer choice has greatly facilitated taxpayer use of hybrids that contain inconsistent domestic and foreign tax entity classifications. Taxpayers have

---

[56] Notice 95–14, 1995–1 CB at 298.
[57] Treas. Reg. § 301.7701–3(a).
[58] PS–43–95, 1996–1 CB 865, 868.
[59] Treas. Reg. § 301.7701–3(b)(2)(i).
[60] Treas. Reg. § 301.7701–2(b)(8).

found that these hybrids create ready-made vehicles for reducing tax. In early recognition of these concerns, the Service warned taxpayers when introducing the check-the-box regulations that it would issue appropriate guidance to prevent hybrids from producing results contrary to the policies of the Internal Revenue Code and US tax treaties.[61]

As stated at the beginning of this chapter, the Service has recently adopted an even more aggressive stance against tax avoidance hybrids. The Service is now targeting not only US tax avoidance but also foreign tax avoidance if the latter leads to worldwide tax rates below regular US rates. This stance implicates larger US international tax policy concerns involving capital import and capital export neutrality. According to the Service, international hybrids violate capital-import neutrality when foreign taxpayers invest in the USA through hybrids in a manner that reduces their worldwide tax rates below regular US rates. International hybrids similarly violate capital-export neutrality when US multinationals invest abroad through hybrids in a manner that reduces their worldwide taxes below regular US rates. Both reductions in worldwide tax are said to violate concepts of neutrality because both reductions create an uneven playing field against their wholly domestic competitors, regardless of whether the reductions are effectuated through avoidance of domestic or foreign tax. Taxpayers for their part contend that US concerns should be limited solely to US tax avoidance, mainly on grounds of jurisdictional authority and international competitiveness.[62]

The discussion that follows describes some of the basic hybrid structures used to produce inconsistent tax consequences, focusing mainly on US–Canadian cross-border structures that avoid foreign tax.[63] These basic US–Canadian hybrid structures fall into two overall categories: (i) inbound and (ii) outbound. Inbound hybrids arise when Canadian taxpayers invest in the USA, thereby implicating capital-import neutrality concerns. Outbound hybrids arise when US taxpayers invest in Canada, implicating capital-export neutrality concerns.

Canadian Entity Classification and Potential US–Canadian Hybrids

Unlike US tax entity classification, Canadian tax entity classification has not become unhinged from general non-tax corporate and partnership principles. Canada taxes Canadian corporations and partnerships according to their

---

[61] PS–43–95, 1996–1 CB at 866; Notice 95–14, 1995–1 CB at 298.

[62] For an article providing an excellent discussion of capital-import and capital-export neutrality concerns, see generally C I Kingson, 'The Coherence of International Taxation' (1981) 81 *Columbia Law Review* 81; see also R S Avi-Yonah, 'The Structure of International Taxation: A Proposal for Simplification' (1996) 74 *Texas Law Review* 1301; J A Roin, 'The Grand Illusion: A Neutral System for the Taxation of International Transactions' (1989) 75 *Virginia Law Review* 919.

[63] Notes 114 and 118 *infra* also describe two examples of how taxpayers can use international hybrids to reduce US tax.

non-tax labels.[64] Canada has general and limited partnerships but does not permit the formation of LLCs. Canada instead requires each partnership to have at least one general partner with unlimited liability.[65]

Canadian reliance on non-tax labels does not extend to its classification of foreign entities. With respect to foreign entities, Revenue Canada has ruled that:

> A corporation is an entity created by law having a legal personality and existence separate and distinct from the personality and existence of those who caused its creation or those who own it. A corporation possesses its own capacity to acquire rights and to assume liabilities, and any rights acquired or liabilities assumed by it are not the rights and liabilities of those who control it.[66]

In other words, a foreign entity will qualify as a taxable corporation if that entity is economically comparable to a Canadian corporation, the main feature being limited liability.[67] Revenue Canada has subsequently ruled that US LLCs fall within the corporate classification due to their limited liability.[68]

Several hybrid possibilities emerge when the USA and Canadian systems are viewed side-by-side. As is already evident, the USA allows LLCs to qualify for tax pass-through treatment while Revenue Canada views an LLC as a corporation. General and limited partnerships, on the other hand, always qualify for Canadian tax pass-through treatment, whereas the USA potentially treats these partnerships as a tax pass-through or a corporation depending on taxpayer choice. Even statutory corporations create potential hybrids. While the USA generally lists Canadian corporations on its *per se* taxable corporation list,[69] the USA excludes Canadian companies with unlimited liability for all their owners.[70] The target of this exception is the Nova Scotia unlimited liability company ('ULC').[71] This exclusion from the *per se* list allows taxpayers to classify Nova Scotia ULCs as pass-through entities for US tax purposes, whereas taxpayers must always classify Nova Scotia ULCs as corporations for Canadian tax purposes because of their company label.[72]

---

[64] R J MacKnight, 'What's in a Name? Classifying Partnerships, Associations, and Limited Liability Companies for Income Tax Purposes' [1993] *Canadian Corporations Tax Management Conference* 21:1, 21:20.

[65] 'Doing Business in Canada', 97 *Tax Notes International* 183–16, 22 Sept. 1997, available in LEXIS.

[66] Interpretation Bulletin, IT–343R—Meaning of the Term 'Corporation' (26 Sept. 1977).

[67] B L Welling, *Corporate Law in Canada: The Governing Principles* 2nd edn., (Toronto, Butterworths, 1991), 82–5; and see H Sutherland *et al.*, *Fraser and Stewart's Company Law of Canada* 6th edn., (Scarborough, Ontario, Carswell, 1993), 17–22.

[68] E.g., Rev. Can. Acc. Doc. 95–23–755 (23 Oct. 1995); Rev. Can. Acc. Doc. 95–21–535 (14 Nov. 1995); Rev. Can. Acc. Doc. 95–05–645 (28 Nov. 1995).

[69] Treas. Reg. § 301.7701–2(b)(8)(i).

[70] Treas. Reg. § 301.7701–2(b)(8)(ii)(A).

[71] 'IRS Issues Final Check-the-Box Regs—Tax Simplification Creates Planning Opportunities' 96 *Tax Notes International* 252–18, 30 Dec. 1996, available in LEXIS; and see B C Spudis and R H Dilworth, 'Lawyers Suggest Changes to Per Se Corporation List', 96 *Tax Notes International* 194–15, 4 Oct. 1996, available in LEXIS (suggesting that the proposed regulations exempt the Nova Scotia ULC from the *per se* corporate list).

[72] J Bernstein, 'Nonresident Investment in Canadian Real Estate', 98 *Tax Notes International*

Cross-border Structures

Inbound Investments (Canadian Investment in the USA)

1. Traditional Structures

As a general matter, most Canadian investment in the USA is performed by Canadian corporations. Canadian corporations traditionally invest in the USA either through a US corporation or a US branch. Both these investments potentially implicate US and Canadian income taxes.

Canadian corporate taxpayers most frequently invest in US active businesses through US subsidiaries. In these circumstances, the US taxes the subsidiary's income at regular US rates of 35 per cent.[73] The USA then imposes a second tax at the Canadian parent level when the US subsidiary distributes this income to its Canadian parent, but this tax is restricted to a 5 per cent rate by virtue of the US–Canadian tax treaty.[74] On the Canadian side, Canada views the wholly owned US subsidiary as a Controlled Foreign Affiliate ('CFA').[75] CFA treatment means that Canada will tax the Canadian parent on CFA income when that income accrues. However, Canada imposes this tax only to the extent the CFA generates passive income or fungible active business income that can easily be transferred off Canadian shores (both of which are technically referred to as 'foreign accrual property income').[76] As for the remaining active CFA business income, Canada taxes these amounts only when actually repatriated to the Canadian parent. Canada even waives this deferred tax if: (i) the CFA repatriates its earnings by way of dividend, and (ii) the CFA is located and has an active business in a country having an income tax treaty with Canada, such as the USA.[77] Canada exempts CFA dividends from treaty countries because Canada assumes that the CFA has already been fully taxed by the treaty country (Canada typically making treaties only with countries imposing comparable rates).[78]

> *Example (1).* Facts: Canco owns all the stock of US Sub. US Sub generates $100 of active, non-fungible US business income. At the end of the year, US Sub distributes its net after-tax earnings to Canco by way of dividend.
>
> Result: US Sub has $100 of income subject to US tax at 35 per cent, leaving only $65 of after-tax proceeds. Canada does not tax Canco on these earnings

---

12–25, 20 Jan. 1998, available in LEXIS; and see 'Nova Scotia Liability Corporation Classified as a Partnership', 96 *Tax Notes International* 205–13, 22 Oct. 1996, available in LEXIS (synopsis and test of Priv. Ltr. Rul. 96–42–019 (18 Oct. 1996)).

[73] IRC § 11(a)–(b)(1).
[74] Art. X(2)(a) of the US–Canadian Income Tax Treaty.
[75] ITA, s 95(1) ('controlled foreign affiliate').
[76] V Krishna, *Canadian International Income Taxation* (Scarborough, Ontario, Carswell, 1995), ch VII.4(d).
[77] ITA, s 113(1)(a); regs 5907(1)(b), (d), (11).
[78] Krishna, *supra* n.76, at ch.VII.4(f)(ii)(A).

as they accrue even though US Sub qualifies as a CFA because the earnings are from active, non-fungible business activities. The USA then taxes Canco when receiving the $65 of after-tax proceeds, but the US–Canadian income tax treaty limits this tax to 5 per cent ($3.25). Canada waives its tax on the dividend because the dividends are from US Sub, a corporation located and having an active business in a treaty country. In the end, Canco has $61.75 of after-tax proceeds ($100–$35–$3.25).

When Canadian corporate taxpayers invest in US branches, the general results are the same with slightly different contours. The USA again taxes the US income at the regular 35 per cent US rate. The USA also imposes a second tax, known as the 'branch profits tax'. This second tax arises at the Canadian parent level when the US branch constructively repatriates after-tax proceeds to the Canadian home office,[79] but this tax is restricted to a 5 per cent rate by virtue of the US–Canadian tax treaty (the same rate as dividends from a wholly owned US subsidiary).[80] Congress created this tax for constructive repatriations to ensure that US tax falls on branch repatriations in the same fashion as dividend repatriations from US subsidiaries.[81] On the Canadian tax side, Canadian corporate taxpayers currently account for branch income and loss as these amounts accrue.[82] Canadian tax on branch income typically amounts to 40 per cent,[83] but Canada provides foreign tax credit offsets for both levels of US tax imposed on the branch.[84]

> *Example (2).* Facts: Canco owns US branch. US branch generates $100 of business income. At the end of the year, US branch distributes its net after-tax earnings to Canco's home office.
>
> Result: US branch has $100 of US income subject to US tax at 35 per cent, leaving only $65 of after-tax proceeds. The USA imposes a second tax on the $65 of after-tax proceeds when repatriated to Canco's home office, but the US–Canadian income tax treaty limits this tax to 5 per cent ($3.25). Canada normally imposes tax at 40 per cent with tax credit offsets for US taxes paid. In the end, Canco has $60 of after-tax proceeds with the US imposing combined taxes of $38.25 ($35 + $3.25), and Canada imposing net taxes of $1.75 ($40 minus the combined $38.25 of US taxes).[85]

---

[79] IRC § 884(a). Constructive repatriation generally arises whenever US branch assets decrease by reasons other than branch losses: see IRC § 884(b). However, the branch tax applies only to US business income earned by foreign corporate investors, not generally from passive investments such as interest: IRC § 884(b).

[80] Art. 10(6) of the US–Canadian Income Tax Treaty.

[81] HR Rep. No. 426, 99th Cong., 2d Sess. 432–3 (1986); S Rep. No. 313, 99th Cong., 2d Sess. 400–02 (1986).

[82] Krishna, *supra* n.76, at ch. VII(2)(b)(i)–(ii).

[83] ITA, ss 123, 123.1, 123.2.

[84] ITA, s 126(2); Rev. Can. Acc. Doc. 9612907 (undated). See generally Krishna, *supra* n.76, at VII.2(b)(iv).

[85] As examples (1) and (2) demonstrate, Canadian investment in US subsidiaries generally creates lower worldwide tax than Canadian investment in US branches. This saving results because the

2. Canadian-owned Classic Hybrids

Until recently, Canadian investors could use classic hybrid entities to reduce their worldwide taxes on US investments far below the typical rates just described. This classic hybrid came in the form of a US LLC that qualified as both a US tax partnership and a Canadian tax corporation.

In the classic hybrid structure, the Canadian parent owned a hybrid entity and a US subsidiary with an active US business. The hybrid also acted as a creditor to the US subsidiary with the respect to US subsidiary notes. The US subsidiary first paid the interest to the hybrid, and then the hybrid paid the interest to its Canadian parent by way of distribution.[86] When the US subsidiary paid interest to the hybrid, the interest expense offset the US subsidiary's business income as long as that subsidiary was not thinly capitalised.[87] The USA did not tax the hybrid on its simultaneous receipt of the interest because the hybrid qualified as a US tax partnership.[88] The USA instead taxed the Canadian parent with the rate restricted to 10 per cent under the US–Canadian tax treaty.[89] The USA also ignored any distributions from the hybrid to the Canadian parent because the USA does not generally tax distributions by partnerships to their partners.[90] On the Canadian side, Canada viewed the hybrid as a foreign corporation qualifying as a CFA. While CFA interest normally qualifies as passive income triggering a constructive dividend, Canada treated the interest as active business income because the Canadian CFA regime treats interest as active when paid from active related parties (in this instance, the active US subsidiary).[91] Canada also failed to tax the interest proceeds when distributed from the CFA hybrid because the CFA hybrid resides in the USA, a treaty country.[92] The net result reduced the group's worldwide tax from full rates to an aggregate rate of 10 per cent.

exemption provided under the CFA system eliminates all Canadian taxes, whereas the Canadian credit under the branch structure eliminates Canadian taxes only to the extent of US taxes paid.

[86] HR Rep. No. 148, 105th Cong., 1st Sess. 550 (1997); S Rep. No. 33, 105th Cong., 1st Sess. 87 (1997).

[87] IRC § 163(a), (j).

[88] IRC § 701.

[89] Art. XI(2) of the US–Canadian Income Tax Treaty. The treaty rate for repatriating US income via interest payments is slightly higher than the 5% treaty rate for repatriating US income via dividends.

[90] IRC § 731(a)–(b).

[91] ITA, s 95(2)(a)(ii). Query whether this aspect of the structure was as Canadian tax-free as many practitioners believed. The CFA regime contains an anti-abuse rule that eliminates active business treatment for related party interest when related party stock is acquired with the principal purpose of avoiding tax: ITA, s 95(6). An internal memorandum from Revenue Canada suggests this anti-avoidance rule may apply to the classic hybrid structure: Rev. Can. Acc. Doc. 971312 (20 May 1997), 98 *Tax Notes International* 87–14, available in LEXIS. However, setting aside this memorandum, most Canadian practitioners believed the CFA anti-abuse rule was aimed solely at situations where a previously existing creditor formed a *de minimis* relationship with a previously existing unrelated creditor, not at the hybrid structure where all the parties are related from start to finish: see D M Sherman, *Canadian Department of Finance Technical Notes* 9th edn., (Scarborough, Ontario, Thomson Professional Publishing, 1997), 677–8.

[92] ITA, s 113(1)(a); Reg. § 5907(1)(b), (1)(d), (11).

Example. Facts: Canco owns all the stock of US Sub and all of Hybrid. Hybrid is a US LLC qualifying as both a Canadian corporation and a US partnership. US Sub is indebted to Hybrid. US Sub generates $100 of active business income and pays $100 of interest to Hybrid. Hybrid subsequently distributes its net after-tax income to Canco.

Result: assuming US Sub is not thinly capitalised, all of US Sub's income is offset by the interest paid to Hybrid. The US tax on Canco for Hybrid's receipt of interest is limited to 10 per cent by virtue of the US–Canadian tax treaty. The USA also fails to tax the distribution from Hybrid to Canco because the distribution qualifies as a tax-free partnership distribution. On the Canadian side, Hybrid qualifies as a CFA. None of its interest income is taxed as it accrues because the interest stems from the active business of US Sub, a related treaty country CFA. In the end, the $100 of income earned by US Sub is subject to only $10 of worldwide tax.

The USA recently enacted new rules to end this tax arbitrage under all its treaties, including the US–Canadian tax treaty.[93] These new anti-avoidance rules reinterpret how the USA applies its treaties to hybrid entities. This reinterpretation essentially eliminates the 10 per cent treaty rate for the hybrid structure in favour of regular US rates. As a result, the classic hybrid structure no longer contains the interest deduction-income mismatch. The USA continues to allow deductions for the interest with the interest fully offsetting taxable income of US Sub, but the USA taxes Hybrid's receipt of interest at full US rates.

The USA justifies this new treaty interpretation by arguing that US tax treaties are predicated on the mutual premise that its tax treaty partners and the USA are asserting full taxing jurisdiction over the same income.[94] US tax should accordingly yield to treaties only when those treaties prevent double taxation. The USA does not intend to have its tax treaties utilised so that foreign taxpayers can operate in US markets at tax rates comparable to that of a tax haven. Consistently with this philosophy, the US does not generally negotiate income tax treaties with tax havens, reserving its treaty network for countries with comparable tax rates.

This change in interpretation has created substantial controversy. Many practitioners strenuously object to the new treaty interpretation on tax policy grounds. They mainly argue that the USA has no right unilaterally to change its interpretation of tax treaties, especially if no US tax is otherwise avoided.[95] Turning to the hybrid structure, practitioners argue that direct interest payments from a US subsidiary to a Canadian parent have the same US tax conse-

---

[93] See generally IRC § 894(c); Treas. Reg. § 1.894–1T(d).

[94] TD 8722, 1997–29 IRB at 4—6.

[95] K S Blanchard, 'Proposed Regs Violate US Tax Treaties', 97 *Tax Notes Today* 132–29, 10 July 1997, available on LEXIS; R Young, 'Limitation on US Treaty Benefits for Payments to Hybrid Entities', 97 *Tax Notes Today* 127–4, 2 July 1997, available on LEXIS; and see J Avakian, 'Hybrid Entity Proposal Worries International Practitioners', 97 *Tax Notes Today* 121–4, 24 June 1997, available on LEXIS.

quence as the hybrid structure—interest payments offsetting the US subsidiary's fully taxed income with the Canadian parent's interest income taxed at a 10 per cent US rate. The hybrid structure leaves this US tax effect in place, only avoiding Canadian tax upon repatriation to the Canadian parent.

US tax authorities seemingly have two policy concerns with the hybrid structure's avoidance of Canadian tax. First and foremost, this hybrid structure violates capital-import neutrality, leaving wholly domestic US taxpayers at a competitive disadvantage with Canadian investors owning US subsidiaries.[96] US taxpayers are typically subject to a 35 per cent tax rate, whereas the hybrid structure allows Canadian investors the benefit of a lower 10 per cent rate. Tax fairness would dictate that both entities should operate on a level tax playing field. Secondly, the classic hybrid structure does in fact effectively deprive the USA of revenue despite taxpayer protestations to the contrary. As shown above, the classic hybrid structure contains a mismatch. For every $100 withdrawn, the parties offset $25 of US tax (the interest deductions offset $100 of US income at 35 per cent rates and create $100 of includible US income at only 10 per cent rates). While this result could occur via direct interest repatriations as practitioners suggest, taxpayers have little incentive to make direct interest repatriations of this kind because Canadian taxes soak up the US taxes saved. Thus, the classic hybrid structure creates the need for a US tax-reducing method of Canadian repatriation that would otherwise not exist.

3. Canadian-owned Reverse Hybrids

Canadian-owned reverse hybrids are currently a less controversial technique than classic hybrids. Under this structure, Canadian taxpayers invest in a US hybrid that elects corporate status for US tax purposes but acts as a pass-through for Canadian tax purposes. The reverse hybrid may come in the form of a non-incorporated US business entity, such as a general or limited US partnership.[97]

Setting aside specialised situations, the reverse hybrid has little overall value for aggressive tax planning with the possible exception of duplicating losses. If Canadian taxpayers invest in a reverse hybrid, Canadian taxpayers can deduct hybrid losses against Canadian taxable income as these losses accrue. This immediate opportunity for deducting losses becomes especially important for new US businesses with anticipated start-up losses.[98] Canadian taxpayers can similarly deduct these losses against US income, even possibly against US income that is unrelated to the activity generating the loss.

---

[96] See L A Sheppard, 'News Analysis—Congress' Cheap Canadian Joke' (1997) 76 *Tax Notes* 1005.

[97] The reverse hybrid cannot come in the form of a single member entity. Single-member LLCs are *per se* corporations for Canadian tax purposes, and US branches do not appear to qualify as entities that can elect US corporate tax status: see Treas. Reg. § 301.7701–1(a).

[98] Krishna, *supra* n.76, at VII.2(b)(i).

Example. Facts: Canco Parent owns all the stock of Canco Sub. Canco Parent and Canco Sub respectively own 99 and 1 per cent of reverse hybrid. Reverse hybrid owns all the stock of US Sub. Reverse Hybrid qualifies as a US partnership for Canadian tax purposes, but the parties elect corporate status for US tax purposes. Canco Parent and Canco Sub respectively generate $99 and $1 of Canadian income from their separate truck-leasing businesses, reverse hybrid generates $100 of loss from its car sales business, and US Sub generates $100 of US income from its motorcycle sales business. Because reverse hybrid qualifies as a corporation for US tax purposes, reverse hybrid can file US consolidated returns with US Sub.

Result: Canco Parent and Canco Sub may deduct the reverse hybrid loss against their $100 of Canadian trucking income because reverse hybrid qualifies as a pass-through entity for Canadian tax purposes. On the US side, reverse hybrid may also seemingly deduct the loss against the $100 of US Sub car income because the consolidated return filing allows reverse hybrid and US Sub to combine profit and loss. Thus, reverse hybrid's single stream of $100 of loss can seemingly offset $100 of unrelated Canadian income and $100 of unrelated US income.

This duplication of a single loss against unrelated income may prove troublesome for US tax authorities. Congress previously enacted rules to eliminate similar forms of loss duplication.[99] In the initial loss duplication setting, taxpayers typically formed a loss corporation with a US place of incorporation and a UK place of management, thereby creating dual residence.[100] This dual residence subjected the loss corporation to worldwide US and UK tax as well as mutual worldwide use of loss. To enhance their losses, the dual corporate resident would file consolidated returns with US and UK corporate groups. When losses arose as expected, the losses offset both US and U.K. taxable income from other members. For instance, if the dual corporate resident generated $100 of loss, the loss would offset $100 of US income from related US members and $100 of UK income from related UK members. Meanwhile, the profitable US and UK related companies would each report their profits to only one country. Multinational foreign groups soon isolated losses for duplication whenever possible, eventually leading profitable foreign groups to reduce their worldwide taxes to nominal amounts.

Although taxpayers contended that the above structure was not a US concern since it only avoided foreign tax,[101] Congress soon acted to prevent what it perceived as an undue advantage for foreigners *vis-à-vis* their wholly US competitors, thereby evidencing the desire to protect capital-import neutrality. Under the dual consolidated loss rules that resulted, US domestic corporations with dual

---

[99] See generally IRC § 1503(d).

[100] S. Rep. No. 313, 99th Cong., 2d Sess. 419–21 (1986).

[101] J B Magee, F S Farmer and R A Katcher, 'The Final Dual Consolidated Loss Regulations: Reassessing the Congressional Mandate', 92 *Tax Notes Today* 252–87, 18 Dec. 1997, available in LEXIS.

residence can no longer use their losses to offset income from other US corporations (or from other business units).[102] A US domestic corporation under this rule includes 'any corporation otherwise treated as a domestic corporation by the [Internal Revenue] Code' as long as that domestic corporation is simultaneously subject to tax by a foreign country on a worldwide or on a residence basis (that is, is subject to foreign tax by virtue of its status as a foreign entity rather than on an item-by-item basis by virtue of source).[103] The dual consolidated loss rules do not deny the loss altogether, just against unrelated US income.[104]

Returning to the structure at issue, it is questionable whether the Canadian owned reverse hybrid falls within the dual consolidated loss rules. While the reverse hybrid qualifies as a domestic corporation under the Code, the reverse hybrid may not be an entity subject to foreign tax by virtue of its residence. The reverse hybrid is subject to worldwide tax only by virtue of the residence status of its owners. Moreover, the regulations address only hybrids that are a component of a US corporation.[105] The rules do not specifically address a US corporation that itself qualifies as a hybrid because the rules predate the check-the-box regulations. As a matter of policy however, the Canadian-owned reverse hybrid is arguably problematic from a US tax viewpoint. This structure encourages foreigners to shift their losses into the US so that losses no longer simply offset foreign income, but US income as well.

Outbound Investments (US Investments in Canada)

1. Traditional Structures

US investment in Canada roughly mirrors the format of Canadian investment in the USA, implicating both US and Canadian income taxes. As a general matter, US corporate taxpayers traditionally make Canadian investments through a Canadian corporation or a branch.

Turning to the specifics, US parent corporations most frequently invest in Canadian active businesses through wholly-owned Canadian subsidiaries. In these circumstances, Canada first taxes the business income at full Canadian rates of 40 per cent. Canada then taxes the US parent when the Canadian subsidiary repatriates the income via dividend with the US–Canadian tax treaty restricting this second tax to 5 per cent.[106] On the US side, the US views the wholly-owned Canadian subsidiary as a controlled foreign corporation

---

[102] Treas. Reg. § 1.1503–2(b)(1).

[103] IRC § 1503(d)(2)(A); Treas. Reg. § 1.1503–2(c)(1)–(2).

[104] For instance, if the dual US–UK resident just described generated $100 of net loss from the restaurant business, the dual resident could still use the loss to offset $100 of its subsequent restaurant income. This form of offset is not deemed harmful because the restaurant income is equally accounted for by two countries. The dual consolidated loss rules apply only when a single loss arises in two countries and that loss separately offsets two streams of unrelated income, each of which separately arises in only one country.

[105] Treas. Reg. § 1.1502–3(c)(4).

[106] Art. X(2)(a) of the US–Canadian Income Tax Treaty.

('CFC').[107] CFC treatment means that the USA will tax the US parent as currently accruing constructive dividends from the CFC if the CFC generates passive income or fungible active business income that can easily be transferred off US shores (both technically referred to as 'subpart F income').[108] Active non-fungible CFC business income does not generate constructive dividends. The USA taxes this income only when repatriated to the US parent, offsetting the US tax with foreign tax credits for Canadian taxes paid by the CFC.[109]

When US corporations invest in Canadian branches, Canada again taxes the business income at full Canadian rates. Canada also imposes a second tax, known as the branch profits tax. This second tax arises at the US parent level when the US branch constructively repatriates its income to the US home office,[110] but this tax is restricted to a 5 per cent rate by virtue of the US–Canadian tax treaty (the same rate as dividends from a wholly-owned Canadian subsidiary).[111] On the US tax side, US corporations currently account for Canadian branch income and loss as those amounts accrue.[112] The USA typically imposes tax on branch income at 35 per cent with foreign tax credit offsets for both levels of Canadian tax imposed on the branch.[113]

2. Nova Scotia Classic Hybrids

The Nova Scotia unlimited liability company (ULC) has become a popular Canadian vehicle for US investors. As described earlier, the Nova Scotia ULC is the only hybrid that can act as a corporation for Canadian tax purposes but as a pass-through for US tax purposes.[114]

One widely used function of the Nova Scotia ULC is to provide US investors with the ability to utilise losses.[115] Unlike a typical Canadian corporate sub-

---

[107] IRC § 957(a).

[108] See IRC §§ 951(a), 952(a)(2), 954.

[109] See IRC §§ 301(a)–(c), 902(a).

[110] ITA, s 219(1). The Canadian branch tax, like the US branch tax, does not generally apply to passive income such as interest: *ibid.*; see *Pullaman* v. *The Queen*, 83 DTC 5080.

[111] Art. X(6) of the US–Canada Income Tax Treaty.

[112] C H Gustafson, R J Peroni and R C Pugh, *Taxation of International Transactions* (St Paul, West Pub Co., 1997), 778–80.

[113] IRC § 901; Treas. Reg. § 1.901–2(b)(2)(iv)(Example (3)).

[114] Treas. Reg. § 301.7701–2(b)(8)(ii)(A).

[115] Another function of the Nova Scotia ULC is to accelerate foreign tax credits. As a pass-through entity for US tax purposes, the US parent of a profitable Nova Scotia ULC not only receives immediate tax on the Nova Scotia ULC's income but also immediate foreign credits for Canadian taxes paid. The benefit of these credits outweighs the burden of the additional income because Canadian taxes are generally higher than US taxes, providing the US parent with excess credits which the US parent can use to offset US taxes on income from other foreign (not US) sources: IRC § 904(a). For instance, assume US Parent owns all the stock of Nova Scotia ULC, and Nova Scotia ULC generates $100 of Canadian appliance sales income subject to $40 of Canadian tax. Under these circumstances, if the parties elect to treat Nova Scotia ULC as a pass-through entity for US tax purposes, US Parent has $100 of additional income with $40 of foreign tax credits. The tax credits completely offset the $35 of additional US tax normally associated with the income. The extra $5 of tax credits could then offset US Parent's tax on other foreign source income, reducing the US tax on that income to a $30 rate.

At first blush, this acceleration of credits appears problematic because the tax credits should

sidiary, the US pass-through nature of the Nova Scotia ULC allows its US owners currently to deduct losses of its Nova Scotia ULC as they accrue. However, Nova Scotia ULC losses fall squarely within the dual consolidated loss rules previously described because they qualify as a foreign hybrid business unit of a US domestic corporation.[116] US investors can accordingly use Nova Scotia ULC losses against unrelated US business income only if the losses do not offset unrelated Canadian taxable income.[117] The dual consolidated loss rules in this context prevent US multinationals from reducing their worldwide taxes below full US rates imposed on their wholly domestic competitors, thereby protecting capital-export neutrality.

As a practical matter, the dual consolidated loss rules rarely apply for US multinationals investing in Canada, since Nova Scotia ULC losses generally cannot offset unrelated Canadian income. No such opportunities to offset Canadian unrelated income readily exist mainly because Canada does not have consolidated return rules that allow losses to offset income of other Canadian corporations.[118]

3. Interest Syphoning Classic Hybrids[119]

The last structure to be discussed involves classic hybrids that syphon income from Canada via interest payments. The basic purpose of this structure is to

seemingly prevent double taxation of underlying Canadian income, not unrelated foreign income. However, use of the Nova Scotia ULC is not problematic when viewed in isolation. First, US Parent would still receive excess credits when subsequently receiving Nova Scotia ULC dividends if US Parent had instead elected corporate status for its Nova Scotia ULC: IRC § 902(a). Secondly, the US tax system already has a complex statutory regime in place that prevents abusive cross-crediting by limiting taxpayer use of credits solely against foreign source income of similar types: IRC § 904(d)(1). Under this regime, excess credits from foreign business income offset US tax only on other forms of foreign business income, not on foreign passive income. These income type restrictions prevent abusive cross-crediting because each income type is generally subject to similar rates of tax in various foreign countries, thereby generally preventing excess credits on high-taxed foreign sourced income from being used as an offset against US tax on low-taxed foreign sourced income: HR Rep. No. 426, 99th Cong., 2d Sess. 335 (1986); S Rep. No. 313, 99th Cong., 2d Sess. 308 (1986). Returning to the example above, the $5 of excess Canadian credits would often have no beneficial impact for US Parent because its business income located in other foreign countries is typically subject to similar high rates of tax.

[116] Treas. Reg. § 1.1503–2(b)(1), (4).

[117] IRC § 1503(d)(1), (3).

[118] B Erard, 'Income Tax Compliance Burden on Canadian Big Business—A Working Paper Prepared for Finance Canada', 98 *Tax Notes International* 73–15, 16 Apr. 1998, available on LEXIS, Part 2—Overview of Tax Structure.

[119] When examining simple US–Canadian cross-border structures, reverse hybrids seemingly do not play any significant role in reducing Canadian tax but may act to reduce US tax. Reverse hybrids in this circumstance appear to accelerate foreign tax credits without the underlying income. For instance, assume US Parent owns all the stock of US Sub. US Parent and US Sub respectively own 99 and 1 per cent of reverse hybrid generating $100 of active Canadian business income. Reverse hybrid qualifies as a Canadian partnership for Canadian tax purposes, but the parties elect Canadian corporate CFC status for US tax purposes. Under these circumstances, the US owners can immediately use the $40 of Canadian tax as credits against US tax. However, the US owners do not have constructive dividends from hybrid's business income because hybrid qualifies as a CFC for US tax purposes. If the US owners instead invested in a pure Canadian corporation, they could only receive the credits when simultaneously receiving the underlying dividend income.

Sophisticated practitioners argue that this structure appears to have current legal support due to

create Canadian interest deductions without US income. Hybrids of this kind qualify as a Canadian partnership for Canadian tax purposes with the parties electing corporate status for US tax purposes. Under this structure, US investors own a hybrid and a Canadian subsidiary with the Canadian subsidiary repatriating its earnings by way of interest to the hybrid. Assuming the Canadian subsidiary is not thinly capitalised,[120] the interest payments offset the Canadian subsidiary's income.[121] Canada then treats the interest as received by US taxpayers because Canada views the hybrid as a partnership, resulting in a 10 per cent tax by virtue of the US–Canadian tax treaty.[122] On the US side, the hybrid qualifies as a corporate CFC. The USA would typically treat the hybrid's interest as passive income generating constructive dividends,[123] but the CFC regime treats CFC interest as active business income if from a related CFC with a place of incorporation and active business located in the same country.[124] The net effect of this structure is to reduce Canadian taxation from full rates to a 10 per cent treaty rate.[125]

> *Example.* Facts: US Parent owns all the stock of US Sub and Canco, a CFC operating an active Canadian business. US Parent and US Sub also respectively own 99 and 1 per cent of hybrid located in Canada. Hybrid qualifies as a partnership for Canadian tax purposes, and the parties elect CFC corporate status for US tax purposes. Hybrid acts as a creditor on a note from Canco. Canco earns $100 of active Canadian business income and pays $100 of interest to hybrid.

changes in Service position: J L Walser and R E Culbertson, '*Encore Une Fois*: Check-the-Box on the International Stage', (1997) 76 *Tax Notes* 403 at 417–8; S K Shapiro, R B Harvey and M S Burke, 'Uses of Hybrid Entities in the International Arena', 96 *Tax Notes Today* 8–44, 11 Jan. 1996, available on LEXIS. Initially, the Service and the courts took the position that US owners could not receive immediate credits for reverse hybrids: *Abbott Laboratories Int'l Co.* v. *United States*, 160 F Supp. 31 (ND Il. 1958), affirmed 267 F 2d 940 (7th Cir. 1959). However, the Service appears to have administratively reversed this result. In Rev. Rul. 72–197, 1972–1 CB 215, US citizens owned a domestic reverse hybrid that qualified as a corporation for US tax purposes but as a pass-through entity for foreign tax purposes. Without referring to *Abbot Laboratories*, Rev. Rul. 72–197 held that the shareholders, not the hybrid receiving the income, were eligible for tax credits since foreign tax law viewed only the shareholders as liable for the tax. In recent recognition that this mismatch of credits and income creates planning opportunities, the Service has issued a notice stating that the Service is 'considering either deferring the tax credits until the taxpayer recognises the income, or accelerating the income recognition to the time at which the credits are allowed': Notice 98–5, 1998–3 IRB 49. But see Internal Revenue Service Restructuring and Reform Act of 1998, Report to Accompany HR 2676, 105th Cong., 2d Sess. 128 (1998) (suggesting that the Service limit the scope of Notice 98–5).

120   ITA, s 18(4).
121   ITA, s 20(1)(c).
122   Art. XI(2) of the US–Canada Income Tax Treaty.
123   IRC § 954(c)(1)(A).
124   IRC § 954(c)(3)(A)(i).
125   This hybrid structure is similar to the inbound classic hybrid. The main difference between the two structures is that the CFC regime does not provide the CFA exemption for dividends from a foreign treaty subsidiary. Therefore, the hybrid in this structure cannot repatriate earnings to the USA without full US tax.

Result: assuming Canco is not thinly capitalised, the $100 of interest completely offsets Canco's $100 of business income. Canada imposes a tax on hybrid's receipt of interest, but this tax is restricted to 10 per cent under the US–Canadian Tax Treaty because Canada looks through the hybrid to the US owners for determining tax. Although Hybrid qualifies as a CFC for US tax purposes, Hybrid's receipt of interest does not qualify as passive income because the interest comes from Canco, an entity that the US views as a related Canadian CFC engaged in a Canadian business.

In a controversial move, the Service recently issued temporary regulations designed to prevent US multinationals from forming interest-syphoning hybrids with their foreign subsidiaries so as to reduce their foreign tax to inappropriately low levels. The new rules provide that CFCs utilising interest-syphoning hybrids in this fashion will no longer receive active treatment on related party note interest, thereby triggering immediate constructive dividend income.[126] Thus, to the extent multinationals save any foreign taxes in the hybrid structures identified by the Service, US tax will apply to soak up most of the difference. The Service justified its actions on the basis of capital-export neutrality. According to the Service, action had to be taken, '[o]therwise, US businesses striving to be competitive in the United States could have been disadvantaged by tax burdens higher than those imposed on their multinational counterparts that availed themselves of hybrid structures.'[127]

These anti-avoidance regulations have since faced heavy opposition.[128] Practitioners seriously questioned whether the Service had the authority to issue these regulations under the current statutory rules. On policy grounds, practitioners also contended their efforts to reduce foreign tax on their foreign subsidiaries is comparable to those efforts made by their competitors. To punish US-owned foreign subsidiaries alone would put US multinationals at a severe disadvantage. Taxpayers have even enlisted Congressional support with a bill that potentially imposed a six-month moratorium on the regulations.[129] In the face of this strong opposition, the Service withdrew its regulations in temporary form and reissued them in proposed form to be effective for all transactions entered into on or after 19 June 1998.[130]

---

[126] TD 8767, 1998–16 IRB 4; Notice 98–11, 1998–6 IRB 18.

[127] Robert E. Rubin, Secretary of Treasury, 'Treasury Defends Guidance on Hybrid Entities', 98 *Tax Notes Today* 63–34, 2 Apr. 1998, available on LEXIS.

[128] E.g., T J Usher, 'Business Group Reiterates Opposition to Tax Treatment of Hybrid Entities', 98 *Tax Notes Today* 103–20, 29 May 1998, available on LEXIS; M Weinberger and H Ruempler, 'Multinationals Balk at Administration's Proposals on Hybrid Transactions', 98 *Tax Notes Today* 53–36, available on LEXIS; S C Todrys, 'NYSBA Responds to Proposed Treatment of Hybrid Branch Arrangements', 98 *Tax Notes Today* 81–30, available on LEXIS; D R Tillinghast, 'An Old-Timer's Comment on Subpart F', 98 *Tax Notes Today* 60–43, available on LEXIS.

[129] Internal Revenue Service Restructuring and Reform Act of 1998, Report to Accompany HR 2676, at 122–8; see also 'Archer's Call for No New Regs on Hybrid Entities Goes Unheeded', 98 *Tax Notes Today* 59–55, 27 Mar. 1998, available on LEXIS (House Ways and Means Committee Chairman requesting that the Service not proceed with regulations).

[130] Notice 98–35, 1998–26 IRB 1.

Interestingly enough, the new anti-avoidance regulations do not apply to the interest-syphoning example described above. The rules were aimed at a related situation where multinationals were using hybrid structures and related party notes to shift business income from high-taxed jurisdictions to tax haven jurisdictions via related party interest payments.[131] The anti-avoidance rules failed to contemplate the shifting of income in the above example, which involves a hybrid located in the same country as the high-taxed foreign business but subject to a low level of tax by virtue of a US tax treaty.

CONCLUSION

The hybrid entity represents the latest round in the ongoing struggle between tax practitioners and the Service. Practitioners initially used the hybrid entity mainly in the domestic US context to reduce tax on limited liability entities from two levels to one. With the economics between limited and unlimited liability status eroded, the Service conceded defeat and provided taxpayers with complete freedom to choose tax entity status. Today, practitioners are attempting to use this freedom in the international arena so as to reduce a single level of tax to little or no worldwide tax.

The hybrid entity now stands in the centre of a continuing debate about US international tax policy. Should the USA acquiesce to taxpayer erosions of worldwide tax or should the USA ensure that worldwide taxes are maintained at rates comparable to domestic US rates? The Service for its part has currently chosen the latter option, becoming a world tax policeman of sorts. Practitioners meanwhile are struggling to keep one step ahead.

At this stage, the Service seems to have strong support from Congress in its fight to protect wholly domestic operations from foreign competitors in terms of capital-import neutrality. However, the Service is currently facing considerable opposition in its fight to protect wholly domestic operations from US multinationals in terms of capital-export neutrality with Congress instead opting for international competitiveness. While the Service has indicated its intent to continue the fight in the latter regard, the Service's initial resolve may be weakening.

---

[131] Temp. Treas. Reg.§§ 1.954–2T, 1.954–9T.

7

Environmental Challenges for Japanese Corporations in the Twenty-first Century: Legal Aspects of Corporate Environmental Risk Management

JUNKO UEDA

INTRODUCTION

Three decades have passed since it was revealed that many industrial pollution victims were suffering from severe mental and physical disorders in particular areas in Japan. Our environmental awareness rose dramatically at that time. What are called 'the four major pollution sites' became well-known between 1967 and 1969 (though one of them was detected as early as 1910, and the other three were observable from at least the middle of this century).

A historical overview of Japan's environmental law and policy could be divided into three distinct decades. The first decade commenced with the government measures taken to settle pollution problems in response to the damages from 'the four major pollution sites'. These measures were done within a legislative framework as well as an administrative one. Some noticeable movements initiated by the government at this stage were the submission of the Constitutional Bill of Protection against Pollution to the Diet (*Kogai Taisaku Kihon Ho*), which passed it in 1967, and the setting up of the Environmental Agency in 1971,[1] which has the powers to prepare bills and rules for environmental protection, to undertake administrative tasks to sustain the environment, and to examine and comment on the other ministries' policies. At this juncture the pollution was known to be caused by industrial activities and was considered only in the context of disputes between the inhabitants influenced by such activities and the corporations. In other words, it was not yet considered a serious problem concerning all the creatures on the earth. Thus, corporations were concerned only about the compliance with the laws and rules.

---

[1] The Environmental Agency is scheduled to be promoted to a higher rank as one of the governmental ministries in the scheme of administrative structure reform.

The next decade was somewhat different from the earlier one. From the mid-1970s and through the 1980s, after the UN Stockholm Conference on Human Environment was held in 1972, there came a world-wide anti-pollution campaign based on the declaration adopted at the conference. In addition, the concept of pollution was expanded beyond particular industrial issues to include the international problems that sometimes occurred, as when, for example, polluted air moved from a point in one country to many other areas across borders, or when the natural environment in developing countries was exploited by the developed countries. Concurrently, world-wide environmental issues, which should be dealt with co-operatively, such as acid rain, depletion of the ozone layer, and global warming came to be closely monitored. At this point, protection of the natural environment became a major world issue and the concept of 'sustainable development' was formulated. This concept refers to the idea that the imposition on the earth's environment from development should be reduced in order to offer future generations the same level of enjoyment of the natural environment as that presently enjoyed.

In the 1990s, the last decade, the protection of the Earth's environment has been continuously pursued, while at the same time allowing for sustainable development. At this stage, corporate managements are aware of the need to prevent their businesses and products from having a negative influence on the natural environment and of the need to pursue co-existence with it. Moreover, in Japan many important pieces of environmental legislation have been introduced, such as the Act on the Improvement of the Use of Recycled Resources (*Saisei Shigen no Riyo ni kansuru Horitsu*) in 1991, the Act on Protection of Wildlife under Threat of Annihilation in 1992 (*Zetsumetsu no Osore no aru Yasei-doshokubutsu no Shu no Hozon ni kansuru Horitsu*), the Environmental Constitutional Act (*Kankyo Kihon Ho*), which replaced the Constitutional Act for Protection against Pollution in 1993, and the Evironmental Assessment Act (*Kankyo Eikyo Hyoka Ho*), which took quite a long time before being established as law in 1997.[2]

In this chapter, I will examine the corporate attitude towards the management of environmental protection. From the above history, it appears that the impact of their business and products on the natural environment is one of the major recent concerns of corporations. Pursuing this point, this chapter focuses on three areas: first, the corporate risk of incurring legal responsibility; secondly, environmental audits; and thirdly, environmental insurance, the second and third of which have been effective risk avoidance means adopted by corporations.

---

[2] For a survey of the history of Japan's environmental policy and legislation see, e.g., Y Abe and T Awaji, *Kankyo-ho* (2nd edn., 1998) 1–27. Even in the 1990s legal theory has not yet confirmed environmental rights as fundamental human rights. This can be seen by the terms of the injunctions granted for the breach of those rights in law suits filed against state or local governments, and against corporations.

ENVIRONMENTAL LIABILITY OF CORPORATIONS AND CORPORATE
MANAGEMENT: LEGAL THEORETICAL APPROACH

This section, prior to explaining corporate environmental management, presents an outline of the theories in the Japanese legal framework according to which liability is imposed on corporations and their managements for environmental damage. As noted above, there have been several legislative measures for the particular purpose of environmental protection in Japan, as in the USA and European countries. It may be said that the prevention of damage by statute is the approach which the technologically advanced countries should take.[3] Yet, while *ex ante* regulation by statute is an effective means of environmental protection, it cannot be expected that a government agency will actively take such steps as accusing corporations of irregularities since the same agency used to give the corporations administrative guidance to aid them in keeping a good relationship with each other. This interdependence between administrative power and corporations might be attributed to the industrial protection policy of the government, and is ubiquitous in Japan. Although these environmental statutes may be used to impose criminal liability on corporations,[4] they have neither been applied nor have they had a preventive effect in the real world. The government's administrators hesitate to use provisions which have never been referred to before. In this respect, imposition of civil liability is much more effective, in that the victims who have strong incentives to impose liabilities on the wrongdoers may well bring an action; although within the Japanese legal framework such actions do not aim at prevention of what might be done in the future, but instead at compensation for what has already been done. In addition, under Japanese law, the tort provisions in the Civil Code can be applied widely through the violation of certain laws, because illegality, which has been interpreted by the courts, is one of the requirements to constitute tort liability.[5] Therefore, this section focuses on corporate liability from the civil aspect.

Development of Tort Theory as a Pollution Remedy

It would be a great improvement in tort theory if precedents were established to allow the pollution victims to sue based on the offenders' strict liability. In the following, I will survey briefly the long process of development towards what are now accepted as the legal principles for pollution remedies.

---

[3] Abe and Awaji, *supra* n.3 at 47.

[4] E.g., Act regarding Criminal Penalties against Pollution Offences Committed upon Human Health (*Hito no Kenko ni kakaru Kogai-hanzai no Shobatsu ni kansuru Horitsu*), ss 2(1) and 3(1).

[5] Civil Code, s 709. This s only provides that a person who causes an infringement of another person's rights should be held liable. However, the phrase 'the infringement of another person's rights' are to be interpreted as 'the violation of law' according to the predominant view of academics and to legal precedent: see S Wagazuma, *Jimu-kanri, Futo-ritoku, and Fuho-koi* (1937), 125ff; and H Suekawa, *Kenri-shingai-ron* (1949), 294ff.

At the time pollution was first recognised as a public issue, which may be traced back to the time of the Japanese industrial revolution in the Meiji era, there appeared a notable case called the *Osaka Alkali* case.[6] It was brought by the peasants who had been complaining about damage to their crops caused by smoke containing sulphuric gas from the Osaka Alkali factory situated near them. In this case, the judges of the Supreme Court (*Daishin-in*) were dissatisfied with the decision of the Court of Appeal (*Osaka Koso-in*), which affirmed the defendant's civil liability under section 709 of the Civil Code, and ordered the Court of Appeal to re-examine the case.

Section 709 provides that one who violates another's right with intention or with fault shall be responsible for paying compensation for the damages that the affected person has incurred. Regarding ordinary pollution litigation, one arguable requirement for tort is fault, not intention, because it is very rare for such effects to be intentionally caused. The fault is interpreted as breach of duty to act. There are two legal theories to constitute such a breach of duty. One is the breach of duty to foresee, and the other the breach of duty to avoid a certain result.[7]

The controversy about breach of duty and its consequences stems from the decision in the *Osaka Alkali* case. The judges in that case favoured the view that the plaintiff cannot seek more than what it costs for the defendant to rectify the result of damage. In other words, the defendant may be immune from his/her responsibility as far as he/she was acting to take the best reasonable steps within his/her capacity according to the nature of his/her enterprise. Some critics argue that the decision was unduly prejudiced in favour of industry. In response to criticisms, judges in some later cases adopted the same approach as the *Osaka Alkali* case but they interpreted the duty to avoid a result by setting very strict standards and allowing room for confirming fault more easily.[8] Whether the court relies upon the former or the latter interpretation, the subjective factor of the requirement of fault, to some extent, can be overcome.

In tort litigation, the burden of proof is imposed on the plaintiff. Therefore, he/she should prove the causal relation between the conduct and the damages. However, in cases of environmental pollution this is too heavy a burden for the plaintiff, because he/she usually does not have any special knowledge about polluting substances and pollution channels nor about the relationship between the pollution and the damage. The pollution cases changed the legal practice regarding this difficulty for the plaintiff in adducing evidence. One way to mitigate the burden of the onus of proof is that if the plaintiff can prove a high possibility of a causal relationship then this is regarded as *prima facie* evidence and

---

[6] Daishin-in judgment of 22 Dec. 1916, 22 Daishin-in Minji-hanketsu-roku 2474.

[7] See, e.g., T Ikuyo, *Fuho-koi-ho* (1993), 33ff.

[8] See Kumamoto District Court judgment of 20 Mar. 1973, 696 Hanrei-jiho 15. Concerning a company's duty to avoid environmental damage, a judge in this case pointed out that if it is expected that the costs of avoiding damage would be higher than those of stopping operating the factories the corporation has a duty to stop operations.

if the defendant cannot contradict it then his/her responsibility is confirmed.[9] Another way to mitigate the burden of the onus of proof is that when the plaintiff succeeds in proving a causal relationship epidemiologically, a causal relationship between pollution and damages may be inferred.[10] In these ways, the courts have tried to lighten the burden imposed on the victim plaintiff, and the liability of section 709 of the Civil Code has become nearly a non-fault one; that is, if a defendant causes certain damage and a plaintiff can prove the possibility of a causal relationship between the conduct/pollution and the damage, not necessarily meeting the strict criterion of a causal relationship between the fault of the defendant in creating the pollution and the damage, the court may well hold in favour of the plaintiff.

Thus, one basic theory about imposing corporate environmental liability is, as referred to in the foregoing paragraphs, what has developed from the civil liability in section 709 of the Civil Code, interpreted and reconstructed as no-fault liability. This principle of non-fault liability was adopted later by some of the administrative anti-pollution laws.

Company Law Theory on Directors', Auditors' and Financial Auditors' Liability

An alternative to imposing environmental liability on corporate management might come from company law theory. Even though general civil liability theory stipulates fair and equal allocation of damages, and obliges corporations to compensate the victims directly in proportion to their responsibility, there is still little discussion on this point. However, one proponent[11] recently argued that the corporate directors deal with a wide range of duties of care for environmental management,[12] and this implies that if they breach this duty in carrying out the company's affairs they must be personally responsible for the damages.[13] On this point, one should bear in mind that the burden of the damages in question, from the company law perspective, falls on the corporations themselves. The argument with respect to director liability means that the corporate directors must personally compensate their corporations, which have incurred damages

---

[9] See, e.g., Maebashi District Court judgment of 23 Mar. 1971, 628 Hanrei-jiho 25; Niigata District Court judgment of 29 Sept. 1951, 22 Kakyu-Saiban-sho Minji-Saiban-rei-shu 1 (compiled in another volume); T Awaji, *Kogai-baisho no Riron* (1978), 35ff.

[10] E.g., Tsu District Court, Yokkaichi Branch, judgment of 24 July 1972, 672 Hanrei-jiho 30; Nagoya Court of Appeal, Kanazawa Branch, judgment of 9 Aug. 1972, 674 Hanrei-jiho 25. See also A Morishima, 'Inga-kankei no Nintei to Baisho-gaku no Gengaku' in *Gendai-shakai to Minpo-gaku* (1992), 235ff. This theory presents an argument for why the collective causal relationship is completely different from the individual one, and why the individual one is not affirmed until the victim's group can show a 4 or 5 times higher probability of injury than the control group.

[11] E Yoshikawa, 'Kigyo no Kankyo-kansa to Torishimari-yaku no Chui-gimu' (1998) 41 *Jochi Hogaku Ronshu* 5.

[12] Commercial Code, s 245.

[13] Commercial Code, s 266(1)–(5).

caused by inappropriate management conduct, based on the fiduciary relationship between the company and the directors. Nevertheless, the argument is interesting in that it can adequately correspond to and subsume the change of social consciousness about the natural human environment, and can ensure consolidation of environmental concerns into corporate management activities. In practice, the environmental managing directors or the environmental management/audit committee, acting as a board committee, are occasionally appointed from amongst the directors.[14] At the least, these directors are unquestionably charged with a duty of care for environmental management. It is taken for granted that shareholders can bring a derivative action for compensation for damages awarded against a company if the company fails to claim compensation against its directors.[15] In addition, if the managing director, acting as an agent of the corporation, causes damage, the corporation must take responsibility for compensating third-party victims.[16] Also, according to section 266–3 of the Commercial Code, directors who have damaged third parties with malicious motives or a high level of fault should also take responsibility for their actions affecting third parties.[17] The relationship between this section of the Commercial Code and section 709 of the Civil Code is controversial.[18]

Japanese company law also imposes liability on company auditors for misconduct based on the fiduciary relationship between a company and its auditors.[19] The auditors, under the Japanese Commercial Code, are corporate officers, and they have a duty to oversee their company's audit activities.[20] Since company auditors do not manage company affairs, the Commercial Code has no provision imposing on them the kind of liability that directors have to compensate the corporation for breach of duty in managing the company's business and fulfilling its legal obligations. While auditors should not have this type of liability, the auditors should be responsible for their audit activities both to the

[14] See, e.g., T Yoshizawa and T Fukushima (eds.), *Kankyo-management-system-kochiku no Jissai* (1996), 77.

[15] Commercial Code, ss 267, 268, 268–2, 268–3.

[16] Commercial Code, ss 261(3) and 78(2); Civil Code, s 44(1).

[17] The onus of proof is interpreted as being transferred to the company directors.

[18] One prominent theory is that s 266–3 of the Commercial Code is a special provision to be applied without regard to s 709 of the Civil Code. The extent or nature of damage for which the directors should compensate is therefore governed by the former, rather than the latter, provision. The proponents of this prominent theory tend to argue that the damages include both direct and indirect damages. Indirect damages refers to the damage third party victims incur; e.g., where a company creditor is unable to obtain repayment from the company then the debtor company is damaged indirectly because the creditor's damage results from the company's insolvency. In such a case the company has already suffered damage from the directors' misconduct: see, e.g., M Kitazawa, *Kaisha-ho* (5th edn., 1998), 439ff. This argument is also applied to an auditor as well as a financial auditor.

[19] Commercial Code, ss 280, 254, 266(5), 266–3(1), 267, 268, 268–2, 268–3.

[20] The audit activities are divided into two types: one is an audit of company affairs, and the other of the company's accounts. Corporations having a share capital of more than 100 million yen must appoint an auditor who does both types of audits. Other corporations have an auditor who does only an audit of the company accounts. It should also be noted that corporations having a share capital of more than 500 million yen must also appoint a financial auditor. This is discussed in the text below.

company and to third-party victims; that is, they should carry out their duties with reasonable care. If damage to the company results from the auditors' actions or neglect, the company shareholders may well bring a derivative suit against them.

The liability of a financial auditor merits consideration. A large company with a share capital of more than 500 million yen must have a financial auditor for the audit of annual accounts. A financial auditor is appointed at the company's annual general meeting from certified public accountants or audit firms. The law that deals with auditors' competence is the Act Regarding Exceptional Rules of the Commercial Code Concerning Auditing and so on, of Companies limited by shares (*Kabushiki-gaisha no Kansa-tou ni kansuru Sho-ho no Tokurei ni kansuru Horitsu*; hereafter referred to as Special Audit Act). However, it involves a theoretical difficulty because it has no provision concerning the relationship between the company and the financial auditor, which identifies the nature of his/her legal position and obligation to the company. In the predominant view, a financial auditor occupies almost the same legal position as an auditor: he/she has a fiduciary relationship with the company. The fact that a financial auditor must be appointed at the annual general meeting, which was stipulated by the amendment of Special Audit Act in 1981, is strong reason to support this view. Therefore, he/she should have responsibility to the corporation in the case of breach of fiduciary duty.[21] There is also a similar provision in the Special Audit Act that a financial auditor shall be responsible to third-party victims for the damage he/she has caused to them.[22] Recently, the practice of conducting financial audits for environmental costs in corporations has gradually spread in Japan.[23] If there is misconduct on the part of the financial auditor in auditing environmental costs, he/she should be responsible to the company and any third party who has incurred damage resulting from a reckless act on the part of the financial auditor.

Thus, the legal theories which make the corporations, their directors, the auditors and the financial auditors liable to some extent play an important role in protecting pollution victims. Concerning these legal theories for corporate management liability, the next section will refer to corporate environmental management, especially to environmental audits in the next section.

CORPORATE ENVIRONMENTAL AUDITS

As can be seen, Japanese legal theory has gradually taken into consideration the protection of pollution victims and has endeavoured to develop and apply new remedial strategies. Correspondingly, corporations have voluntarily established

[21] M Tatsuta, *Shin-ban Chushaku Kaisha-ho* (1988), 572.

[22] Special Audit Act, s 10.

[23] Kankyo-cho (ed.), *Kankyo-Hakusho* (1998), 166ff; '*Special Issues: Kankyo-cost-kaikei no Jissen-teki-kadai*' (1998) 50 Kigyo-kaikei 18, at 18ff.

their own environmental management systems. It is essential for corporate existence to avoid economic loss due to judicial proceedings or administrative measures resulting from failure to set up adequate environmental management. Moreover, even if a company is not legally responsible, it is willing to practise environmental management for the purpose of pursuing its goodwill or gaining social appreciation for good environmental management. Eventually this will make sustainable development affordable for the whole of society. This section, will focus on environmental audits in Japanese corporations, as they have attracted a good deal of international attention, especially in the USA and Europe where these management practices have spread widely since the 1970s and where the decision about whether or not to have business relations may depend on the establishment of a good environmental management scheme. Additionally, if corporations are intending to invest in new frontiers, prior environmental risk assessment of the land, which is called a pre-acquisition audit, is necessary.[24] The EU's Eco-Management and Audit Scheme (EMAS), started from April 1995,[25] is well known and has been taken up as a model in management practice in Japan.[26]

Environmental audits are activities in which a company itself checks its compliance with environmental legislation and rules, and evaluates the risk and impact of its business on the natural environment.[27] The definition of the concept of an environmental audit is, according to the International Organisation for Standardisation (ISO), a 'systematic, documented verification process of objectively obtaining and evaluating audit evidence to determine whether specified environmental activities, events, conditions, management systems, or information about these matters conform with audit criteria, and communicating the results of this process to the clients'.[28] According to the International Chamber of Commerce (ICC), an environmental audit is 'a management tool comprising a systematic, documented, periodic and objective evaluation of how well the organisation's management and equipment is performing in meeting the goal of safeguarding the environment by: (i) facilitating management

---

[24] R B German, 'Real Estate Preacquisition Audits' in F N Edwards (ed.), *Environmental Auditing: The Challenge of the 1990s* (Calgary, University of Calgary Press, 1992), 157ff.

[25] The Eco-Management and Audit Scheme of the EU is applied to each Member State by Reg. 1836/93 [1993] OJ L168/1: see L Krämer, *EC Treaty and Environmental Law* 3rd edn., (London, Sweet & Maxwell, 1998) 8–9.

[26] Since the EMAS started in Germany, the fore runner among the EU Member States in this respect, in Autumn 1995, Japanese subsidiaries in Germany have gradually adopted the practice. It has influenced Japanese corporations by being implanted and rapidly absorbed by corporate management: see T Yoshizawa and T Fukushima (eds.), *Kigyo ni okeru Kankyo-Management* (1996), 5ff. For a discussion of Germany's environmental audits within the EU legal framework, see H-W Rengeling, *Integrierter und Betrieblicher Umweltschutz* (Schriften zum deutschen und europäischen Umweltrecht: Band 7, 1995), 207ff.

[27] J Butler, 'Environmental Audits: A Corporate Necessity' in Edwards, *supra* n.24, at 10–11.

[28] International Organisation for Standardisation, 14010—*Guidelines for Environmental Auditing—General Principles* (Geneva, Oct. 1996) art 2.9.

control of environmental practices; and (ii) assessing compliance with company policies, which would include meeting regulatory requirements'.[29]

However, patterns and schemes of environmental audits vary from company to company according to what the company needs to achieve most. In relation to who takes the initiative in these activities, it is possible to divide them into what are called top-down audits, which are initiated by the management, and bottom-up audits, which are primarily undertaken by members of each section. They can also be classified by purpose: compliance audits are those in which the purpose of auditing is mainly to check compliance with regulations and policies; management audits are made for the purpose of the evaluation of the efficiency or validity of the management; and comprehensive audits are a combination of the former two. Additionally, in practice, a number of other complicated types have appeared.

In Japan, environmental management was introduced late compared with its introduction into the USA and Europe; however, in the 1990s it has spread rapidly. Between December 1997 and May 1998, 418 corporations including public sector corporations adopted internationally standardised eco-management systems in accordance with the ISO 14001.[30] One good model for Japanese practice can be cited here, see figure 1. Japanese large-scale electric, mechanical, chemical or automobile corporations used to have such schemes as indicated by the following personnel structure.

Proceedings

The ISO 14001 started from October of 1996 through the JIS (Japanese Industrial Standards), which was set up within the Ministry of Commerce and Industry.[31] The ISO 14001 is, in fact, called JIS Q 14001 in Japan. The ISO guideline treats a wide range of environmental management matters. It is divided into four parts: introduction, coverage, standards, definitions, and the requirements of environmental management. The procedure of environmental management may comprise a PDCA (plan-do-check-act) cycle,[32] as shown in the figure below, and environmental audits would play an important role at the stage of check. Therefore, in the last part of the requirements for environmental management in the guidelines, environmental audits are treated in detail.[33]

Environmental audits are handled in three different phases: pre-audit activities, auditing activities and post-audit activities. In pre-audits, when appointing the auditors, whether or not such persons are external independent

---

[29] P T Budzik, 'Environmental Auditing: A Management Process' in Edwards, *supra* n.24, at 28.

[30] *Nippon Keizai Shimbun*, 4 July 1998 (evening edition). The number of accreditations by ISO 14001 in Japan was calculated at more than 1,000 in June 1998 and was the highest number of such accreditations in the world: *Nippon Keizai Shimbun*, 17 Aug. 1998.

[31] ISO 14001 took effect in Sept. of 1996, one month before JIS was put into practice in Japan.

[32] Yoshizawa and Fukushima, *supra* n.26, at 17–18.

[33] ISO 14001, *supra* n.28, at art 4.5.4.

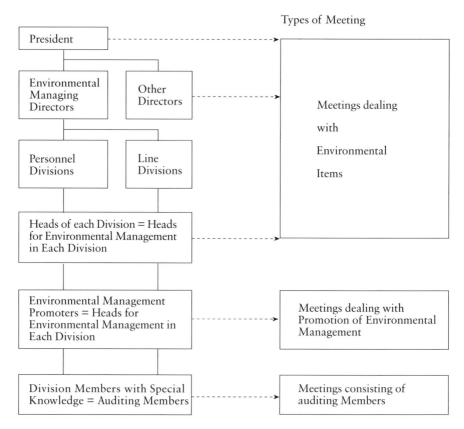

Figure 1. Example of Environmental Management Structure : The NEC Tohoku Corp.

Source: T Yoshizawa and T Fukushima (eds.), *Kankyo-Management-System-Kochiku no Jissai* (1996), at 63.

professionals is a point for consideration. Also included are: an examination of the audit purposes, audit items and audit process; a review of legislation, regulations and rules; a check of the report of the previous year; a visit to the sites, and so forth. In auditing practice, gathering all the documents and records required for inspection in a principal office or main branch is an efficient way to deal with this time-consuming process.[34] Visiting and investigating the main sites as well as the related ones, hearing from all the staff members concerned, collecting information, recommending measures for compliance, improving management schemes and enhancing the division personnel's environmental awareness are all included in the proceedings at this stage.

---

[34] D Chollak, 'Environmental Auditing Standards and Activities' in Edwards, *supra* n.24, at 58.

The post-audit includes preparation for the audit report and follow-up of the investigation in order to create a better eco-management system and to check continuously its validity within the company. The audit report may be produced by the environmental auditors in almost the same manner as the financial audit report, including sections concerning introduction, coverage of audits, findings and conclusion.[35] Therefore, it should be prepared with reasonable care and skill and, if it is not done in this way, the company directors would be primarily responsible for the breach of duty of care and their participation in any resulting misrepresentation.[36] The environmental auditors might also be liable

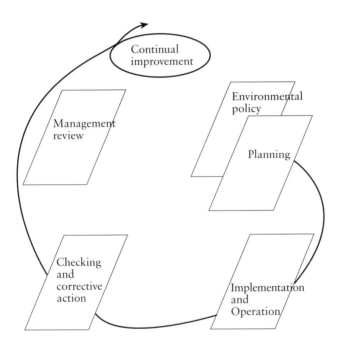

Figure 2. Model for ISO Environmental Management Procedure

Source: International Organisation for Standardisation, ISO 14001—Environmental Management Systems—Specification with Guidance for Use (Geneva, Oct. 1996), Introduction.

---

[35] See H W Blakeslee and T M Grabowski, *A Practical Guide to Environmental Audits* (New York, Van Nostrand Reinhold Co., 1985).

[36] This point has not yet been discussed in Japan. However, in some other countries where environmental auditors failed to prepare environmental reports in good faith it would not be possible for company directors to rely on a due diligence defence. Furthermore, auditors, as well as the company and its directors, are likely to be subject to civil liability for misrepresentation: see H P Cleghorn, 'Post-audits: Consultant's Perspective' in Edwards, *supra* n.24, at 84; G L Boucher, 'Post-audits' in *ibid.*, at 91, 93, 94; see generally, W P Keeton (ed.), *Prosser and Keeton on Torts* 5th edn., (St Paul, West Pub Co., 1984) 725ff.

for this. This issue is discussed below in the part of this chapter dealing with the liability of environmental auditors.

For security reasons, the audit report is reviewed by counsel and copies of it are distributed only to a limited number of persons, such as the directors, officers, the head of the environmental management branch and legal advisers. The company must introduce a follow-up self-audit scheme to advance and reconstruct the eco-management system according to the report, even if no serious problems have been detected. This follow-up is strongly recommended because the circumstances affecting corporations, such as corporate environmental policies, environmental legislation and regulations, and staff members may continuously change.[37] In this sense, environmental audits are needed to allow for checks and corrections at any time.

Positive Effects

Needless to say, it is convenient in many ways to carry out environmental audits in corporations. First, environmental audits which show how corporate enterprises obey environmental regulations and which evaluate environmental risk objectively may enhance employees' environmental awareness and knowledge about environmental regulations and corporate internal environmental policies. This educational effect with respect to employees can be most important in the case of environmental audits[38] as the directors and officers may come, as a result, to conduct their affairs with due diligence and skill corresponding to the enhancement of the employees' consciousness. Secondly, environmental audits offer corporations an opportunity to review their eco-management schemes, and this ensures the improvement of the schemes.[39] Thirdly, the attitude of corporations in undertaking the audit system and carrying out management activities with great care for our natural environment is well accepted by the business world, and corporations with such an attitude will have a good reputation on account of it. Ultimately, this may strengthen the trade relationship of such companies with other companies.[40] Finally, macroscopically, since environmental audits are positioned at the cross-point of environmental subsistence and continuous development of a sound economy, it is essential for corporations to do business with regard to the protection of the environment with the goal of sustainable development.[41] Corporate incentives on profit maximisation and on better eco-management systems under the same *laissez-faire* conditions enable corporations to be highly competitive with each other in free trade, with the

---

[37] Cleghorn, *supra* n.36, at 87.

[38] G H Holliday, 'How to Prevent Criminal Prosecution of Senior Management' in Edwards, *supra* n.24, at 186.

[39] É Giroux, 'L'entreprise et l'audit environnemental: perspectives de développement national et international dans les secteurs de l'environnement et du commerce' (1997) 38 *Les Cahiers de Droit* 77, at 77–9.

[40] *Ibid.*, at 79–81.

[41] *Ibid.*, 83–4, 118.

result that only corporations with high adaptability to sustainable development will be able to survive.

Negative Effects on Corporations Security and Confidentiality

There are also problems with environmental audits that are worth consideration. One possible disadvantage is that the environmental audits cause serious delay to corporate projects and result in a reduction of proceeds. In addition, it is pointed out that the advantages and the costs of implementing the environmental audits are still vague. Another possible disadvantage for employees is that they may well be discouraged in doing their jobs as a result of the strain of always being under the supervision of 'watchdogs'. However, those negative effects could be overcome in the long term because once corporations improve their environmental management practices, they will be able to save the costs of environmental economic loss[42]; and as the enlightenment and environmental awareness of the workers are increased, they can understand the importance of the supervision of the business affairs and get along with the watchdogs. Sometimes, under the supervision of auditors, they may even work harder to participate in the activities of environmental protection.

Securing sensitive information in an audit report on the other hand, is a major problem. In general, the disclosure of corporate information to the public should be encouraged, especially for information concerning the public interest. However, the necessity to protect corporate privacy must be discussed seriously as environmental audits are voluntarily conducted. In Japan, unlike some other countries,[43] this point has not yet been of interest in either practice or theory, although there is a possibility of seizure of audit reports under the authority of a search warrant and their use in legal proceedings as incriminating evidence in relation to the environmental offences of a corporation.[44] The government is at present planning to introduce a new bill for the mandatory disclosure of information regarding the emission of harmful gases at each operation site.[45] Although the protection of public health is now much more respected and the disclosure of this kind of information is necessary, this topic of security of sensitive corporate information should be opened to debate, and the sooner the better.

---

[42] *Ibid.*, at 88.

[43] In relation to North America, see e.g. M I Jeffery, 'Environmental Strategies for the 1990s: A Canadian Perspective' in International Bar Association (ed.), *Environmental Liability* (London, International Bar Association, 1991), 102; and F J Veale, Jr, 'Evaluating Potential Environmental Liabilities' in Edwards, *supra* n.26 at 329.

[44] So far as environmental impact assessments are concerned, reports prepared by the corporations involved on the environmental impact of any new development projects are open and available for inspection by the public in accordance with the Environmental Impact Assessment Act, s 27.

[45] *Asahi Shimbun*, 30 Nov. 1998. This proposal has now been realised as law. 'An Act for the Pollutant Release and Transfer Register (Tokutei-kagaku-Busshitsu no kankyo eno Haishutsu-ryo no Haaku-to oyobi kanri no kaizen no Sokushin ni kanshutsu Horitsu)' was promulgated in July 1999 and will be effective within 9 months of promulgation.

Competence, Qualifications and Liability of Environmental Auditors

The environmental auditors are appointed from internal staff as well as external professionals. The first audits used to be processed by external independent auditors for fair and skilful evaluation. The practice of environmental auditing requires expertise in various fields and, in order to fulfil this complicated task, environmental auditors need to be highly qualified persons. Some companies have internal rules of their own concerning the qualification of such auditors, and some other companies require the internal auditors to be accredited according to the ISO 14001 guidelines. I will briefly discuss the ISO criterion for guidelines on the assessment and registration system of qualified auditors first, and then discuss auditors' liability.

Verifiers of Auditor Systems

At present, based on ISO 14001, the accreditation procedures for verifiers of audit systems have been established in Japan. As shown in Figure 3, there are two different functional bodies: one for assessment and registration of verifiers, and another for training future verifiers. To be a verifier, one must take part in the training course given by the training body, after which one may become an applicant. In parallel with these two bodies, there is also a body for review and registration of firms and factories. It examines their eco-management schemes and applies to the accreditation body for the registration of the eligible firms and factories. The review and registration body itself applies its own accreditation procedures. The body has its own verifiers, and they apply to the assessment and registration body for evaluation of whether or not their qualifications are suitable for the higher rank of verifiers. The accreditation body controls these three bodies.

The verifiers are divided into three ranks, namely, lead verifier, verifier and deputy verifier. To be a verifier or a lead verifier, adequate experience in environmental practices including the various aspects of technology, related regulations, management and audit proceedings is required. The accreditation of verifiers is valid for one year for the renewal of identification cards and for three years for registration. As mentioned above, the environmental auditing of each firm and factory of a corporation should be handled by the verifiers of a review and registration body, or by individual registered verifiers, or should at least be reviewed by those verifiers.

Legal Liability

From the legal aspect, environmental auditors may in theory be liable in certain cases. In the case of internal self-audit, as the auditors are usually the employees of a corporation, if they damage the company by their misconduct, they are

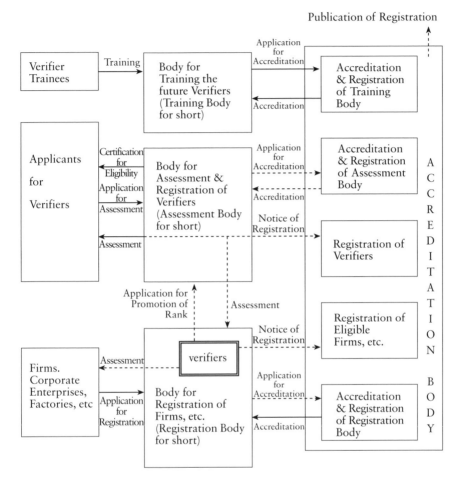

Figure 3. ISO Accreditation and Registration Schemes

Source: T Yoshizawa and T Fukushima (eds.), *Kigyo ni okeru Kankyo-Management* (1996), at 54.

liable to the company for the breach of duty according to the employment contract,[46] and also in tort if the requirements reviewed above are met. If the employee auditor's misconduct causes certain types of damage to third parties (for example, the shareholders and the creditors) the employer (the company) will be primarily liable according to the employer liability theory,[47] and then the employer may claim recourse to the employee. The level of duty of care which

[46] Civil Code, s 415.
[47] Civil Code, s 715.

is imposed on the employee auditors might be higher than that for other employees who have no special knowledge of environmental audits. The following discussion of the civil liability of external professional auditors will include this point in detail.

The case of external accredited environmental auditors/verifiers needs separate consideration from that of internal ones. As the auditors have professional qualifications, they must carry out their task with due diligence, following contract law theory. When external auditors handle the auditing in a company, they enter into an auditing contract with the company, and all the terms and duties of the auditors are derived from the contract. In practice, the external auditors' liability for their conduct is extremely limited or completely excluded according to the terms of the contract.[48] So far as it is subject to the wording of the contract, there will be no problem about the liability of external environmental auditors. However, inasmuch as the auditors accredited by certain professional bodies undertake the auditing task, the present practice of environmental audits with clauses regarding restraint or exclusion of legal liability have to be reconsidered.

According to a purely theoretical approach, the auditors owe a duty to carry out audits with due diligence, but the nature of this duty varies with the purpose and the method of auditing. Where the purpose of auditing is the observation of facts and the evaluation of findings, the auditors are charged with *obligations de résultat*. In contrast, if the purpose of the auditing is the representation of the auditing opinion and preparation of a report, *obligations de moyens* might be imposed on them.[49] This means that the requirements for establishing breach of duty differ in the two types of obligations. Where the auditors have the former obligation, the breach of duty will not be established until it is ascertained that the result of the conduct contains certain defects, however, it will be enough to establish a breach of duty in the latter case without considering the result where someone performs recklessly.[50] In both cases, as mentioned earlier, the duty of care which the auditors owe as professionals is an important consideration; that is, if the environmental auditors do not conduct auditing activities with the due diligence that is required of a person in that type of position, they incur civil liability for this.

The matter of the civil liability of professionals in Japan is worth considering, and may arise in cases involving environmental auditors[51]; however, particular examination of their liability is necessary. Furthermore, there are other areas of possible legal liability which must be considered, such as: matters of risk and insurance to cover auditors' legal liability; confirmation of the system of reviewing audit reports; the preparation of rules on professional ethics; and the clari-

---

[48] Giroux, *supra* n.39, at 109.

[49] H Endo *et al.*, *Minpo (6) Keiyaku-Kakuron* (4th edn., 1997) 247.

[50] *Ibid.*

[51] Concerning the civil liability of professionals in Japan, see, e.g., Senmon-ka-Minjise-kinin-kenkyu-kai (ed.), *Senmon-ka no Minji-sekinin* (1994), and T Kawai *et al.*, *Senmon-ka no Minji-sekinin* (Symposium), (1995) 57 *Shiho* 3ff.

fication of who should be risk-takers within a company. Where damage as a result of these types of activities is caused to the company or third parties intentionally or culpably, then tort liability may arise.

THE ROLE OF INSURANCE IN ENVIRONMENTAL RISK MANAGEMENT

Insurance is also involved in the risk management of corporate environmental damage. It is voluntarily acquired by corporations to make them secure against economic loss, and has spread widely in the business world corresponding to the increase in the risk of environmental damage. In Japan, Environmental Impairment Liability (EIL) insurance, which covers compensatory liability for bodily injuries and damage to property of third parties from environmental contamination, as well as clean-up costs mandated by laws and rules, has been available since 1992,[52] and it has had the useful function of ensuring the compensation capacity of corporations to the third parties which have been damaged.

Nevertheless, in general, insurance policies to cover the liability imposed on corporations for environmental damage involve some difficulties or problems. First, the environmental economic loss tends to be limitless and it is hard even to estimate precisely.[53] Insurance systems are unfamiliar with this and find it difficult to evaluate the risk appropriately and distribute it amongst the insured. Secondly, since environmental policies and legislation have changed continually, insurance policies must also frequently be reviewed to be in line with such reforms.[54] Thirdly, as the likelihood of insurable accidents resulting in environmental damage is not obvious, if the insurer has less information than the insured, adverse selection can easily occur. When that happens the premium is raised because an insured with a high risk must remain in the insurance market. This implies that a substantial screening of potential insured parties based on a scientific approach, rather than on an historical risk review, will be needed to transfer risk.[55] Finally, moral hazard is also a problem. With respect to environmental insurance, there is criticism that the existence of insurance can induce carelessness and irresponsible, even illegal, performance by the directors.[56]

In order to prevent these problems from occurring, insurers in Japan used to investigate and evaluate the potential risk of the future insured parties and select them carefully before entering into a strict contract. This practice has its advantages. For example, in underwriting EIL insurance, the insurers force insured companies intending to invest in new areas to investigate the risk of the

[52] H Morikawa, 'Waga-kuni ni okeru Kankyo-osen-baisho-sekinin-hoken no Hikiuke-hoho: Yakkan-naiyo to Underwriting-Shuho' (1992) 539 *Hoken-gaku Zasshi* 107.

[53] *Ibid.*, at 108.

[54] J Tanega, 'Implications of Environmental Liability on the Insurance Industry' (1997) 8 *Journal of Environmental Law* 117.

[55] *Ibid.*, at 188.

[56] *Ibid.*, at 119; and see Morikawa, *supra* n.52, at 109.

acquisition of land and enterprises and to obtain information about the environmental regulations relating to the land. This is one of the important steps in environmental management as part of the pre-acquisition audit, and it is expected that the requirement of EIL insurance may well be an impetus to environmental audits.[57] It is a great pleasure to see that eco-management and insurance interact with each other in this way; and it enables us to enhance the efficiency of our economy by saving the costs due to environmental harm while concurrently accomplishing sustainable development.

CONCLUSION

As has been seen, it is noticeable that the environmental liability imposed on corporations has become almost like no-fault liability as a result of judicial precedents and that, in the end, corporations' environmental strategies have developed dramatically. Moreover, it is possible for directors, auditors and financial auditors to be held personally liable for their misconduct in relation to companies and third parties according to company law theory. This could also be a strong stimulus for them to take reasonable steps to ensure environmental protection.

A number of corporations have recently applied for ISO 14001 accreditation for good environmental management. However, this trend has been brought about, not only by incentives for risk aversion, but also by a great enhancement of their environmental awareness. This will continue in the twenty-first century, which may be called the century of the environment.

Environmental audits, coupled with insurance, will be the core activities to ensure environmental progress towards sustainable development in the highly competitive free trade business environment. Meanwhile, legal issues about environmental management, as mentioned above, such as the extent to which the confidentiality of the audit information is ensured, review of the environmental verifiers system, environmental auditors' civil liability with respect to auditing activities, the internal environmental liability system and the preparation of rules of professional ethics, and so on, should be furthered as part of interdisciplinary studies by all interested persons.

---

[57] Yoshikawa, *supra* n.11, at 27.

8

Takeover Bids in Japan

MAMI SAKAUE

INTRODUCTION

Recently in Japan there has been a notable increase in the number of company restructurings through M&A activity. The term 'M&A' in a narrow sense means mergers and acquisitions, which encompasses share acquisitions (including takeover bids, that is, TOB or tender offers[1]) and assignments of assets (including transfers of undertakings). The purpose of this chapter is to summarise the regulation and characteristics of TOB in Japan.

CONTENT AND CHARACTERISTICS OF TOB REGULATION

The Transition

Substantive provisions to regulate TOB came into effect in 1971 (the 1971 Law) when a Bill was passed to amend the Securities and Exchange Law (the SEL) which forms the main body of law regulating securities transactions in Japan. Until then no TOB had taken place in Japan. However, there was a need to prepare for possible TOB by foreign companies in the near future. Therefore the 1971 Law provided for the TOB system.[2]

However, the 1971 Law was not yet fully developed and had many problems. To take an example, it adopted an advance notification system. As a result, the offeror could not try to persuade the target company's shareholders to accept the offer until ten days after sending the offer documents to the Minister of Finance. A ten-day waiting period was thought necessary by the Minister of Finance. As the TOB was a new system for Japan, the Minister of Finance wanted to have enough time to inspect the offer documents.[3] At the same time,

---

[1] See Japan Investment Promotion Council, Coordination Bureau, Economic Planning Agency, *Tainichi M&A no kasseika wo mezashite (Aiming for the Activity of M&A between Foreign and Japanese Companies)* (Securities Bureau, Ministry of Finance, 1996), at 9.

[2] I Kawamoto and Y Otake, *Shoken Torihikiho dokuhonn (A Textbook of Securities and Exchange Law)* 3rd ed., (Tokyo, Yuhikaku, 1998), at 74.

[3] T Suzuki and I Kawamoto, *Shoken Torihikiho (The Securities and Exchange Law)* (Tokyo, Yuhikaku, 1984), at 174.

the waiting period gave the target company the opportunity to mount a defence against any hostile (or unwelcome) offer. To take another example, the 1971 Law stipulated that when a non-resident offeror commenced a TOB, the offeror had to appoint a Japanese bank or Japanese securities firm resident in Japan to act as a proxy to send the offer documents to the Minister of Finance on the offeror's behalf. That was disadvantageous to non-residents. In contrast, Japanese companies were actively involved in M&A in foreign countries. These factors led to considerable criticism that TOB by foreign companies in Japan were restricted. Consequently, the SEL was amended drastically in 1990 (the 1990 Law) to harmonise the Japanese TOB system with foreign TOB systems (particularly the UK and the US systems), internationalise stock markets and protect investors.[4]

One of the most significant changes in the TOB concerned the point at which an offer must be made. Formerly any shareholder holding 10 per cent of the voting rights of the target company was required to make an offer (see below for further details). However, with the introduction of the disclosure system (commonly known as 'the 5 per cent rule') when the 1990 Law came into force, the threshold figure was reduced from 10 per cent to 5 per cent. The 5 per cent rule requires that once a shareholder's holding exceeds 5 per cent of the voting rights of the company, the shareholder must submit a report to the Minister of Finance disclosing the holding.[5] The aim in amending the threshold figure was to give companies whose shares are being bought slowly and in secret advance notice that they may be the target of a TOB.

Another amendment to the SEL was the repeal of the advance notification system. The 1990 Law also made a change concerning non-residents. While retaining the requirement under the 1971 Law that a non-resident offeror must appoint a resident as a proxy to submit the offer documents, the 1990 Law provides that anyone who lives or has an office in Japan can be a proxy.

To summarise, although Japanese law contains provisions which are similar to provisions in the UK and the USA, it can said that some aspects of Japan's TOB system are unique.

Outline of TOB regulation

Definition

Section 27-2(6)of the SEL defines a TOB as 'an offer to buy shares, or an invitation to sell shares, made by notice to an unspecified number of the general public, and the subsequent sale of those shares off-market'. An off-market purchase

---

[4] J Naito, 'Kabushiki Koukai Kaitsuke Seido no Kaisei (Amendment of the Takeover System)' [1990] 1219 *Shojihomu* at 2; S Matsui, *Shoken Torihihiko (The Securities and Exchange Law)* (Tokyo, Chuon keizai Sya, 1993), at 42.

[5] SEL, s 27–23(1).

is a purchase effected by private contract. Later I will briefly discuss the meaning of the words 'an unspecified number of the general public'.

The Scope of TOB Regulation

Under the SEL, when a person acquires shares off-market, that person will in principle be obliged to make a TOB offer.[6] There are, however, a number of exceptions to this.

It is important to note that the term 'off-market' not only excludes the exchange market but also the 'over-the-counter' (OTC) market. Exchange trading is conducted in accordance with the self-regulatory rules of the Stock Exchange. Similarly, OTC trading is conducted under a set of self-regulatory rules. This self-regulation has achieved fairness and transparency. Consequently, in principle, both exchange trading and OTC trading are outside the scope of TOB regulation. However, this point raises a problem concerning the scope of application of the TOB regulations to which I will refer again later.

There are cases where a person who acquires shares off-market is not obliged to make an offer. One example is where the shares are purchased from a 'small number' of vendors (meaning not more than ten vendors). To ascertain whether a purchase meets this test the number of vendors selling shares to the purchaser in the transaction in question is added to the number of vendors who have sold shares to the purchaser in the previous 60 days. However, even where the number of vendors is ten or less, the purchaser will still be required to purchase the shares by a TOB if the purchase would result in the purchaser holding one-third or more of the voting rights of the target company. That ratio (one-third of the voting rights) has an important bearing on the control of the company as it is the threshold for preventing the passing of an extraordinary resolution.[7]

The cases where a purchaser must make a TOB offer can be summarised as follows:

(a)   an off-market purchase which would result in the purchaser's shareholding carrying between 5 per cent and one-third of the voting rights of the target company, where the number of vendors selling shares to the purchaser in the transaction in question and during the 60 days prior to that transaction totals more than ten.

(b)   an off-market purchase which would result in the purchaser's shareholding carrying one-third or more of the voting rights of the target company, regardless of the number of vendors.

(c)   a purchase on the securities exchange, where prior to the purchase the purchaser already had a 50 per cent or greater holding in the target company, and the number of vendors selling shares to the purchaser in the transaction in question and the prior 60 days is more than ten.

---

[6]   SEL, s 27–2(1).
[7]   Naito, *supra* n.4, at 4.

The cases in paragraphs (a) to (c) can be represented in a simple diagram as follows:

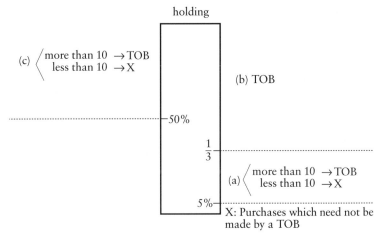

Purchases which must be made by TOB

Purchases which must be made by a TOB

Characteristics of the TOB System

The first important characteristic of the TOB system is that the acceptance in full of a TOB does not necessarily result in the offeror's shareholding carrying 100 per cent of the voting rights of the target company (that is, a '100 per cent offer'). The SEL does not oblige the offeror to make a 100 per cent offer. Consequently, 'partial offers' (that is, offers for less than 100 per cent of the target company's shares) are made more often than 100 per cent offers.

In the United Kingdom, Rule 9 of the City Code on Takeovers and Mergers provides that where any person acquires shares which, together with any shares held or acquired by others acting in concert with him, carry 30 per cent of the voting rights of the target company, in principle, that person must extend offers to all remaining shareholders of any class of equity shares whether voting or non-voting (the so-called 'mandatory bid').[8] Under the UK Code, a 30 per cent holding represents *de facto* control of the target company. In contrast, Japanese SEL is more advantageous for the offeror as there is no obligation on the offeror to acquire any more shares than the offeror wants.

At this point I should also mention section 27–13(5) of the SEL. Section 27–13(5) seeks to ensure that all shareholders of a target company are treated

---

[8] See M Tanabe, 'Igirisu ni okeru Shihaikabu no shutoku keisei' ('The Mandatory Offer in the English City Code') (1986) 16 (3–4) *Kobe Gakuin Hogaku* 81–120.

equally by the offeror. It provides that in the case of a partial offer, if the vendor shareholders tender shares in excess of the number sought by the offeror, the offeror must purchase shares from the shareholders in the same proportions as the numbers of shares that are tendered by the shareholders.

The second characteristic of the Japanese TOB system is, as stated above, if a purchase of shares would result in the purchaser acquiring one third or more of the voting rights of the target company the purchase must be made through a TOB offer. Under the UK Code Rule 9, a purchaser acquiring 30 per cent or more of the shares of a company is deemed to have *de facto* control of that company, and therefore is obliged to make a TOB offer giving all of the remaining shareholders the opportunity to sell their shares. In contrast, under Japan's SEL a purchaser is obliged to make a TOB offer if the purchase would result in the purchaser's shareholding carrying one-third or more of the voting rights of the target company.

There are, however, circumstances in which the Japanese purchaser can avoid the obligation to make a TOB offer. One example is where the purchaser switches from an off-market purchase to a purchase on the stock exchange. In this case, as discussed above, a TOB is not required, even where the purchase would give the purchaser one third or more of the voting rights of the target company. Another example is where the purchaser plans to buy shares from ten or more vendors within a 60-day period (which, as noted above, would ordinarily necessitate a TOB), but is able to reduce the number of vendors to fewer than ten (without necessarily reducing the number of shares being purchased). In this scenario the purchaser does not have to make a TOB offer.

These situations arise because in TOB regulation the SEL makes a distinction between the stock exchange (including the OTC market) and off-market purchases. Many academics are of the view that the 1990 Law 'obliges' a purchaser to make a TOB offer.[9] I disagree with that view because under the 1990 Law the purchaser has opportunities to avoid making a TOB offer, as I have explained.

The third significant characteristic of the system is that there is no provision in Japan's SEL concerning purchase price. Consequently, an offeror is free to decide the offer price. Where an offeror wishes to purchase as many shares as possible, it is likely that the offer will be in cash at a higher price than the market price. However, even where the purchase price is lower than the market price the purchase is still lawful.

In the light of this it is interesting to consider the criteria upon which an offeror bases the calculation of the offer price. Based on an analysis of TOB cases in 1998 the criteria can be divided into two types. These are: (a) the average of the market price during a fixed period of time; and (b) the average of the market price in one day. An example of type (a) was the offer by Showa Denko Co. for SDS Biotic Co., where the offer price of 1,550 yen was based on the

---

[9] J Naito, 'Kabushiki Koukai Kaitsuke Seido no Kaisei' ('Amendment of the Takeover System') (1990) 1208 *Shojihomu* 5.

average of the market price over the previous year (1,549 yen). When compared with the last market price before the offer announcement, this represented a premium of 74 per cent.[10] Another example of type (a) was the offer by TOYOTA Motor Co. for Daihatsu Motor Co. (the offer period was from 31 August until 21 September), where the offer price of 519 yen was based on an average of the closing price from 3 August until 27 August (514 yen).[11] An example of type (b) was the offer by TI Group Co. for Nippon Marin Techno Co. There the offer price of 580 yen was based on the closing price on 17 April (366 yen), representing a premium of 58.46 per cent.

Where a TOB is made for the purchase of shares in the offeror company itself (that is, a share buy-back) it is common for the offer price to be based on the closing price on the last business day before the board of directors' decision to make the offer.

Security Interests and TOBs

As noted above, if a purchase of shares would result in the purchaser holding one third or more of the voting rights of the target company, the purchaser must effect the purchase through a TOB. However, where a creditor would acquire one-third or more of the voting rights of a company as a result of the exercise of rights under a security interest, the question arises whether the creditor should be required to exercise those rights by means of a TOB offer. There is a view that, as this is merely the exercise of rights under a security interest, the creditor should not be obliged to make a TOB offer.[12] I disagree with this view for two reasons.[13]

First, under Japanese law a purchaser acquiring one third or more of the voting rights of a company is required to make a TOB because a one-third holding is considered a substantial holding. The law is concerned with the quantity of shares held after an off-market purchase, not the means by which the shares are acquired. Also, an intention on the part of the purchaser to secure control of the target company does not in itself necessitate a TOB. Secondly, I believe that if the acquisition of shares by the exercise of security interest rights does not require a TOB offer, cases that are substantially the same would produce different results. Consider the following scenarios. One scenario is where a debtor is insolvent and therefore does not have the ability to pay certain debts when

---

[10] For further details of these cases, see '100% Kogaisha no tameno Kabushiki Koukai Kaitsuke Jirei' ('Takeover Cases which will make a Target Company a 100% Subsidiary Company') (1998) 171 *Shiryoban Shojihomu* 33–85.

[11] *Nikkei Shinbun*, 8 Aug. 1998.

[12] K Kanzaki, 'Koukai Kaitsuke Seido no Tekiyou Hani' ('Applicable Areas of the Takeover System') in M Kishida, A Morita and S Morimoto (eds.), *Gendai Kigyou to Yuukasyouken no Houri (Principles of Law on Modern Companies and Securities)* (Tokyo, Yuhikaku, 1994), at 202.

[13] For further details on this, see M Sakaue, 'Koukai Kaitsuke ni okeru Tanpokabu no Houritsu Mondai' ('The Legal Problem of the Shares as a Target of the Security Interest on Takeover') (1992) 106 (6) *Minshohou Zasshi* 825–44 (Part 1) and (1992) 107(1) *Minshohou Zasshi* 70–87 (Part 2).

they fall due. With the debtor's consent, a creditor acquires shares as a security interest before the due date (scenario A). Another scenario is where a creditor acquires shares as a security interest on the due date (scenario B). If the exercise of rights under a security interest does not require a TOB the creditor in scenario B does not have to make a TOB offer whereas the creditor in scenario A does. This is inconsistent, allowing some creditors to avoid the law.

THE CURRENT SITUATION AND ISSUES FOR THE FUTURE

TOBs to Acquire the Offeror's Own Shares

As a result of amendments to the SEL and the Commercial Law in 1994, and further amendments to the Commercial Law in 1997, a purchase by a company of its own shares off-market (that is, a share buy-back) falling within any of the following categories must be made by means of a TOB:

(a) a share buy-back to allow a transfer of shares to directors or employees;
(b) a share buy-back to allow a redemption of the shares on a special resolution of a shareholders' meeting;
(c) a share buy-back to allow a redemption of the shares authorised by the company's articles of association.

Most TOB offers in fact fall within one of these three categories.

Listed (or public) companies and OTC registered companies can acquire their own shares through stock exchange or OTC trading as well as through a TOB. So, why is it that these companies use the TOB method relatively frequently? In April 1996, Asahi Beer Co. acquired its own shares for the first time by means of a TOB. A report published by Asahi explained why they had chosen to proceed by a TOB.[14] The following reasons were given:

(i) Compared with buying its own shares on the stock market, the TOB enabled Asahi to buy many shares in a short period of time without the need to manage insider information issues.
(ii) The longer the offer period is, the greater the risk of suspicion that the purchasing process has been manipulated. However, as the TOB procedure is stipulated in detail in the legislation, suspicion of manipulation of the procedure is unlikely.
(iii) Speculative buying would decrease the number of available Asahi shares and result in a rapid increase in the share price. If that were to occur Asahi would not be able to buy its shares at a low price. Also, there would be suspicion that Asahi had attempted to manipulate the market.

---

[14] Y Kakegai, 'Asahi Beer ni okeru Jikokabushiki Syoukyaku ni tuite' ('Redemption of their own shares at Asahi Beer Co.') (1996) 131 *Gekkan shihon Shijou (Monthly Capital Market)* 76–83.

The Likelihood of Hostile Takeovers

In Japan there have not as yet been any instances of the typical hostile takeover. A typical hostile offer is a takeover offer made without the approval of the target company. The board of directors of the target company recommends to its shareholders that they reject the offer. In Japan there are only two types of offer. One is a share buy-back offer (where the offeror wants to buy its own shares). The other is a 'friendly' offer. A friendly offer is an offer that will proceed with the target company's co-operation. In some friendly offers the offeror makes the offer after having secured the approval of the target company's shareholders (in particular, institutional investors with large holdings in the target company).[15] In the case of an offer exercising rights under a security interest, before making the offer the creditor may obtain the debtor's agreement that the debtor will accept the offer by transferring the shares constituting the security interest.

Hostile takeovers have not occurred in Japan for two reasons.[16] First, hostile takeovers are held in poor regard by Japanese. Secondly, there is considerable mutual or cross-shareholding between listed companies in Japan. Most listed companies belong to a group of companies where the shares in each company are owned by other companies within the group ('*keiretsu*'). For example, company A holds 30 per cent of the issued share capital of company B and 30 per cent of the issued share capital of company C. Similarly, company B holds 30 per cent of the shares in companies A and C, and C holds 30 per cent of the shares in A and B. In this way a majority of the shares of each company is held by 'friendly' shareholders. If company X were to make an offer to acquire control of company A, B and C (which together hold a majority of A's issued share capital) would not accept, preventing X from gaining control of A.

However, the level of cross-shareholding between Japanese companies is slowly declining. Cross-shareholding has become a high risk investment, with falls in share prices resulting in losses for many 'friendly' (group) companies. In particular, share prices of financial institutions have fallen,[17] leading to a number of life insurance companies selling their holdings.[18] Recently it was reported in the news that Haseko Corporation had decided to sell all of its shares in financial institutions by the end of March 1999.[19] In this way, a kind of fortification that has defended companies against hostile offers is collapsing.

[15] See *supra* n.10, at 34ff.
[16] See M Tatsuta, *Shoken Torihikihou (The Securities and Exchange Law)* (Tokyo, Yuhikaku, 1994), i, at 230–1.
[17] *Nikkei Shinbun*, 21 July 1998.
[18] *Nikkei Shinbun*, 10 July 1998.
[19] *Nikkei Shinbun*, 22 Nov. 1998.

Measures to Defend Against Hostile Offers

The following measures can be taken to defend against a hostile offer:

(a) the board of directors of the target company can circulate their views on the offer to their shareholders;
(b) the target company can purchase its own shares;
(c) where the offeror seeks to inspect the target company's record of share-holders (on the basis that the offeror is a shareholder and therefore entitled to inspect), the target company can refuse permission (provided the target company can prove that the offeror has an unjust intention or purpose in seeking to inspect);
(d) the target company can merge with, or transfer undertakings to, another company; and
(e) The target company can issue further shares to a third party.[20]

Of these measures, (e) has the greatest prospect of success, although it does present one serious problem. In general, a board of directors is authorised to issue shares not only to all shareholders but also to a particular shareholder or third party. However, an issue of shares to a third party at an extremely 'profitable' price (that is, considerably lower than the market price) requires a special resolution of a shareholders' meeting[21] in addition to a resolution of the board of directors.[22] This kind of case is, though, an exception. In general the board of directors decides the matter.

Thus, when company A has a large shareholding in company B, and the board of directors of company B decides to issue shares to a third party resulting in a dilution of A's holding, the question arises whether the issue is lawful. If company B issues the shares to raise equity finance, the issue is lawful. On the other hand, if company B issues the shares in order to dilute company A's holding, and the directors of company B continue to hold the management rights, the issue is unlawful. This latter scenario would constitute 'an issue of shares in an unfair way' under section 280–10 of the Commercial Code, and the shareholders could take action to stop the issue. In that action the shareholders (company A in the example above) would have to prove that company B's objective in issuing the shares was to dilute the shareholders' (company's) holdings. However, this is difficult because company B always insists that it needs to raise funds and that is the reason for the share issue. The question then arises: how does one

---

[20] S Nishimura, 'Koukai Kaitsuke ni taisuru Bouei' ('Defence Tactics Against Takeover Bids') in K Kanzaki (ed.), *Kigyoubaishuu no Jitsumu to Houri* (*Practice and Principles of Law of M&A*) (Tokyo, Shojhomu Kenkyukai, 1985), 294; H Aratani, 'Kigyou Baishu Shudan no Hourironteki Kentou' ('Legal Theoretical Examination of Protection Against Takeovers') (1991) 36 (1–3) *Hukuoka University Review of Law* 247.

[21] Commercial Code, s 343.

[22] Commercial Code, s 280–2I(8).

determine company B's true objective. According to what is known as the main purpose theory, when a share issue to raise equity finance would result in the dilution of a particular shareholder's holding an analysis should be done to ascertain the main purpose of the issue. Professor Hiroshi Suzaki of Kyoto University argues that in the struggle for control of a company, shares in that company can only be issued to a third party where two factors exist. First, there must be a need to raise finance. Secondly, the issue must be reasonable. The burden of proof is on the company.[23]

TOBs Which will Make the Target Company a 100 per cent Subsidiary

In 1998, there were three TOBs where the objective of the offer was to make the target company a 100 per cent subsidiary of the offeror (a '100 per cent offer'). In all three cases that objective was not achieved. Showa Denko Co.'s offer for SDS Biotic Co. resulted in Showa acquiring 97.59 per cent of SDS's shares. The offer by NCR Holdings Co. for Japan NCR Co. resulted in NCR Holdings acquiring 97.14 per cent of the shares of Japan NCR. And the offer by TI Group PLC for Nippon Marin Techno Co. resulted in TI acquiring 89.59 per cent of Nippon Marin's shares.

In the UK, section 429 of the Companies Act 1985 provides that where an offeror has acquired not less than 90 per cent of the shares of the target company, the offeror may give notice in the prescribed form to the remaining minority shareholders that the offeror wishes to acquire their shares. Subject to certain exceptions, the offeror is then entitled and bound to acquire the remaining shares on the terms of the offer. This is called a 'compulsory sale' or 'compulsory acquisition'.[24] In contrast, the Commercial Law and the SEL in Japan contain no similar provision. Therefore, notwithstanding that the offeror wants to acquire all of the target company's shares, if a shareholder does not wish to sell, the offeror's objective cannot be achieved.

Recently, a paper was published proposing the introduction of a new system whereby one company (company B) can become a 100 per cent subsidiary of another company (company A).[25] One method that has been proposed for achieving this is a share (stock) exchange system. Under this system company B could become a 100 per cent subsidiary of company A by the shareholders of company B exchanging their shares in B for shares in company A. The other suggestion is that offerors be given a right of compulsory acquisition, and likewise

---

[23] H Suzaki, 'Hukousei na Shinkabu Hakkou to sono Kisei' ('The Unjust Issue of Shares and its Regulation' (1986) 94(5) *Minshohou Zasshi* 561.

[24] For further details of a compulsory acquisition, see M Tanabe and M Sakaue, 'Igirisu ni okeru Kabushiki Koukai Kaitsuke no Houkisei' ('Regulation of Takeover Bids in the UK') (1991) 44(6) *Investment* 34.

[25] M Nakahigashi, 'Kabushiki Shutokugata no Kigyou Ketsugo' ('Business Combinations by Stock Acquisitions') (1997) 171 *Nagoya University Journal of Law and Politics* 125.

that minority shareholders be entitled to require the offeror to purchase their shares. The government has decided to introduce the share exchange system and came into force on October 1, 1999.

9

Legitimating Global Corporate Power

FIONA MACMILLAN

INTRODUCTION

This chapter considers the extent to which recent developments in relation to the liberalisation of international investment might be effecting the emergence and legitimisation of a global corporate sector or, at least, a corporate sector which wields global power. The chapter commences by considering the meaning of the concept of globalisation in the context of the financial and investment markets and the extent to which this concept may be distinguished from that of internationalisation. It is then argued in the second substantive part of the chapter that while internationalisation has been a prevailing norm of corporate behaviour and regulation in the modern era it may be giving way to more globalised forces. The third part of the chapter gives an overview of the relevant provisions of the General Agreement on Trade in Services (GATS) and the draft Multilateral Agreement on Investment (MAI). The discussion in this part focuses on the role which these two international agreements are likely to play in the process, and consequent legitimisation, of the corporate sector's movement from internationalisation to globalisation. The chapter concludes with a call for a stronger regulatory response to the globalisation of private power.

INTERNATIONALISATION VERSUS GLOBALISATION

The expression 'globalisation' has been described as a portmanteau word,[1] meaning different things to different people in different places and contexts. In this chapter globalisation will be used in contradistinction to the notion of internationalisation.[2] Walker, Mellor, Fox and Francis[3] have identified key differences between the concepts of globalisation and internationalisation. One is

---

[1] G Walker, S Mellor, M Fox and S Francis, 'The Concept of Globalisation' (1996) 14 *Company and Securities Law Journal* 59.

[2] See also generally, e.g., P J Lloyd, 'The Nature of Globalisation' in Economic Planning Advisory Commission Paper No 5, *Globalisation: Issues for Australia* (Mar. 1995).

[3] Walker *et al.*, *supra* n.1.

'that globalisation denotes a process of *denationalisation*, whereas internation-alisation refers to the co-operative activities of *national* actors'.[4] They also note that globalisation concerns itself with the interests of all humanity while inter-nationalisation looks to the national interest.[5] (Hence the notions of global human rights, global peace and soforth.) A consequence of these distinctions between the two concepts is that where globalisation occurs it amounts to 'the erosion and irrelevance of national boundaries'.[6]

The concurrence of a number of factors has resulted in a global, rather than an international, market for capital. In a nutshell, the major forces here have been economic liberalisation, deregulation and advances in rapid communica-tion technology[7]:

> Deregulation and financial liberalisation have put down barriers that restricted the flow of capital across national borders. Restrictions on exchange rates and capital markets controls have been eliminated in many countries. Greater reliance has been placed on market forces to allocate capital and price the value of firms. Along with these factors, rapid pace in information and communication networks has contributed to accelerate the process of data analysis and information dissemination. Moreover, fast-moving communication technologies have facilitated the trade of currencies and securities across national borders around the clock, which has lead to increased finan-cial activities and enhanced arbitrage opportunities between markets.[8]

Wriston has emphasised, in particular, the importance of technology in the development of global financial markets:

> Technology has made us a 'global' community in the literal sense of the word. Whether we are ready or not, mankind now has a completely integrated, international financial and information marketplace capable of moving money and ideas to any place on this planet in minutes. Capital will go where it is wanted and stay where it is well treated. It will flee from manipulation or onerous regulation of its value or use, and no government power can restrain it for long.[9]

It does not seem to be contentious to assert that the significance of major cor-porations as players in these globalised capital markets lends a global lustre to many of their activities. Is this enough, however, to lead to the conclusion that a global corporate sector exists?

---

[4]   Walker *et al.*, *supra* n.1 (emphasis as in original).
[5]   *Ibid.*
[6]   *Ibid.*
[7]   Walker *et al.* would also add to this list 'the rise of global business strategies', privatisation and 'the rise of the institutional investor': *ibid.*, at 60.
[8]   D K Ghosh and E Ortiz, 'The Changing Environment of International Financial Markets: Introduction' in D K Ghosh and E Ortiz (eds.), *The Changing Environment of International Financial Markets* (New York, St Martins Press, 1994) 1, at 4–5.
[9]   W B Wriston, *The Twilight of Sovereignty* (New York, Schribner, 1992), at 61–2.

There can be little doubt that the financial markets, while being perhaps the most obvious example, are not the only global markets in which corporations act. It is arguable that other markets in which members of the corporate sector trade are also global, in the sense that the relevant commodities move around with little respect for the national borders which they cross. Further, corporations are often involved in global business strategies:

> Globalisation is an important emerging business mandate relevant to virtually all businesses. It is an Information Economy, as opposed to an Industrial Economy, business concept. Modern communications enable businesses to operate in multiple countries with diverse shapes and forms of organisation and control. They make it possible to send information to any part of an organisation instantaneously, enabling every part to know what every other part—and the organisation as a whole—is doing all the time.[10]

On the other hand, at least prior to any conclusion of the MAI it is arguable that, notwithstanding the involvement of corporate players in global markets and strategies, no corporation can be regarded as truly global. There are two prongs to this argument: one relates to the juridical nature of the corporation and the other relates to commercial realities. So far as the arguments concerned with the juridical nature of the corporation are concerned, whichever theoretical basis is adopted to describe the juridical nature of the corporation it is not possible to escape the conclusion that any single corporation is a national entity. It is traditional to identify three different theories to explain the juridical nature of the company.[11] The concession[12] or fiction[13] theory regards the company as an artificial entity created and supervised by the state.[14] Modern variations on the theory, such as the communitarian or corporatist theory,[15] which (amongst other things) move away from the notion of incorporation as a privilege, nevertheless affirm the idea that the corporation is a creation of the state. The second

---

[10] P Bradley, M Housman and P Nolan, 'Global Competition and Technology' in P Bradley, M Hausman and P Nolan, *Globalization, Technology and Competition: The Fusion of Computers and Telecommunications in the 1990s* (Boston, The Harvard Business School Press, 1993), 4. The role which the possession and communication of information or knowledge plays in the strategies of international corporate players is emphasised by a range of social and cultural commentators: see, e.g., J F Lyotard, *The Postmodern Condition: A Report on Knowledge* (trans. G Bannington and B Massumi, 1984), at 3.

[11] For a general discussion of the theories and their consequences, see F Macmillan Patfield, 'Challenges for Company Law' in F Macmillan Patfield (ed.), *Perspectives on Company Law:1* (London, Kluwer Law International, 1995) 1, at 7–15.

[12] See, e.g., S Bottomley, 'Taking Corporations Seriously: Some Considerations for Corporate Regulation' (1990) 19 *Federal Law Review* 203, at 206–8.

[13] See, e.g., M Stokes, 'Company Law and Legal Theory' in W Twining (ed.), *Legal Theory and the Common Law* (Oxford, Blackwell, 1986) 155, at 162.

[14] For variations on the concession/fiction theory, see W W Bratton, 'The New Economic Theory of the Firm: Critical Perspectives from History' (1989) 41 *Stanford Law Review* 1471, at 1475.

[15] Stokes, *supra* n.13, at 178; D Millon, 'Communitarians, Contractarians, and the Crisis in Corporate Law' (1993) 50 *Washington and Lee Law Review* 1373.

commonly postulated theory is the contractual model[16] which, in its modern economic manifestation, perceives the company as a nexus-of-contracts between the various people involved in it.[17] While this theory would seem to suggest that the company exists irrespective of state intervention, its proponents cannot easily resist the argument that state intervention is necessary in an enabling capacity (nor can they easily explain the existence of mandatory rules in company law).[18] The position is similar with respect to the third theory, the natural entity theory.[19] Its proponents argue that by acting together to create a company those who formed it create, as a result of the nature of things, an entity separate from themselves. Nevertheless, this separately constituted entity does require enabling intervention from the state in order to operate. Ultimately, therefore, the capacity of a company to operate, if not its very existence, is dependent on the state. In these circumstances it was difficult to see how any corporate entity could be regarded as global in any legally meaningful sense.

Commentators have also doubted whether corporations can be regarded as global in a commercially meaningful sense. Following is a sample of the views of international experts consulted by Fleenor[20]:

> A truly global company operates not only on a worldwide basis, but coordinates its activities across national borders. Hence, 'global' refers not only to geographical scope, but also to the cross-border integration within the company. Very few firms have worldwide sales, but more importantly very few companies are able, or find it necessary, to engage in extensive cross-border coordination. Thus, few companies have purely global strategies and matching organisational structures. When most people say 'global' all they really mean is 'very international'.[21]

> A global company is one in which the corporation and its management have been transformed into an entity in which it is difficult to discern a single country bias. Today, very few if any corporations qualify as global; that is, a company without a country.[22]

Fleenor herself stated: '[t]he global corporation is a fable. It cannot be defined because it simply does not exist'.[23]

As suggested by the foregoing material, when many people speak of global corporations they are really thinking of multinational corporations. Certainly, there is a good argument for what has been described as 'conceptual blurring'[24] with respect to multinationals:

[16] See, e.g., Stokes, *supra* n.13.

[17] W W Bratton, 'The Nexus of Contracts' Corporation: A Critical Appraisal' (1989) 74 *Cornell Law Review* 407.

[18] E W Orts, 'The Complexity and Legitimacy of Corporate Law' (1993) 50 *Washington and Lee Law Review* 1565, at 1569.

[19] See, e.g., Stokes, *supra* n.13, at 162–3.

[20] D Fleenor, 'The Coming and Going of the Global Corporation' (1993) 28 *Columbia Journal of World Business* 6.

[21] Ron Meyer in *ibid.*, at 8.

[22] Sheldon Weinig in *ibid.*, at 8.

[23] *Ibid.*, at 8.

[24] Walker *et al.*, *supra* n.1, at 60.

[I]nsofar as a multinational operates in many nations and integrates its activities across borders via a strategy based on the interests of the group as a whole, it is an example of globalisation. On the other hand, insofar as a multinational pursues a strategy of maximising the interests of each entity within the group within the national boundaries in which it operates, it could be viewed as an example of internationalisation.[25]

Prior to the conclusion of the MAI, the strongest argument in favour of the existence of a global corporate sector hinges upon the business activities of a very small group of multinationals the operation of which might have been said to have transcended the merely international and embraced the global. Hovering in the background, however, is the fact that, while the activities of a corporate group may well have been global or international, the legal structure of the group recognises national borders. This tends to suggest that it is probably more appropriate to regard the group as internationalised rather than globalised. Nevertheless, it is important not to overlook the fact that the globalisation of markets has already given rise to the type of business strategies which have tended to internationalise corporate power and, as a result, make the relationship between the corporate sector and the governments of nation states problematic.[26]

GLOBALISATION THROUGH INTERNATIONAL AGREEMENT

The burning question now is whether or not the conclusion that the multinational corporate sector is better described as international than global will still hold good in the new era ushered in by the GATS and possibly to be fundamentally consolidated by the MAI.[27] If the MAI is finally concluded in a form which resembles in any way the present negotiating text[28] its significance in terms of the present enquiry will be immense. However, it is important not to let the (now somewhat quieter) fanfare over the MAI obscure the foundation of

[25] *Ibid.*

[26] See Lyotard, *supra* n.10, at 5: 'the problem of the relationship between economic and State powers threatens to arise with a new urgency'.

[27] Exactly when this new era will commence (assuming that it commences with the conclusion of the MAI) is unclear. Under the original negotiating schedule the terms of the agreement were due to be settled in Apr. 1998, however the Apr. 1998 negotiations stalled as a result of failure to reach agreement in relation to a number of different issues: see *Report by the Chairman of the Negotiating Group*, 28 Apr. 1998, http://www.oecd.org/daf/cmis/mai/repor98.htm. The next meeting of the negotiating group took place in Oct. 1998: see *Opening Statement by Mr. Donald J. Johnston, Secretary General: Consultations on the Multilateral Agreement on Investment*, 20 Oct. 1998, http://www.oecd.org/news_and_events/release/nw98–100a.htm. This meeting closed in stalemate with delegates agreeing 'on the importance of devoting additional time to take stock of . . . concerns and to assess how to accomplish the goal we all share of developing a multilateral framework of rules for investment': *Chairman's Statement, Under Secretary of State Stuart Eizenstat (USA): Executive Committee in Special Session*, 23 Oct. 1998, http://www.oecd.org/news_and_events/release/nw98–101a.htm.

[28] MAI Negotiating Text (as at 24 Apr. 1998).

trade liberalisation, especially financial services liberalisation, laid in the GATS.

The GATS is described by its promoter, the World Trade Organisation (WTO), as 'the world's first multilateral agreement on investment, since it covers not just cross-border trade but every possible means of supplying a service, including the right to set up a commercial presence in the export market'.[29] Like the MAI, the GATS embraces the principles of national treatment[30] and Most Favoured Nation treatment (MFN)[31] in relation to the supply of services. The principle of national treatment requires member states to treat services and services suppliers of another member as least as favourably as it treats its own national services and service suppliers. MFN, on the other hand, requires members not to discriminate between services and service suppliers emanating from other member states. A difference between the MAI and GATS is that the level of permissible derogation from these principles is probably considerably greater than that which will prevail under the MAI.[32] Unlike the relevant MAI provision,[33] exemptions from and limitations of the principles of national treatment and MFN are built into the relevant GATS provisions. The principle of national treatment has differential application for members.[34] The principle of MFN is explicitly subject to a member's ability to maintain a measure inconsistent with that principle subject to compliance with an Annex to the GATS specifically dealing with MFN exemptions.[35] In relation to financial services, the possibility of complete derogation from the MFN principle was permitted.[36]

The general definition of 'services' under GATS includes 'any services in any sector', but excludes 'services supplied in the exercise of governmental authority'.[37] This exclusion covers services which are not supplied on a commercial or competitive basis.[38] These partial exemptions for services provided by govern-

---

[29] WTO, *General Agreement on Trade in Services—The Design and Underlying Principles of the GATS*, http://www.wto.org/wto/services/services.htm.

[30] GATS, Art. XVII.

[31] GATS, Art. II.

[32] This, of course, is likely to be a reflection of the considerably wider membership of the WTO compared to the membership of the OECD. The WTO currently has 134 member states, with Estonia about to make it 135 (see http://www.wto.org/wto/about/organsn6.htm), compared to the OECD's 29 members (see http://www.oecd.org/about/general/member-countries.htm).

[33] See *infra* n.46.

[34] See GATS, Art. XVII(1): '*In the sectors inscribed in its Schedule, and subject to any conditions and qualifications set out therein*, each Member shall accord to services and service suppliers of any other Member, in respect of all measures affecting the supply of services, treatment no less favourable than that it accords to its own like services and service suppliers' (emphasis added).

[35] GATS Art. II(2) and Annex on Art. II Exemptions.

[36] GATS, Second Annex on Financial Services.

[37] GATS, Art. I(3)(b).

[38] GATS, Art. I(3)(c). So far as financial services are concerned, this provision excludes:
  (i)   activities conducted by a central bank or monetary authority or by any other public entity in pursuit of monetary or exchange rate policies;
  (ii) activities forming part of a statutory system of social security or public retirement plans;
  (iii) other activities conducted by a public entity for the account or with the guarantee or using the financial resources of the Government: GATS Annex on Financial Services, para 1(b).
The exclusions from the definition of service in paragraphs (ii) and (iii) are subject to the

ment are an important point of distinction between the GATS and the MAI which, as will be seen, does not make similar broad-based exclusions for government investors. As an example of the scope of the GATS, reference may usefully be made to the matters covered by the financial services obligations. These include, for example, insurance and insurance related services, and banking and a range of other types of financial services relating to matters such as foreign exchange, securities underwriting, derivatives and asset management.[39] In relation to these services members may enter into certain specific commitments[40] as set out in that member's Schedule.[41] There is provision for modification of these Schedules.[42] As will be apparent from the discussion below, in comparison to the MAI there is greater scope for individual nations to water down their commitment.

One of the most recent GATS developments is in relation to financial services and is embodied in the Fifth Protocol to GATS. The Protocol was agreed in December 1997. It was open for ratification by WTO members until January 1999 with the new commitments under the Protocol expected to enter into force by the beginning of March 1999.[43] The negotiations for the Fifth Protocol gave WTO members the opportunity to change the obligations they had undertaken in relation to financial services in the GATS Interim Agreement on Financial Services which was concluded in July 1995. Overall, the negotiations for the Fifth Protocol resulted in substantial liberalisation of trade as a number of parties withdrew or reduced the scope of their exemptions from the principle of MFN treatment.[44] The WTO's own summary of the new environment of financial services liberalisation as a consequence of the Fifth Protocol to GATS is as follows:

> The new commitments contain inter alia significant improvements allowing commercial presence of foreign financial service suppliers by eliminating or relaxing limitations on foreign ownership of local financial institutions, limitations on the juridical form of commercial presence (branches, subsidiaries, agencies, representative offices, etc.) and limitations on the expansion of existing operations. Important progress was also made in 'grandfathering' existing branches and subsidiaries of foreign financial institutions that are wholly- or majority-owned by foreigners. Improvements were

activities in question not being conducted in competition with a public entity or a financial service supplier: GATS Annex on Financial Services, para 1(c).

[39] GATS, Annex on Financial Services, para 5(a), which contains an inclusive list of the financial services covered.

[40] GATS, Part III.

[41] GATS, Art. XX.

[42] GATS, Art. XXI.

[43] WTO, 'The Results of the Financial Services Negotiations under the General Agreement on Trade in Services (GATS)', http://www.wto.org/wto/services/finance_background.htm.

[44] For the new commitments and exemptions of member countries, see *Schedules of Specific Commitments and Lists of Art. II Exemptions to be Annexed to the Fifth Protocol of the General Agreement on Trade in Services*, http://www.wto.org/wto/services/finsched.htm. For a country-by-country summary of the new commitments, see WTO, 'Non-attributable Summary of the Main Improvements in the New Financial Services Commitments', 26 Feb. 1998, http://www.wto.org/wto/services/finsum.htm.

made in all three of the major financial service sectors—banking, securities and insurance, as well as in other services such as asset management and provision and transfer of financial information.[45]

There is, therefore, significant potential for WTO members to participate in substantial trade liberalisation as a result of the GATS and, in particular in the area of financial services, the Fifth Protocol to GATS.

While the concept of services under GATS is a relatively wide one it is arguable that the OECD's MAI focuses on a much broader range of activities. It also provides signatories with substantially less opportunity for derogation from the prescribed commitments. The central plank of the MAI is to require signatory states not to discriminate between investors. As under the GATS, this is to be achieved through the principles of national treatment and MFN treatment.[46] The principle of national treatment will require signatory states to treat foreign investors at least as favourably as it treats its own national investors for the purposes of its laws and regulations on investment. MFN treatment, on the other hand, requires signatory states not to discriminate between investors or investors emanating from other MAI member states. With respect to both national treatment and MFN treatment the prohibition on discrimination extends to 'the establishment, acquisition, expansion, operation, management, maintenance, use, enjoyment and sale or other disposition of investments'.[47] The notion of 'investment' under the MAI is defined widely and means, in the current available negotiating text, '[e]very kind of asset owned or controlled, directly or indirectly, by an investor'.[48] 'Investor' is also widely defined to include natural persons and 'a legal person or any other entity constituted or organised under the applicable law of a Contracting Party, whether or not for profit, and whether private or government owned or controlled and includes a corporation, trust, partnership, sole proprietorship, joint venture, association or organisation'.[49] The MAI, however, is not just about non-discrimination.[50] It also imposes what are described as 'specific disciplines'[51] on contracting parties.[52] Effectively, these are uniform rules imposed on contracting parties which limit their freedom to legislate in a number of areas touching on investments

[45] *Supra* n.43.

[46] MAI Negotiating Text (as at 24 Apr. 1998), Art. III.

[47] *Ibid.*

[48] MAI Negotiating Text (as at 24 Apr. 1998), Art. II(2). This definition is followed by an inclusive list of 'investments', the inclusion of some of which has proved contentious.

[49] MAI Negotiating Text (as at 24 Apr. 1998), Art. II(1).

[50] In passing it might be noted that the advent of the MAI hardly reinforces the already very dubious proposition that non-discrimination is a type of motherhood principle. Perhaps this is another example of what postmodernist scholars have described as the failure of the meta-narrative: see N Andrews, 'What Would Sir Samuel Griffith Have Said? Postmodernism in the 1990s Company Law Classroom' (1998) 5(2) *E-Law—Murdoch University Electronic Journal of Law*, http://www.murdoch.edu.au/elaw/issues/v5n2/andrews522.html.

[51] OECD, 'The Multilateral Agreement on Investment: Frequently Asked Questions and Answers', http://www.oecd.org/daf/cmis/mai/faqmai.htm.

[52] See MAI Negotiating Text (as at 24 Apr. 1998), Art. III.

under the agreement. These include matters such as immigration laws regulating the entry into a contracting state of investors and key personnel,[53] investor participation in the privatisation of public enterprises,[54] as well as a whole cartload of restrictions referred to in the MAI as 'performance requirements'.[55] A brief trawl through these performance requirements gives some idea of the level of restraints on domestic legislation which are envisaged by the agreement. In general terms, the requirements in the current negotiating text prevent a contracting state from enforcing any of the following types of restrictions: export requirements; domestic content requirements; territorial restrictions on the acquisition of goods or services; export, import or foreign exchange restrictions; territorial sales restrictions; technology transfer restrictions; rules on location of head offices; requirements relating to minimum levels of research and development; requirements relating to a minimum level of national employees; requirements for domestic participation in joint ventures; and requirements relating to domestic equity participation. There is provision in the current negotiating text for some general exemptions from these requirements,[56] as well as the possibility of negotiating country-specific exemptions.[57] The scope of the various different types of exceptions and exemptions is one of the areas of controversy in the current negotiations.[58]

In all, as indicated above, the GATS is probably more limited in scope than the MAI both in terms of the range of activities which it affects and in the range of affected participants. In particular, the partial exemption for government suppliers of services reduces its scope and consequent effect. Further, the level of permissible derogation by members from its obligations is greater than that which is allowed under the current version of the MAI. However, provisions such as those on progressive liberalisation[59] and on increasing the participation of developing countries[60] bolster the normative force which the WTO wields against such derogation. The scope may be narrower and the obligations possibly weaker, but the GATS has a much larger potential membership than the MAI is likely to have in its early days.[61] Having said this, the negotiations over the MAI have shown that the OECD members are evangelistic about securing non-OECD signatories to the agreement.[62] Also, while the OECD has a more

---

[53] *Ibid.*
[54] *Ibid.*
[55] *Ibid.*
[56] Including exemptions for putting into effect temporary safeguards to protect certain types of national interests: MAI Negotiating Text (as at 24 Apr. 1998), Arts III and VI.
[57] *Ibid.*, Art. IX.
[58] See *Report by the Chairman of the Negotiating Group*, 28 Apr. 1998, *supra* n.27.
[59] GATS, Part IV.
[60] GATS, Art. IV.
[61] See *supra* n.32.
[62] See, e.g., OECD, 'The Multilateral Agreement on Investment: Frequently Asked Questions and Answers', *supra* n.51, at para 14.

select membership than the WTO, it numbers the world's most powerful economies amongst those members.[63]

The GATS and the MAI are powerful tools of globalisation, the former perhaps more potentially limited than the latter. Nothing in either agreement has the effect of removing the legal requirement that a corporation have a home jurisdiction in which it is registered. However, the direct effect of these agreements, especially the MAI, is to render almost meaningless the distinction between a corporation registered in a particular jurisdiction and a corporation registered outside that jurisdiction. It is tempting to argue that the provisions of the MAI, in particular, have a destructive effect on national sovereignty across a wide range of areas. The OECD seem sensitive about this criticism and is at pains to point out that that MAI will be 'fully consistent with the sovereign responsibility of governments to conduct domestic policies'[64]:

> The MAI will not immunise foreign investors from domestic laws. It will not remove the authority of domestic courts, tribunals and regulatory authorities over foreign investors and their enterprises.

> The MAI will not deprive national governments of their sovereign right to promote economic development, encourage a cleaner environment, protect cultural diversity and other public policy goals through regulations or incentive programmes, *so long as they do not discriminate.*[65]

The actual terms of the MAI may well be consistent with the OECD's protestations. The significant point, however, is that the relatively unfettered market for international business investment introduced by the MAI, and supported by agreements such as the GATS, is likely to have the effect of depriving national governments of any real remaining autonomy across a whole range of areas, such as taxation rates, labour standards, health and safety issues (to name but a few). The reason for this, in a nutshell, is that due to the lifting of restrictions on establishment of enterprises in other member states, international business organisations will be free to move from jurisdiction to jurisdiction. Once every jurisdiction is effectively a market for investment, it will need to take steps to make itself attractive to potential investors.

There are two other aspects of the MAI which may impact dramatically on the issue of national autonomy and sovereignty. One of these relates to the enforcement provisions of the MAI and the other to the provisions on withdrawal from the agreement. Article V of the MAI negotiating text contains the agreement's dispute-settlement procedures. What is notable about these procedures in the context of concerns about national sovereignty is that the Article

---

[63] Of course, if it is the case that the MAI negotiations are revived under the auspices of the WTO, then this would have the capacity to result in much more extensive liberalisation obligations imposed on a much broader range of members.

[64] *Supra* n.51.

[65] *Ibid.* (emphasis added). Nevertheless the issue of national sovereignty was still a bone of contention in last year's Oct. negotiations: see *Chairman's Statement, Under Secretary of State Stuart Eizenstat (USA): Executive Committee in Special Session, supra* n.27.

contains not only state against state dispute-settlement procedures, but also investor against state procedures.[66] This gives a corporate entity a limited[67] but direct right to rein in allegedly defaulting nation states, along with all the strategic advantages that such a right confers. So far as the matter of withdrawal from the MAI is concerned, the current draft provisions further reinforce the argument that entry into the MAI will result in a substantial loss of national sovereignty. MAI signatories commit themselves for an initial five-year period; after that they may withdraw on six months' notice. After withdrawal, however, the obligations under the MAI last for 15 years in relation to investments made prior to withdrawal.[68] It is, perhaps, overkill to observe that this period is considerably longer than the life of most democratically elected governments and that, accordingly, the withdrawal rules of the MAI make sensible domestic planning in relation to participation in the MAI problematic. All this is very likely to mean that national boundaries will become irrelevant to the operations of international corporate players. As the national boundaries fade away in terms of legal regulation this will be likely to be mirrored by an increase in the level of truly globalised corporate strategies and operations.

At base, the general and specific concerns which militate against continuing down the road of the GATS and the draft MAI in their present forms, are about the issue of substantial loss of national sovereignty. This is not just about whether individual nation states have bound, or will bind, themselves by treaty to excessive limits on their legislative power. It is also, perhaps more importantly, about an adjustment in the relative power balance between nation states and international corporate entities.[69] The Interim Report on the MAI of the Australian Parliamentary Joint Standing Committee on Treaties[70] observes that '[t]he overwhelming number of submissions [made to it] oppose or express concerns about particular aspects of the MAI'.[71] In so far as such concerns address

---

[66] Compare the GATS procedures in Art. XXIII, which give only state against state rights.

[67] MAI negotiating text (as at 24 Apr. 1998), Art. V(D) applies to disputes 'concerning any obligation which the Contracting Party has entered into with regard to a specific investment of the investor through: (i) An investment authorisation granted by its competent authorities specifically to the investor or investment, (ii) a written agreement granting rights with respect to [categories of subject matters] on which the investor has relied in establishing acquiring, or significantly expanding an investment'.

[68] MAI negotiating text (as at 24 Apr. 1998), Art. XII.

[69] This would not be a new development but would, arguably, amount to the acceleration of a process which has characterised the late 20th century: see further R J Barnet and J Cavanagh, *Global Dreams: Imperial Corporations and the New World Order* (New York, Simon & Schuster, 1994); E W Orts, 'The Legitimacy of Multinational Corporations' in L E Mitchell (ed.), *Progressive Corporate Law* (Boulder, Westview Press, 1995), 247; E W Orts, 'Shirking and Sharking: A Legal Theory of the Firm' (1998) 16 *Yale Law and Policy Review* 265, at 286 and 286n; E W Orts, 'The Future of Enterprise Organization' (Book Review) (1998) 96 *Michigan Law Review* 1947, at 1962.

[70] Parliament of the Commonwealth of Australia, Joint Standing Committee on Treaties, *Multilateral Agreement on Investment: Interim Report* (14th Report, Canberra: Australia Government Publishing Services, May 1998). For the final report, see Parliament of the Commonwealth of Australia, Joint Standing Committee on Treaties, *Report 18: Multilateral Agreement on Investment—Final Report* (Canberra: Australian Government Publishing Service, Mar. 1999).

[71] *Interim Report*, *supra* n.70, at para 1.43.

matters of national sovereignty, they relate to matters including 'the environment, labour standards and employment conditions, culture, media and communications, quarantine, social policy including health care and education, the rights of indigenous Australians and human rights'.[72] Many of these have also been a matter of widespread international concern, particularly the issues of the environment, labour rights and national culture.[73] In relation to protection of the environment and protection of labour rights, the argument that a 'race to the bottom' is inevitable in a world dominated by global corporate entities has been pervasive.[74] It should, of course, be acknowledged that so far many of the compromises in the GATS obligations reflect popular concerns about these types of matters. For example, it is interesting that while the GATS includes an Annex on Telecommunications and there is a Protocol dealing with the application of this Annex, the Annex specifically exempts from its scope 'measures affecting cable or broadcast distribution of radio or television programming'.[75] This may well be a response to concerns about the erosion of national cultural identity which would follow the lifting of restrictions on matters such as domestic ownership and domestic content requirements for television and radio broadcasting.[76] Nevertheless, the current stance of GATS on these matters could easily change. It can hardly be contentious to say that it is well known that there is pressure from powerful corporate interests to see these types of restrictions removed as part of the liberalisation of global investment.

[72] *Interim Report, supra* n.70, at para 1.47.

[73] These three matters, along with the issue of sovereignty, were specifically stated by the negotiators to require further consultation after the Oct. 1998 OECD negotiations, which suggests that they were perceived as forming major stumbling blocks to the successful conclusion of the agreement: see *Chairman's Statement, Under Secretary of State Stuart Eizenstat (USA): Executive Committee in Special Session, supra* n.27.

[74] A mountain of literature (presumably on recycled paper) has been generated over these issues. For a few pithy examples see: P C Newman, 'MAI: A Time Bomb with a Very Short Fuse' (1998) 111(9) *Maclean's* 51; P Rauber, 'All Hail the Multinationals!' (1998) 83(4) *Sierra* 16; S Zeller, 'A Pact Bagged—The Naderites, Greens and Unions are Roiled by the Multilateral Agreement on Investment. The What?' (1998) 30(10) *National Journal* 531; National Tertiary Education Union, 'An Introduction to the Multilateral Agreement on Investment', http://www.edunions.labor. net.au/nteu/debates/multlat3.html and 'ACTU Decision: Multilateral Agreement on Investment', http://www.edunions.labor.net.au/nteu/debates/multlat1.html; Friends of the Earth, 'A Bill of Rights for Multinationals?', http://www.foe.co.uk/foei/tes/link14b.htm; 'The Multilateral Agreement on Investment' (1998) 15(2) *The Environmental Forum* 46. Cf. Annex 2 to the MAI negotiating text (as at 24 Apr. 1998). For a wide-ranging discussion on the possible consequences for a nation state in joining the MAI, or any similar agreement, see P Ranald, *Disciplining Governments? What the Multilateral Agreement on Investment would mean for Australia* (Public Sector Research Centre and Evatt Foundation, 1998).

[75] GATS, Annex on Telecommunications, Art. 2(b).

[76] It is worth noting in this context that it is also arguable that the definition of services in the GATS (see *supra* nn.37 and 38 and accompanying text) excludes public services broadcasters from the purview of obligations since such services are generally supplied by government on a non-commercial and non-competitive basis.

CONCLUSION

To its proponents at least, the MAI may be seen as a logical and irresistible response to the problems posed by globalisation.[77] There is no question, however, that the MAI and members of its supporting cast, such as the GATS, restrike the balance of power between the international corporate sector and the political power of any individual nation state. The emasculation of the regulatory power of the nation states as a consequence of the trade liberalisation agreements seems likely to have a symbiotic relationship with the rate at which their socio-economic power will be eroded by the increasing power of the corporate behemoths. It seems that the socio-economic power of these multi-national corporate groups is enhanced by the mere fact of their multinational operation. This is partly a factor of their size and influence across a number of jurisdictions. Such groups may, for example, be able to insulate themselves from other market pressures in one jurisdiction by relying on the strength of their market in another jurisdiction. The competitive advantages gained by multinationals as a result of their tendency to isolate and fragment their markets along national lines[78] are often gained at the expense of things we purport to care about, such as consumers, workers, the environment, cultural policy and soforth. This effect can only be increased as these corporate groups become global and the rival power of the nation states declines.[79]

This decline in the power and significance of the nation state and the corresponding growth of rival powers in the form of a global corporate sector have, obviously, profound implications for notions of corporate regulation. We will need at some stage to grapple with the fact that once corporations become truly global it will not be possible to regulate them without some type of global, or at least supranational, regulatory structure.[80] The problem with agreements such as the GATS and the MAI, but especially the latter, is that they give rights and benefits to corporate entities without imposing any obligations on them or putting in place any structure to regulate them. The result of this is the creation of unaccountable and autonomous blocs of private and potentially global

---

[77] See, e.g., F Cotti, 'Foreign Policy and Globalisation', Address by the President of the Swiss Confederation, 15 Dec. 1997, *Geneva and International Report*, http://w3.iprolink.ch/gnir/ html/cover_story1.html. See also OECD, supra, n.51.

[78] For just one example of this, see F Macmillan, 'Copyright and Culture: A Perspective on Corporate Power' (1998) 3 *Media and Arts Law Review* 71.

[79] At present a strong argument can be made that the use of multinationals which may be made by national governments in the exercise and pursuit of their own foreign policy initiatives confers significant power on such corporate groups: see further, A Chayes, 'The Modern Corporation and the Rule of Law' in E S Mason (ed.), *The Corporation in Modern Society* (Cambridge, Harvard University Press, 1959, reprinted 1980) 25. It will be interesting to see how the power dynamics of this relationship are altered in the post-MAI era.

[80] See further, in the specific context of corporate disclosure rules, F Macmillan, 'Corporate Disclosure On-Line: An Appropriate Response to Globalisation?' (1998) 21 *University of New South Wales Law Journal* 514.

power. We should not be prepared to accept such unaccountable power as legitimate.[81]

The prospects for achieving some kind of supranational, international or global regulatory regime in order to legitimate the power of the corporate sector in the brave new world of the GATS and MAI are not all that encouraging. Already nation states have allowed corporate entities to achieve significant unaccountable socio-economic power on the international stage with barely a murmur. In 1976 the OECD promulgated its *Guidelines for Multinational Enterprises*[82] and under the current negotiating text of the MAI these will form an Annex to the MAI.[83] However, as the name implies the so-called obligations in these *Guidelines* are voluntary and will remain so if the MAI is concluded in a form approximating the present negotiating draft. In addition to lack of political will, attempts to introduce some type of supranational regulatory regime for corporations will be dogged by difficulties familiar to those attempting harmonisation in other areas of regulation, the most obvious of these being the difficulties of operating uniform systems of regulation in jurisdictions with differing legal and economic systems.[84] Nevertheless, the dangers of failing to introduce a supranational or global regulatory regime are great, bearing in mind the power wielded by multinational and global business entities.

The passage towards such a global regulatory regime is most likely to be achieved by way of supra-national agreements. Ironically, the MAI is just such an agreement, yet it can hardly be regarded as much of a comfort to those concerned about the growth of unaccountable blocs of private power which will transcend the power of national governments. What went wrong? The answer may be that the MAI is a wrong step in the right direction. It is a wrong step because it concerns itself with constraining the power of the nation states, rather than the power of international business concerns, at a time when the former are arguably already weaker than the latter.[85] However, the direction is right because it amounts to a recognition that the legal environment for international

---

[81] See further, e.g., Bottomley, *supra* n.12, at 215; J E Parkinson, *Corporate Power and Responsibility* (Oxford, Clarendon Press, 1993), esp. ch. 1; Chayes, *supra* n 79; *Curtis Publishing Co. v. Butts*, 338 US 130, 163 (1967), *per* Warren CJ; Macmillan Patfield, *supra* n.11, at 11–15.

[82] Reissued in 1997.

[83] MAI negotiating text (as at 24 Apr. 1998), Art. X.

[84] Important light may be shed on this matter by W W Bratton and J A McCahery, *Comparative Corporate Governance and the Theory of the Firm: The Case Against Global Cross Reference*, the forthcoming publication of which is noted in G A Mark, 'The Role of the State in Corporate Law Formation', ch. 1 of this volume, at n.15, and awaited by the author of this chapter with some eagerness.

[85] See *supra* n.69. It is interesting to note that 18th century thinkers, including Montesquieu and Sir James Steuart, recognised the power of international business as being a more than sufficient counterweight to the power of despots and other autocrats: see A O Hirschman, *The Passions and the Interests: Political Arguments for Capitalism before its Triumph* (Princeton, Princeton University Press, 1977), esp part 2. At the close of the 20th century we seem to have chosen to load the dice in favour of international business and against democratically elected and accountable governments of nation states.

business entities requires action at the supra-national level. A right step in the right direction now would be a supra-national agreement which concerned itself with adequate mechanisms for the regulation and accountability of international and global corporate power.

10

Australia and the UK on the Quest for Best Corporate Governance Practice

FIONA ELLETT

INTRODUCTION

Corporate governance, or the way in which companies are monitored and controlled,[1] has become popular largely due to the corporate excesses and failures of the 1980s and early 1990s. Many of these corporate excesses resulted in serious corporate failure, with concomitant economic effects. Often these excesses were not illegal; however, they crossed a general sense of propriety and moral decency. The fact that they were not illegal required a renewed investigation into the regulatory framework available to deal with these issues.[2]

Rules of corporate governance are required, as power without accountability can promote abuse. Separation of ownership from control in large listed companies means that mechanisms must be implemented to ensure that corporate performance is maximised.[3] There is no magic solution for all companies in all countries. All that can hope to be achieved is a delicate balancing of competing objectives to help companies operate at their optimum. This will involve a balancing of different forms of regulation, a balancing of profitability against accountability, and a balancing of competing interests between the constituencies of the firm.

Australia and the UK are currently evolving in terms of best practice in corporate governance. Both countries have undergone reforms recently to improve their corporate governance regime. However, both have far to go to promote optimal corporate governance arrangements for listed companies. This chapter will briefly comment on some of the reforms of corporate governance in Australia and the UK in light of the recent Corporate Law Economic Reform Bill 1998 (CLER Bill) released in Australia.

---

[1] The definition used in Australian Stock Exchange, *Disclosure of Corporate Governance Practices by Listed Companies: Discussion Paper* (1994), at 1.

[2] N Jackson, 'Organisational Chiaroscuro: Throwing Light on the Concept of Corporate Governance' (1995) 48(8) *Human Relations* 875.

[3] P Barratt, 'Corporate Governance and the Role of Australia 2010' (1995) 121 *Business Council Bulletin* 12, at 13.

The Corporate Law Economic Reform Program (CLERP) has proposed Australia's latest reform of corporate governance. CLERP was announced by the Treasurer on 4 March 1997 and represents a sweeping programme to develop a policy framework for corporate law reform.[4] Specifically, a CLERP paper was released entitled 'Directors' Duties and Corporate Governance'[5] with the aim of promoting optimal corporate governance structures without compromising flexibility and innovation.[6]

The CLER Bill, incorporating most of the CLERP proposals, was introduced into the House of Representatives of the Commonwealth Parliament and had its first and second readings on 2 July 1998.[7] It was then referred to the Parliamentary Joint Committee on Corporations and Securities. However, the Committee's deliberations were cut short by a federal election being called, which also caused the CLER Bill to lapse. A new version of the CLER Bill was introduced into Parliament on 3 December 1998. On 10 December 1998 the Senate resolved to refer the matter again to the Committee for report by 22 April 1999. The CLER Bill can be expected to come into operation is 1 July 1999. However, it has been delayed. When the CLER Bill was brought before the House of Representatives and the Commonwealth Parliament for debate on 3 July 1999, the Minister did not reveal an expected commencement date. Realistically, the earliest it can commence is the beginning of 2000.

THE PROPOSED REFORMS

Briefly, the major reforms proposed by the CLER Bill include:

- clarifying directors' obligations:

  - extending the duty to exercise care and diligence,[8] making it clear that the duty must be assessed by looking to the particular circumstances of the officer involved;

  - altering the duty to act honestly[9] to include the fiduciary principles that directors must exercise their powers and discharge their duties in good faith in the best interests of the company, and for a proper purpose;

- introducing a statutory business judgement rule;

---

[4] Corporate Law Economic Reform Program, *Policy Reforms* (Canberra, Australian Government Publishing Service, 1998), at iii.

[5] Corporate Law Economic Reform Program, *Directors' Duties and Corporate Governance: Facilitating Innovation and Protecting Investors* (Canberra, Australian Government Publishing Service, 1997).

[6] Corporate Law Economic Reform Bill 1998: outline to the Bill at http://www.aph.gov.au.

[7] 'Corporate Law Economic Reform Bill 1998' (1998) 15 *Butterworths Corporation Law Bulletin* para 246.

[8] Currently Corporations Law, s 232(4).

[9] Currently Corporations Law, s 232(2).

- giving legislative authority to the board of directors to delegate its powers, and clarifying its liability for reliance on the information provided by others;
- allowing the company to indemnify officers for most legal expenses;
- introducing a standard form of due diligence defence; and
- introducing a statutory derivative action.

Most of the reforms in this area do not purport to change the law. They merely make the law more certain. For example, it is arguable that the courts already use a type of business judgement doctrine.[10]

It is interesting to note that the UK is also currently undergoing reform in this area in the form of a wide-ranging review of the legal framework under which business operates.[11] This review was launched by the UK Department of Trade and Industry (DTI) in March 1998. It does not appear that UK law with respect to the rights and duties of shareholders and directors will change drastically as a result of this review. The UK reliance on judge-made law appears to be working well for the UK, although it would not be suitable for Australia following the uncertainties created in the wake of *Daniels* v. *Anderson*.[12]

CURRENT REGULATORY FRAMEWORK

Australia

Australia currently has a very weak system of ensuring that companies are adopting best practice in corporate governance. Corporate governance practices are regulated by the Australian Stock Exchange (ASX) via the Listing Rules. These rules state that a company merely has to include '[a] statement of the main corporate governance practices that the entity had in place during the reporting period'.[13] Appendix 4A to the Listing Rules does contain an indicative list of corporate governance principles that may be considered when complying with this rule, however there is no requirement to take the list into account.

On 9 February 1998 the ASX introduced a Guidance Note designed to assist listed entities when preparing their corporate governance statement under Listing Rule 4.10.3.[14] It expands the indicative list of corporate governance matters contained in Appendix 4A, and provides insight into interpretations of these matters. However, it does not change the fact that the Australian approach merely requires disclosure of *any* form of corporate governance practices. It does not require mandatory compliance with any specified benchmarks, nor does it require disclosure of voluntary compliance with any specified benchmarks. This can create problems for both the company trying to operate at an

---

[10] J Farrar, 'Corporate Governance, Business Judgement and the Professionalism of Directors' (1993) 6(1) *Corporate and Business Law Journal* 1, at 20.

[11] See also D R Macdonald, 'Recent Developments in UK Company Law', Ch 13 of this volume.

[12] (1995) 16 ACSR 607, 13 ACLC 614.

[13] ASX Listing Rule 4.10.3.

[14] Australian Stock Exchange, *Guidance Note: Disclosure of Corporate Governance Practices*, 2 Feb. 1998, point 1.

optimal level and the investor trying to gauge the suitability of a company's governance practices.

CLERP recognises that it is essential to Australia's international competitiveness and economic growth that effective corporate governance practices are established and maintained.[15] Yet, CLERP's policy is not to introduce any legislation in this area. CLERP states that practices should be monitored by the ASX and other various bodies. However, it does not propose to enforce this in any way. The process of monitoring is a passive one and this 'reform' does not provide any clear benefit to the corporate governance cause.

CLERP believes that the government should 'encourage' rather than 'prescribe' rules for appropriate corporate governance practices, but it does not give guidance about what these may be. It believes that competitive economic, commercial and international pressures will ensure this. However, if these fail then it will impose rules.[16] This 'wait and see' approach highlights the infancy of Australian corporate governance regulation. This approach gives no certainty to the area, and sanctions *ad hoc* development of principles. This is especially dangerous for Australia's international competitiveness in light of the UK's initiatives in the area, which appear to strike a balance between external forces and the need for regulation.

The United Kingdom

Unlike Australia, UK reforms of corporate governance regulation have focussed on systematically developing codes of best practice. During the 1990s, three successive committees have been commissioned to review and reform corporate governance practices, namely the Cadbury Committee,[17] Greenbury Committee[18] and most recently the Hampel Committee.[19] The Committees have each been concerned with developing a standard benchmark for corporate governance practices against which companies must disclose compliance. The recent Combined Code of Best Practice (the Hampel Code) embodies practices which have been identified as being able to contribute to the better functioning of companies. It also contains a broad set of principles for companies to adopt in order to ensure good corporate governance.[20]

The London Stock Exchange (LSE) Listing Rules 12.43A(a) and (b)[21] require companies to make a statement in their annual report regarding their compli-

[15] Corporate Law Economic Reform Program, *supra* n.5, at 71.
[16] *Ibid.*
[17] The Committee on the Financial Aspects of Corporate Governance, *Report of the Committee on the Financial Aspects of Corporate Governance* (1992), chaired by Sir Adrian Cadbury.
[18] The Greenbury Committee released a report entitled *Directors' Remuneration: Report of the Committee on Executive Remuneration* (1995), chaired by Sir Ronald Greenbury.
[19] Committee on Corporate Governance, *Final Report* (1998), chaired by Sir Ronald Hampel.
[20] The Combined Code, as developed by the Hampel Committee.
[21] The Combined Code and new Listing Rule 12.43A were published on 25 June 1998.

ance with the Combined Code. The Listing Rules also require some aspects of this compliance statement to be reviewed by the auditors.[22] This statement must explain the company's application of the Code's principles or give an explanation of its failure to comply with any of the provisions during any part of the accounting period.[23]

COMPARING THE UK AND AUSTRALIAN APPROACHES TO DISCLOSURE

Similarities

The rules are similar in that:

- both countries' Listing Rules will encourage some public scrutiny of the way that companies conduct their affairs[24];
- both Listing Rules are based on the premise that self regulation, rather than statutory enforcement, is the best way to improve the way companies are managed. They also manifest a belief that it is financial markets rather than the regulators that are likely to provide the most effective external controls where companies fail to reach acceptable standards of corporate governance[25];
- both merely require the disclosure of corporate governance principles, not strict compliance with any particular set of principles[26];
- both have identified some type of benchmark; and
- both provide guidelines which are not lengthy nor complex.

Differences

The Australian and UK systems have some stark differences. The UK system is not entirely self-regulatory. It has a prescribed, but voluntary, Code of Best Practice. UK companies must disclose their compliance with the developed Code of Best Practice.[27] However, failing to comply with the Code is not a

---

[22] See the final para of Listing Rule 12.43A. Now the Auditing Practices Board, *Auditors' Responsibility Statements* and *Auditors' Reports on Corporate Governance* (June 1998) proposes a comprehensive auditors' responsibility statement to be included in annual accounts, and removal from the Listing Rules of the requirement for auditors to review compliance with certain aspects of the Combined Code: see further, Law Commission of England and Wales, *Company Directors: Regulating Conflicts of Interest and Formulating a Statement of Duties* (1998), at para 1.35. On this matter, see also Macdonald, *supra* n.11.

[23] Listing Rule 12.43A(a) and (b). The Principles are contained in Part 1 of the Combined Code and the Provisions are contained in Part 2 of the Combined Code.

[24] T Clarke, 'Corporate Governance after Cadbury' (1993) 6(3) *Executive Development* 28.

[25] V Finch, 'Board Performance and Cadbury on Corporate Governance' [1992] *Journal of Business Law* 581.

[26] That is, there are no mandatory rules for corporate governance practices.

[27] Being either the Cadbury Code and Greenbury Code or the Combined Hampel Code.

breach of the LSE's rules. A company which does not meet the Code, but discloses that fact and gives reasons, will still satisfy the rules.

In Australia, companies are free to disclose any corporate governance practices. Appendix 4A and the Guidance Note to Listing Rule 4.10.3 provide an 'indicative list' and recommendations for disclosure. However, unlike with the LSE Listing Rules, Australian companies do not need to disclose their compliance with this list. This is a much weaker solution. Both countries require disclosure of their corporate governance practices; however, only the UK provides a strong benchmark against which companies must disclose their practices. Australia's current system represents a poor attempt to ensure that companies are carrying out best practices.

SUCCESS OF THE PROPOSED REFORMS

CLERP aims to ensure that regulation facilitates economic activity and development in business and capital markets.[28] The impetus for CLERP, and the CLER Bill, was the concern over Australia's ability to compete internationally, especially in the increasingly aggressive environment of Asia and the Pacific.[29] As these reforms are yet to be implemented, it is not entirely clear how effective they will be in facilitating expansion of Australia's capital markets.[30] However, the fact that they do not purport to change the law, but merely make it more certain, seems to suggest that the reforms will not result in any radical improvements. Nonetheless, the CLER Bill's moves to reform directors' duties and other corporate governance issues illustrate that Australia is willing to take some of the necessary steps to improve corporate governance. Australian company law is still developing on its quest for best practice.

In some respects the new DTI reforms of UK company law are moving slowly behind the Australian. Australian reforms are of particular importance to the UK due to the limited litigation in the UK dealing with corporate governance issues, and the extent to which courts in that country have drawn on Australian authorities in recent years.[31] In some areas UK reform recommendations do not yet encompass the same degree of reform as their Australian counterparts. The law of directors' duties in the UK is still largely based on case law. UK reform proposals are indicating that UK law will remain largely common law based; however, the major DTI reforms now underway may take a different approach.

---

[28] I Campbell, 'Corporate Law Economic Reform Program: Accounting Standards' (1997), http://www.treasury.gov.au/Treasurer/Speeches/Framework/Default.asp.

[29] R Baxt, 'Company Law Reform by No Half Measures—The CLERP Program Really "Takes Off" (1998) 26 *Australian Business Law Review* 217.

[30] Corporate Law Economic Reform Program, *supra* n.5, at 10.

[31] R Tomasic, 'Modernising the Rules of Corporate Governance—The AWA Case on Appeal' (1995) 5 *Australian Journal of Corporate Law* 487, at 491.

THE OVERALL IMPACT ON BEST PRACTICE

In terms of ensuring that companies implement their own best practice corporate governance standards, the CLER Bill provides nothing.[32] Its only impact on corporate governance is the enhanced certainty it brings to the law of directors' duties. The CLER Bill's clarification of directors' duties[33] should lead to improved corporate governance practices and market confidence. This clarification will also lead to a reduction in agency costs as directors will be free to take calculated business risks to maximise company profits. They will have the certainty required to be confident in acting innovatively.

The CLER Bill proposals have been well received by many. However, it appears that implementation of the reforms is not likely to result in any change in the regulation of company directors in Australia.[34] Conversely, there is a concern that the government may have gone too far and that the proposals actually soften the law in an unacceptable manner.[35] It seems that most of the reforms merely codify the existing common law position (such as the statutory business judgement rule). Their only benefit to corporate governance is their impact on certainty to allow directors and shareholders to act with more confidence, knowing their duties and rights.

CONCLUSION

Good corporate governance will not necessarily be able to deter the activities of unscrupulous entrepreneurs. Those determined to act in a fraudulent or dishonest manner should be dealt with by criminal laws. Good corporate governance will ensure that companies have the best opportunities to operate at their optimum. This is dependent on the willingness of boards and management to comply with the best practice requirements. Corporate governance is about substance over form. Company management must be responsible for their own fate.[36]

The reforms of directors' duties and shareholders' rights in the CLER Bill appear to be a positive step forward in providing certainty for the roles of these parties. This will in turn impact favourably on the internal governance of

---

[32] Especially since its only recommendation is that corporate governance matters be continuously monitored, without any regulation. See Corporate Law Economic Reform Program, *supra* n.5, at 71.

[33] Referring to all matters contained in Corporate Law Economic Reform Program, *supra* n.5, and codified by CLER Bill.

[34] C Grose, 'Directors' Duties and Corporate Governance', *Freehill Hollingdale & Page: In Time*, 28 Oct. 1997, at 1.

[35] Baxt, *supra* n 29, at 217.

[36] L Factor, 'Corporate Governance of Listed Companies in WA' (1996) 6 *Australian Journal of Corporate Law* 380.

companies. However, it cannot overcome the fact that a comprehensive corporate governance framework is missing.

Future reforms of corporate governance in Australia should promote a broad corporate governance framework. This will consist of a combination of statutory, market, judicial and self-regulation within a defined, mandatory framework. It should enable and encourage institutional investors to take an active role in the companies in which they invest, and boost the confidence of global investors in Australian companies. Corporate governance in Australia is still in its infancy stage. In order to ensure rapid improvement regulators and companies should always be focused on the quest for best practice.

11

Japan's Current Move Towards Corporate Statutory Reform: Is it a Breakthrough to a New Era ?

JUNKO UEDA

INTRODUCTION

Japan, in the wake of its 'bubble economy', has been plagued by stagnant corporate performances and a sluggish stock market. The corporations have not yet recovered the financial loss which they incurred from excessive borrowing and unrestrained investment during the bubble period. Moreover, the decline in corporate net proceeds has caused depreciation of share prices, which has been ascribed to the release of shares held by the corporations in themselves. A reduction of cross-shareholdings has occurred, as a matter of course, with the release of the shares and has resulted in further depreciation of share prices.

The aftermath of these extremities and the depreciation of share prices have put Japanese financial institutions into a crisis. They have been unable to recover their credits or to offer new or further lending. The last couple of years have seen the bankruptcies of financial institutions including major banks, securities and insurance companies. In 1998 two distinguished banks became nationalised for a certain period of time. Furthermore, corporations have been rocked by many scandals. Illegal corporate actions such as insider trading, window-dressing and payoffs to *sokaiya* racketeers were revealed in 1998. Inevitably, Japanese corporations have been burdened with restructuring and rehabilitation for sound management.

With this economic background, there has been serious discussion about fundamental corporate issues and a prominent move toward corporate law reform initiated by Diet members, even though for Diet members themselves to start the legislative process independently with administrative members was rather unusual in the past in Japan. In this report I will review the current legal issues concerning business enterprises.

ENACTMENT OF SPECIAL LEGISLATION

In 1998, two time-limit acts were passed as emergency measures for the rehabilitation of the Japanese economy: one for cancellation of shares from capital reserve and the other for re-appraisement of land on the balance sheets of public corporations.

The Act for cancellation of shares permits corporations to buy back shares from their shareholders through the appropriation of their capital reserve, and it allows the cancellation of the repurchased shares. In 1994, an amendment of the Commercial Code enabled corporations to buy back shares using the profits available for dividends, and to cancel the repurchased shares with a resolution of the annual general meeting (AGM). This means that the corporations can buy back their shares regardless of the percentage of repurchased shares out of total issued shares, but only with a resolution of the AGM and by using profits available for dividends. In addition, buying back shares for employees' benefits using the profits available for dividends was also permitted; however, in contrast to the case of cancellation, there is an upper limit of 3 per cent on the percentage of repurchased shares out of total issued shares. In line with these amendments, special legislation was enacted in 1997 permitting the cancellation of shares repurchased with the profits available for dividends. This was intended to facilitate the procedure for share buy-backs and cancellation of shares by resolution of the board of directors within the framework of the conditions and the procedures in the articles of association of each company. The special legislation in 1998 expanded these conditions further, developing on past amendments of the Commercial Code and the special legislation of 1997. It may meet the needs of the real business world in the sense that it enables corporations to purchase shares using not only profits but also capital reserves, and to do this by resolution of the board of directors without requiring a resolution of the AGM. While the effect of share buy-backs from capital reserve is analogous in some respects to buy-backs using the profits available for dividends and to reduction of share capital, the procedures for carrying them out are unlike those relating to share buy-backs from profits and to reduction of share capital. Some arguments have been derived from this point. From the legal perspective, the following points are worth consideration.

First, the Act to simplify the repurchasing of shares appears to have been introduced as a provisional means only for the purpose of protecting share prices against further declines, and ultimately for rebuilding a sound economy. Without a legal review or discussion about possible theoretical problems with the institutional revision, it is difficult to explain why there are procedural differences between the existing equivalent provisions and the revised ones, even though the underlying conditions are similar. Secondly, while the earlier legislation set strict conditions for the appropriation of funds, this special Act relaxes these conditions and permits buy-backs from capital reserve. It seems to have gone beyond the earlier taboo. Finally, in contrast to the procedure for reduction of share capital, which requires a special resolution from the shareholders' meeting, it is possible for the companies to buy back their shares with only a resolution of the board of directors. Although this simplified procedure is flexible and convenient for management, it must still be carefully considered because share buy-backs from particular shareholders out of capital reserve are a major concern for the other shareholders as well as company creditors. The conditions of purchase such as number, price, time, and so on should be reviewed and approved at least by the shareholders.

An extended legal theoretical approach to these problems is necessary, and special legislation should be handled on an exceptional basis. This means that it is neither to be respected as laying down principles nor to be regarded as having an impact upon the Commercial Code since it was introduced only as an emergency measurement for the ultimate purpose of the resurgence of Japanese economy.

PROPOSED CORPORATE LEGAL REFORM REGARDING PARENT–SUBSIDIARY COMPANIES

The present Commercial Code's conditions regarding parent–subsidiary companies have been under review and examination at the Division of Commercial Law of the Council for Reviewing the Legal System (*Ho-sei Shingi-Kai Sho-ho Bu-kai*) of the Ministry of Justice, which has been considering matters related to the release of pure holding companies in the amendment of the Anti-trust Law in 1997. The Division of Commercial Law at the Council for Reviewing the Legal System disclosed controversial points (*Ron-ten*) about the existing system to the public, and subsequently many opinions, criticisms or proposals were presented by various societies. The controversial points can be divided into two parts: one concerns the procedure for establishing parent–subsidiary relationship; and the other concerns the protection of shareholders and creditors in the parent–subsidiary relationship.

It is argued that the procedure for setting up a holding company should be given flexibility in line with granting permission to take advantage of pure holding company status in the Anti-monopoly Act. From this perspective, the controversial points concern the availability of setting up a parent company by exchanging shares between two companies: that is, shareholders of company A invest in company B with payment in kind for their shares of company A. Then, company B becomes a parent company of A and the shareholders of company A become shareholders of company B. The controversial points also refer to the method of flotation of a parent company such as triangular merger and compulsory acquisition. However, as the exchange of shares between two companies is the most convenient in practice, the controversial points relate mostly to that method.

Protection of the shareholders and creditors of each company against the conditions expected to occur in this situation must be considered, because if a parent company *de facto* consigns certain of its affairs to a subsidiary, the shareholders of the parent *de jure* cannot monitor those affairs by voting or through the execution of the rights given for the checking and correction of management activities. As for the shareholders and creditors of the subsidiary, if the subsidiary is obliged to follow the direction of the parent, the subsidiary has to take part in its corporate affairs, even when there is a conflict of interest affecting its shareholders and creditors. It is suggested that protection of the rights of the shareholders of a subsidiary should be respected.

First and fundamentally, as the controversial points suggest, the present definition of the parent–subsidiary relationship must be reconsidered. Secondly, corresponding to the point raised regarding the protection of shareholders of a parent, shareholders of the parent should execute their rights in its subsidiary directly. The way to implement their monitoring function when the activities of the parent are transferred to its subsidiary are, for instance, to require a resolution at a shareholders' meeting of the parent company before the parent company votes at shareholders' meetings of its subsidiary, to give the shareholders of the parent company the right to inspect books and records of the subsidiary, to allow them to bring a statutory action against the subsidiary, and so on. Thirdly, a further problem regarding the protection of the shareholders and creditors of a subsidiary has to do with the right of the shareholders of a subsidiary to check the parent's affairs. In addition, these controversial points deal with such matters as the right of shareholders of a subsidiary to inspect books and records of its parent, in case damage has been caused to the subsidiary because of a reckless act of the directors of its parent. In such cases, either the parent or its directors should be held liable, and the auditors (possibly financial auditors as well) of a subsidiary should have the power to require the parent to report its affairs and to investigate its business affairs and financial status in detail.

The opinions and criticisms of the public were to be reviewed, and a draft bill including the procedure for setting up the parent company by exchanging shares was being prepared by the Council for Reviewing the Legal System of the Ministry of Justice in January 1999. At the time of writing, this draft bill has not yet become an amendment bill to the Commercial Code; however, it will be submitted to the Diet as an amendment bill shortly.

CORPORATE GOVERNANCE

Corporate governance is still a hot issue in Japan as well as in other countries, in the face of continued economic depression and corporate scandals. Throughout the year, practical endeavours for reconstituting boards of directors have been carried out. The major corporations have gradually introduced a system of executive officers to split the functions of present directors in two: administration of corporate affairs and monitoring. Efficient corporate management and monitoring to ensure the maximisation of profits for shareholders might be a main concern in the argument about corporate governance.

The Liberal Democratic Party (LDP) has been keen on the amendment of the Commercial Code regarding auditors and the derivative suit system. The LDP released a memorandum on the Amendment of the Commercial Code, with a specific reference to Corporate Governance, in September 1997, and then published its code again in June 1998 after revision based on criticisms and opinions arising from public debate. Academics and businesspersons have also organised forums or research groups for the purpose of discussing these matters. One of these, the Japanese Corporate Governance Forum published a final report, which seems to be more in line with the US model.

While the LDP's old version of the code deals with many points concerning institutional problems about auditors and derivative suits, the new one focuses on particular points and is, accordingly, more persuasive. The revised proposed code refers to the following points. As a purpose for revising the Commercial Code it mentions general trends of the Japanese economy such as lower payout ratio, cross-shareholdings between related companies, a greater number of total issued shares, offering of certain interests to particular shareholders, and so on, that have resulted in companies taking little account of their general public shareholders. Concerning the matter of light treatment of public shareholders, it proposes taking such steps as improving the auditors' legal position and reviewing the procedures for derivative suits. This proposal follows the US governance model.

Under the new proposal of the LDP, the legal position of auditors would be the same as that of outside directors in the USA. Generally the provisions concerning auditors, in terms of the percentage of outside auditors out of total auditors, tenure and power, are improved and expanded. External auditors are mandated in public companies and it is proposed that more than half of the auditors should be outsiders. Furthermore, the auditors may play a very important role when a company itself brings an action against its directors upon its shareholders' request or when a derivative suit against the company directors is filed directly by its shareholders in cases where the company failed to bring a suit against its directors upon its shareholders' request.

In the proposal, in a derivative suit, only persons who are or have been shareholders at the time of misconduct or malpractice by the directors can bring a derivative action. The company auditors are to be representatives of the company when a derivative action is brought against the directors and the auditors have a discretion whether or not the company should initiate the procedure. The LDP's proposal extends the term that auditors can take to consider the initiation of proceedings by the company and, further, it enables them to join a derivative suit on the defendants' side on a supplementary basis if they regard the suit as unreasonable.

Under the proposed new code, the board of directors can submit an item to the shareholders' meeting enabling the directors culpable for misconduct to be immune from liability for damages, however, the consent of the board of auditors is required before such an item can be submitted.

REFORM FOR RESURGENCE OF FINANCIAL INSTITUTIONS

Problems with the reconstruction of financial institutions, on the whole, are rather serious and in need of emergency measures because they are directly related to the nucleus of a reform to produce economic resurgence.

In June 1998, a voluminous Act regarding the reform of the financial system was passed in the Diet and came into effect in December of the same year. It deals with a wide range of financial business including the amendment of bank law, securities law, securities trust law, trust business law, insurance business law, and so on, as part of what we call the 'Financial Big Bang'. This reform included a change from a licensing system to a registration system in the securities business (while maintaining a licensing system both in the banking business and in the insurance business), liberalisation of fees for selling and buying securities on commission, deregulation of eligible securities for market trading and allowing banking and insurance corporations to engage in investment trust selling, which had been carried on only by securities corporations. As alternatives to crossover between financial businesses, the setting up of holding companies to include all such businesses, as well as subsidiary companies to handle other businesses, is provided for. A regulation against short selling, as an amendment to the securities law, had been scheduled to come into operation concurrently with these other revisions; however, it came into force two months earlier in response to the world-wide hedge-funds crisis. Coupled with these statutory reforms, there has been a move towards the proposal of a new law, the Financial Services Act. In support of this reform tendency, a discussion group to consider new financial trends (*Atarashii Kinyu no Nagare ni kansuru Kondan-kai*) was organised, and it published a report in June 1998.

The most noticeable events among financial reforms may have been the foundation of new supervisory agencies in the government both in June and in December of 1998. One is called the Board of Supervision of Financial Business (*Kinyu- Kantoku- Cho*) to separate clearly the functions of planning and making proposals about financial business and the functions of supervising, monitoring and investigating. The other agency is the Committee for the Rehabilitation of Financial Institutions (*Kinyu-Saisei-Iin-kai*) whose function is to check and take corrective action for financial institutions in tight cash positions. The nationalisation of one bank, noted above, was based on a decision by this Committee (formally, by the Prime Minister who had representative power until the Committee was fully set up).

FUTURE PROSPECTS

So far, I have been reviewing the recent noticeable trends towards corporate statutory reform in Japan. Past years have seen a number of superficial and hasty legal changes, such as have never been observed before. Some laws obviously have an emergency purpose and are halfway solutions for economic sluggishness. Still, they require further legal discussion even after their time of operation.

The need for new regulations suitable for and able to adjust to the new business environment, and which can also cover this period of economic difficulties, has been widely recognised. However, discussions leading towards an effective statutory framework should never be hastily concluded, even in times of rapid and acute change in the socio-economic trends.

Postscript

There has been progress since this report was completed in January, 1999. At the proof stage, the most notable change is that a draft bill enabling the setting up a parent company by share exchange was submitted to the Diet in March, 1999 as a bill, and passed as an amendment to the Commercial Code in August of the same year. As for the reform of the auditor system and derivative suits, a draft bill has been prepared and put out for public debate. However, it is expected that it will still take a long time for this draft to become an amendment for the submission to the Diet.

12

Improving Nigeria's Investment Climate: Recent Developments

C O OKONKWO

INTRODUCTION

For Nigeria, as for most independent African countries, political independence did not bring with it economic independence. It was left for these countries to initiate measures for putting the economy into the hands of their nationals.[1] In Nigeria the policy of indigenisation of industries/businesses came in the 1970s—the period of the oil boom when Nigeria's economy was buoyant and the country had substantial foreign reserves. This policy was pursued through the Nigerian Enterprises Promotion Decrees 1972 and 1977, respectively. These Decrees specified three categories of enterprises. The first category (category 1) was reserved 100 per cent for Nigerians. The second category (category 2) required not less than 60 per cent Nigerian equity participation, while the third category (category 3) required at least 40 per cent Nigerian equity participation. The overall effect was to limit foreign participation in some enterprises.

By 1989 a great need was felt for the inflow of foreign capital. Accordingly, a reversal of policy was embarked upon. The Nigerian Enterprises Promotion Decree 1989 abrogated the aforementioned categories 2 and 3. Category 1 was retained. An alien could own any business in this category provided he held a minimum equity of 20,000 naira. This was the beginning of an 'open door' policy for attracting foreign investment. Such a policy was inevitable. The global economic recession had hit Nigeria hard, the devaluation of its currency, the huge external debt, political instability and high incidence of corruption, its poor human rights posture—all of these combined to make Nigeria an unattractive market for foreign investment.

Before the 1989 Enterprises Decree, the Industrial Development Coordination Committee Decree (IDCC) was promulgated.[2] Its aim was to remove all the formidable administrative bottlenecks and delays which confronted

---

[1] See, e.g., the Ghanaian Capital Investment Decree 1973 (NRCD 141), Investment Policy Decree 1975 (NRCD 329) and Ghanaian Investment Code, (PNDCL 116).

[2] No 36 of 1988. This was repealed by s 30 of Decree No 16 of 1995. The functions and duties of the IDCC were taken over by the NIPC, discussed below.

potential foreign investors by bringing under one establishment the functions of the various ministries needed to be consulted by the investor.

In pursuit of the new open door policy, two other decrees have since been promulgated. They are the Nigerian Investment Promotion Decree (No 16) of 1995 (the NIPC Decree)[3] and the Foreign Exchange (Monitoring and Miscellaneous Provisions) Decree No 17 of 1995 (the FEMM Decree). What follows is an examination of the incentives and assurances which the two Decrees hold out for foreign investors in order to attract much needed foreign capital into the country.

THE NIPC DECREE

This Decree establishes the Nigerian Investment Promotion Commission (the Commission) as an agency of the Federal government for monitoring and co-ordinating all investment promotion activities to which the Decree applies. Its functions include:

(a) initiating and supporting measures designed to enhance the investment climate in Nigeria;
(b) promoting investments in and outside Nigeria;
(c) collating and disseminating information about investment opportunities and sources of investment capital as well as offering advice on the choice or suitability of partners in joint venture projects;
(d) identifying specific projects and inviting interested investors to participate in them;
(e) providing and disseminating up-to-date information on incentives available to investors;
(f) assisting incoming and existing investors by providing support services.[4]

A foreigner may now invest in and participate in the operation of any enterprise in Nigeria including those dealing with petroleum resources.[5] The production of arms and ammunition, the production of and dealing in narcotic drugs and psychotropic substances, production of military and parliamentary wear and accoutrement, including those of the Police, Customs, Immigration and Prison Services[6] were however excluded. By section 28 of the Decree, the Commission shall provide a new enterprise with such assistance and guidance as it may require and shall act as liaison between the enterprise and the relevant government departments, agencies and public authorities.

---

[3] This Decree repealed the IDCC Decree, having taken over the responsibilities listed under it.
[4] NIPC Decree, s 4.
[5] 'Petroleum resources' which was initially included in the prohibited negative list is now free for full foreign investment because s 3 of the NIPC (Amendment) Decree No 3 of 1998 removed petroleum resources from the negative list.
[6] See NIPC Decree, ss 17, 18 and 32.

Incentives

In order to promote identified strategies or major investments, the Commission is empowered, in consultation with appropriate government agencies, to negotiate specific incentive packages.[7] Generally however, the Decree offers a number of specific incentives and assurances, as follows.

(1) By section 24 thereof, a foreign investor is guaranteed unconditional transferability of funds in freely convertible currency through an authorised dealer of:

    (a) dividends or profits (net of taxes) generated by the investment;

    (b) payments in respect of loan servicing where a foreign loan has been obtained;

    (c) the remittance of proceeds (net of taxes) in the event of sale or liquidation of the enterprise.

(2) One of the fears of foreign investors in Africa is the risk of nationalisation or expropriation. The Decree seeks to assuage this fear by providing that no enterprise shall be nationalised or expropriated by any Nigerian government.[8] And no person who owns, wholly or partly, the capital of any enterprise shall be compelled by law to surrender his interest in the capital to any other person.[9]

(3) No enterprise shall be acquired by the government unless it is in the national interest or for a public purpose and under a law which provides for the payment of fair and adequate compensation and a right of access to the courts by the investor for the determination of his rights and the amount of compensation due to him. Any such compensation shall be paid without undue delay and with authorisation for its repatriation in convertible currency.[10]

(4) Any dispute between a foreign investor and the government shall be settled amicably, but if this fails it will be submitted to arbitration within the framework of any bilateral or multilateral agreement on investment protection to which the federal government and the investor's country are parties, or in accordance with any other national or international machinery for the settlement of investment disputes agreed on by the parties. If there

---

[7] NIPC Decree, s 22. In Ghana a similar objective of attracting foreign investment through relaxation of controls and offer of incentives is pursued: see the Ghana Investment Promotion Centre Act 1994. For comment on this Act see A Guobadia, 'Issues in Facilitating Foreign Investment for National Development in Nigeria' (1998) 2 *Modern Practice Journal of Finance and Investment Law* 38, at 50.

[8] NIPC Decree, s 25(1)(a).

[9] NIPC Decree, s 25(1)(b).

[10] NIPC Decree, s 25(2) and (3). *Cf* s 40 of the Constitution of the Federal Republic of Nigeria, 1979.

[11] NIPC Decree, s 26.

is disagreement between the federal government and an investor as to the method of settling any dispute, the International Centre for Settlement of Investment Disputes Rules shall apply.[11]

This Decree eases off a good number of restrictions and constraints in foreign exchange dealings and makes it much easier than hitherto to bring in and take out foreign currency from Nigeria. It thus complements the incentives and assurances offered the foreign investor by the NIPC Decree and helps to create a favourable investment climate in Nigeria.

The Decree creates an autonomous Foreign Exchange Market (the Market) for the conduct of transactions in foreign exchange.[12] Any foreign exchange purchased from the Market may be repatriated from Nigeria without any further approval.[13]

A person may invest in any enterprise or security in Nigeria, with foreign currency or capital imported into Nigeria through an authorised dealer in freely convertible currency,[14] in respect of:

(a) dividends or profits (net of taxes) attributable to the investment;
(b) payments in respect of loan servicing where a foreign loan has been obtained; and
(c) the remittance of proceeds (net of all taxes) in the event of sale or liquidation of the enterprise.[15]

A foreign investor may open and operate a domiciliary account designated in foreign convertible currency with an authorised dealer. No money imported for the purpose of the Decree shall be liable to seizure, forfeiture or expropriation by the federal or a state government.[16]

Any person, including a foreigner, may invest in, acquire or dispose of, create or transfer any interest in securities and other money market instruments whether denominated in foreign currency or not. Similarly, anyone may invest in securities traded on the Nigerian capital market or by private placements in Nigeria.[17]

These liberal provisions are designed to attract the inflow of foreign capital into the Nigerian economy. Other recent relevant measures include the 1997 bud-

---

[12] FEMM Decree, s 1.
[13] FEMM Decree, s 13.
[14] FEMM Decree, s 15(1).
[15] FEMM Decree, s 15(4).
[16] FEMM Decree, s 17.
[17] FEMM Decree, s 26(2).

getary policy of exempting certain goods from Value-Added Tax (VAT) in order to encourage investment in some preferred areas of the economy,[18] the abolition of Capital Gains Tax on stocks and shares with effect from 1 January1998, the abolition of excise duty as an incentive to local manufacturers and the creation of Export Processing Zones (EPZ).[19] Such additional incentives are reviewed periodically as economic exigencies demand.

Lack of basic infrastructure, the problem of corruption and economic crimes, an unstable banking sector, as well as political instability, all contributed to the unfavourable investment climate which has plagued Nigeria in the last few years. The present military regime is making a serious effort to recover money stolen under the immediately preceding Abacha regime. Substantial sums of money in foreign currency have already been recovered. Numerous prosecutions and recoveries under the Failed Banks Decree No 18 of 1994 are rapidly restoring sanity to the banking sector of the economy.

The activities of fraudsters who specialise in duping foreigners (the offence popularly known as '419') are being energetically tackled under the Advance Fee Fraud and Other Fraud Related Offences Decree No 13 of 1995. The 1968 Companies Act which was found inadequate for the practice of corporate law in a dynamic economy has been replaced by the more modern Companies and Allied Matters Act 1990.[20] Furthermore, the Petroleum (Special) Trust Fund (PTF) established under Decree No 25 of 1994 to manage proceeds from the sale of petroleum products,[21] is seriously engaged in constructing roads, bridges and other infrastructure nationwide.

On the political scene, the sudden death of the late dictator seems to have paved the way for the restoration of democracy and political stability in Nigeria. Elections have been held and a new democratically elected government was sworn in on 29 May 1999. The recent tour of the world by the new Head of State, designed to restore international confidence in Nigeria seems to be achieving its purpose—judging at least from diplomatic and other official comments.

All indications are that Nigeria is poised for a future of increased economic and corporate activity as we enter the next millenium.

---

[18] The goods include fertiliser produced locally, tractors and other agricultural implements. Included are plant and machinery imported for use in the Export Processing Zone: see Guobadia, *supra* n.7, at 45.

[19] See the Nigerian Export Processing Zones Decree No 63 of 1992. These Zones are designed to encourage the inflow of capital for the production of goods for export. Industries in the Zones are exempted from all federal and states taxes, levies and rates and enjoy customs duty exemptions in respect of certain imported goods such as raw materials, capital goods, consumer goods etc.

[20] For the major handicaps of the 1968 Act in so far as control of foreign investment is concerned, see O A Osunbor, 'Nigeria's Investment Laws and the State's Control of Multinationals' (1988) 3 *International Centre for Settlement of Investment Disputes Review* 38, at 48 ff. One Nigerian Enterprises Promotion (Issue of Non Voting Equity Shares) Decree 1987 which sought to attract foreign investment in Nigerian securities without involvement in control has been repealed.

[21] The proceeds referred to here are 'less the marketer's margin'.

13

Recent Developments in
UK Company Law

D R MACDONALD

INTRODUCTION

The pace of British company law reform is accelerating. The last three years have seen the publication of the Hampel Report on Corporate Governance,[1] the consequent promulgation by the London Stock Exchange of a Code of Best Practice and amended Listing Rules,[2] consultation papers and a report on shareholders' remedies and directors' duties from the English and Scottish Law Commissions,[3] and the initial stages of a major Company Law Review under the auspices of the Department of Trade and Industry (DTI). The Review has now produced a wide-ranging consultative paper on the future of British company law reform.[4] This chapter aims to consider some of these developments in the light of the issues raised in the Review consultative paper.

THE CONTEXT OF REFORM

These recent steps reflect longer standing moves for reform. Much of the impetus, institutionally, has come through the DTI. Its ongoing review of company law has, over the last decade, produced numerous consultation papers aiming to reduce technical regulatory requirements[5] and to ensure that legal forms of business organisation reflect modern business needs.[6] Most recent, in this vein, are

---

[1] *Committee on Corporate Governance: Final Report* (1998).

[2] *Principles and Combined Code of Best Practice* (June 1998); Listing Rule 12.43A.

[3] Law Commission of England and Wales, *Shareholder Remedies*, Consultation Paper No 142 (1996), Report No 246 (Cm 3769, 1998); Law Commission of England and Wales, *Company Directors: Regulating Conflicts of Interests and Formulating a Statement of Duties*, Consultation Paper No 153/Scottish Law Commission Discussion Paper No 105 (1998).

[4] *Modern Company Law for a Competitive Economy: the Strategic Framework* (Feb. 1999), available (along with supporting research papers on comparative law) from http://www.dti.gov.uk. References in this chap. to 'the Review' are to this paper unless the context indicates otherwise.

[5] For instance on *Share Buybacks* (URN 98/713, May 1998).

[6] In particular, *The Law Applicable to Private Companies* (URN 94/529, Nov. 1994) which discusses, as well as a possible new form of small company (at length), also shareholder remedies, shareholders' agreements and limited partnerships.

proposals for a new limited liability partnership intended for use within self-regulated professions such as that of accountants.[7] These reflect the introduction of this form in Jersey and elsewhere (whither UK partnerships might wish to relocate) and the professions' strongly expressed fear of unlimited liability for professional negligence. This overtakes the Law Commissions'[8] ongoing consideration of the reform of partnership law generally.

How to improve standards of and procedures for corporate governance has been another major theme. Hence the Law Commission projects, carried out under reference from the DTI, and further DTI consideration of the effect on shareholders' rights of the growing use of nominee holdings as a consequence of electronic share dealing.[9] These apart, the main thrust has been on self-regulation, so far[10] largely through Stock Exchange-enforced disclosure requirements for listed public companies (albeit with a statutory underpinning[11] and the thinly veiled threat of more extensive legislation in the longer term if this method is perceived to fail). Thus the Hampel Report reviews and builds on earlier codes of best practice in the Cadbury and Greenbury Reports,[12] and the resulting 'Combined Code' is 'given teeth' by the requirement, in the Stock Exchange Listing Rules,[13] that listed companies report generally on compliance with it; that auditors review certain specified aspects of that compliance (such as the company's 'internal control' mechanisms); and, indirectly, through the statutory requirement[14]—itself a relatively recent innovation, but not confined to listed companies—that the auditors' report draw attention to inconsistencies between statements in the directors' report and the accounts. This method depends heavily for its effectiveness (first) on clearly agreed criteria on what the disclosure requirements actually mean, and (secondly) on active—particularly institutional—shareholder influence. The latter is said to be increasing.[15] There have however been concerns about 'creative compliance' (giving unhelpfully bald disclosures, for example on remuneration policy) and a 'box-ticking'

---

[7] *Limited Liability Partnerships*, Consultation Paper (URN 97/597) (Consultation Document including draft Bill and regulations: URN 98/874).

[8] This is a joint project by the English and Scottish Law Commissions. While the statutory framework is the same—the Partnership Act 1890—Scots law differs significantly, e.g., in that Scots partnerships have legal personality.

[9] *Private Shareholders: Corporate Governance Rights* (URN 96/983, Nov 1996). As this notes, the trend reflects the use of sheltered tax-free investment schemes (Personal Equity Plans) as well as the CREST dealing mechanism.

[10] Professional organisations will be central to creditor protection under the proposed limited liability partnership regime.

[11] Under the Financial Services Act 1986, ss 142(6) and 145(2), the Stock Exchange's power to make listing rules, and under them to suspend securities from listing, receives statutory recognition.

[12] In 1992 (*Report on the Financial Aspects of Corporate Governance*) and 1995 (*Directors' Remuneration*) respectively.

[13] Listing Rule 12.43A(b); also para (c), considerably amplifying the Code, requires a remuneration report and specifies its contents. These largely restate pre-Hampel provisions.

[14] Companies Act 1985, s. 235 (3).

[15] R Smerdon, *A Practical Guide to Corporate Governance* (London, Sweet & Maxwell, 1998) usefully discusses developments.

mentality.[16] Hampel tried to address these variously by pleas for more helpful disclosures and, much more fundamentally, by the requirement (now in the Listing Rules[17]) that companies' annual reports not simply disclose any non-compliance with the Combined Code but also include a narrative statement of how they have applied its principles 'providing explanation to enable [their] shareholders to evaluate how the principles have been applied'. As this last requirement has only applied since the end of 1998 it is too soon to assess its effect. There are also ongoing concerns about how effective the auditors' current corporate governance review function is, with the profession itself mooting that it be reduced, but the Review, by contrast, suggesting that it might be increased.[18] However, given that one of the most practically significant disclosure (and auditor comment) requirements concerns companies' 'internal control' mechanisms, it is potentially very important that Hampel signalled their extension to all aspects of control (not merely financial) and that guidance on effective control mechanisms has now been issued.[19] Again, of course, these developments only apply to listed companies.

Other factors are influencing change. While harmonisation at the European Union level is currently moving slowly—the draft Fifth Directive, which touches on directors' liability, shareholders' remedies and company board structure, is unlikely to be finalised in the near future—other aspects, such as a proposed European Company, are further advanced.[20] More negatively, existing directives[21] are recognised as imposing restraints on the Review's suggested simplification of requirements for incorporation documentation, changes to company capital, lodging of accounts and share structure (though the Review moots the possibility of seeking those directives' amendment). The European Convention on Human Rights, more important now as a result of its imminent incorporation into domestic UK law (which will allow it to be enforced through the UK courts), may limit possible reforms to corporate governance and certainly imposes procedural restrictions on investigation of corporate wrongdoing.[22]

At a domestic UK level, the pace of reform reflects the election of a Labour Government in 1997 and associated political factors. The Review marks a clear attempt at co-ordinated wide-ranging reform with a strong conceptual underpinning. The Government's aim of 'a framework of company law which is

[16] Hampel Report, *supra* n.1, paras 1.12–1.14, 4.15; A Belcher, 'Regulation by the Market: The Case of the Cadbury Code and Compliance Statement' [1995] *Journal of Business Law* 321.

[17] Listing Rule 12.43A(a).

[18] Auditing Practices Board, *Auditors' Responsibility Statements* (June 1998); Review, *supra* n.4, para 6.21.

[19] Institute of Chartered Accountants in England and Wales, *Internal Control: Guidance for Directors of Listed Companies*, Consultation Draft (Apr. 1999) (the 'Turnbull Report').

[20] Note European Commission, *Consultation Paper on Company Law* (1997), with associated consultation in UK by DTI, and DTI, *The European Company Statute*, Consultative Document (URN 97/786, July 1997).

[21] The First, Second, and Fourth Dirs.

[22] See Review, *supra* n.4, ch 3 and Annex C; also paras 5.3.12 (company formation), 5.3.19 (objects), 5.4.12, 5.4.28 (capital maintenance).

up-to-date, competitive and designed for the next century, [and] which facilitates enterprise and promotes transparency and fair dealing'[23] sums it up. The
'competitiveness' theme is not new, but the emphasis on 'stakeholder' ideas of
corporate governance is: 'modern companies work not only with their investors,
but with the community at large . . . it is no longer unusual to emphasise that a
good company should address the interests of all its constituencies in this
way'.[24] Concern for standards in public life generally has also led separately to
proposals for reform of the funding of political parties and, more specifically,
for companies to be required not merely—as now—to declare political donations in their annual report but also to seek shareholders' prior approval for
them; again legislation is possible in the longer term.[25]

The introduction of a Scottish assembly should not have a large impact, as
Scots company law differs relatively little from English and its control will be
reserved to the UK Parliament rather than devolved to the assembly.[26] However,
differences in court procedures will be relevant to reform of shareholder remedies. Separate statutory provisions are needed in order to introduce a statutory
derivative action and—a significant innovation in Scotland—allow its costs to
be indemnified from company funds.[27] Active judicial case management will be
central to a streamlined unfair prejudice remedy: while in England this will rest
on the new civil procedure system, an analogous Scottish reform has already
been in place and working effectively for some years.[28]

THE TIME SCALE FOR REFORM

The Review project is clearly seen as a government priority. Its timetable is,
admittedly, challenging. It is being carried out through a central steering group
and working groups on specific topics; these comprise members of the legal profession (including the Chairman of the English Law Commission), academics
and others from the business world. The Review Strategy Paper, besides identi-

[23] *Modern Company Law for a Competitive Economy*, Consultation Document (Mar. 1998),
Foreword by Margaret Beckett, President of the Board of Trade.

[24] Margaret Beckett, 5 Mar. 1998, cited in Smerdon, *supra* n.15.

[25] *Fifth Report of the Committee on Standards in Public Life* (the 'Neill Committee')(Cm 4057,
1998), Recommendation 34, noted by Review, *supra* n.4; and see now DTI, *Political Donations by
Companies* (Apr. 1999, URN 99/757), broadly adopting the Neill proposals. See also 'Shareholders
Set to be Given Final Word on Political Gifts', *Financial Times*, 25 Mar. 1999, noting the support
for these proposals of *inter alia* the corporate governance research consultants PIRC (Pensions and
Investments Research Consultants Ltd).

[26] Scotland Act 1998, Sched 5, para C1. There are however significant differences in relation to
company charges (which are a devolved matter).

[27] See Law Commission Report No 246, *supra* n.3, Appendix D. The policy, and substantive
result, will be the same in both jurisdictions.

[28] For England, see the 'Woolf Report', *Access to Justice, The Final Report* (July 1996, in operation Apr. 1999); for Scotland, see A C Hamilton, 'Commercial Actions in the Court of Session',
Journal of the Law Society of Scotland, Mar. 1999, at 20 (Lord Hamilton is the full-time commercial judge in the Court of Session).

fying issues and setting out overall strategy, examines topics chosen for their central importance (the scope of company law—essentially the 'stakeholder' issue—and the needs of small companies) or 'because they seemed promising areas in which to begin' for reasons of practical importance, logical priority, or as guinea-pigs for law reform (regulatory jurisdictions, company formation, company powers, capital maintenance, and electronic communications and information). It also floats initial comments on other topics (accounting and international issues). Meanwhile, the Review moves to consider more broadly legal forms of business activity and the full range of corporate governance problems. This second stage will clearly overlap heavily with—or overtake[29]—the Law Commission's work on directors' duties, shareholders' remedies and partnership. Significant empirical research is also planned on all these topics in order to provide a sound practical basis for reform. It is hoped that the final report will appear in the spring of 2001.

THE SHAPE OF LAW REFORM

Principles and Objectives

Advocates of company law reform have noted the need for it to identify and reflect clear identifiable principles in order to succeed. Those enunciated by the Review and, earlier, the Law Commissions differ in detail but share certain broad themes.[30]

The Review sees as its objectives *modern company law for a competitive economy*, which to achieve this must attempt an optimal *balance between freedom, the risk of abuse, and regulatory standards*; reform must be comprehensive and coherent (while recognising the special needs of small companies) and reflect recent commercial change.

To this end the Review states broad principles which the reformed law should meet. First, it should aim to facilitate transactions by encouraging transparent effective markets which will, by their operation, exert pressure to ensure accountability to outside interests. So regulation should be avoided unless markets fail to achieve this. Any regulation should be cost-effective, with implications as to enforcement (via self-regulation, civil and criminal remedies in ascending order of likely cost). A logically related principle is the need to ensure that regulatory jurisdictions are properly demarcated. In similar vein the Law Commission had, in addition, spoken of sanctity of contract, respecting

---

[29] Already, as regards *Directors' Duties*, the Law Commission has agreed not to pursue the issue of decriminalising Part X of the Companies Act 1985 (directors' conflicts of interest—see below), while the whole format of the ultimate Report is evidently under consideration: see Review, *supra* n.4, para 7.20.

[30] For the Law Commission principles, see Consultation Paper No 153, *supra* n.3, Part 2; and see Review, *supra* n.4. ch 2.

directors' commercial judgement, imposing appropriate sanctions and ensuring 'ample but efficient' disclosure and 'adequate but not excessive' regulation.

Secondly, the user should be able to find out easily what the law is. It should be accessible, usable and comprehensible, avoid complexity so far as possible, meet business needs and (here the Law Commission expands more explicitly on what is implicit in the Review) aim for certainty so as to avoid litigation.

The Law Commission added other 'principles' which give rather more explicit guidance on the actual content of the reformed law. Shareholders and the board of directors should have separate roles; the former should not interfere unnecessarily with the latter; and the 'internal management' and 'proper plaintiff' rules should be affirmed.

Commentators criticised the Law Commission principles as 'not articulating the fundamental values which company law ought to achieve and . . . being insufficiently penetrating and analytical'.[31] The Law Commission felt, in defence, that as its project mooted reforms to a limited aspect of company law to contribute in due course to the wider Review, it had to assume that companies' current legally-permitted socio-economic role remained as now. This is understandable in that particular context, and the Review does reopen that assumption by raising the wide issue of the role of the company in society and 'stakeholder' theories. That said, both Law Commission and Review do appear to start from the basis that markets operate efficiently, information disclosure will solve most ills and management autonomy is to be defended. Not all commentators will agree.[32] The Review offers the opportunity to make a point of rigorously scrutinising these important issues. Also, most of the principles, while uncontroversial in isolation, beg the question how they are to be balanced if and when they conflict. Thus, say, sanctity of contract or management autonomy may be overridden in the interests of minority shareholder protection; and it has been pointed out[33] that the Law Commission proposals actually lean this way more strongly than the principles, barely stated, might suggest.

Making Law Reform Coherent and Comprehensive

As we have seen, coherency and comprehensiveness are stated to be important to the Review. By contrast the Commission projects have been relatively restricted and piecemeal (though not small) in their scope. This is largely not the Commission's fault: the ambit of its terms of reference, its relatively small

---

[31] The Law Commission's summary; see, e.g., D Sugarman, 'Reconceptualising Company Law' in B A K Rider (ed.), *The Corporate Dimension* (Bristol, Jordans, 1998) 179; (on the initial Review consultation document) J Dine, 'The Comprehensive Review of Company Law: The Consultative Document' (1998) 19 *The Company Lawyer* 82.

[32] See Belcher, *supra* n.16; C Villiers, 'Self Regulatory Corporate Governance—Final Hope or Last Rites?' (1998) 3 *Scottish Law and Practice Quarterly* 208, at 218.

[33] Sugarman, *supra* n.31, at 227.

resources and the wish to avoid unnecessary duplication of DTI work, made this likely. The Commission is, of course, well aware of the point.[34] However, the effect was perhaps unfortunate. Various topics which might arguably have merited discussion in relation to either directors' duties, or shareholders' remedies fell into neither: reform of the rules on ratification of directors' wrongdoing is the most noteworthy—both because the Law Commission noted the difficulty, and because of its continuing role in the proposed new statutory derivative action[35]—but there are others, such as weighted voting rights and the interests of employees, which were also omitted as outside the scope of the Law Commission's terms of reference. At a higher level, there is the question of legal forms of business organisation. These need at some point to be considered *en bloc*: partnership (limited or otherwise), small (or, more specifically, close) companies' constitutions, and the use of limited liability generally. As it is, the divided approach to partnership reform has already been noted[36]; the Review, like the DTI some years ago,[37] takes a more holistic approach, though starting with a more liberal preconception of whether or not access to limited liability should be encouraged.

Making the Law Accessible

The issue of accessibility of the law raises, first, the question of the structure of reform. What will the resulting legal regime look like? The Review is based on considerable comparative legal research. While it makes reference to developments in other European Union states, its emphasis seems fairly firmly on an 'Anglo-American' tradition of company law: its inspiration comes, on the face of it, strongly from the Canadian, New Zealand and now Australian law reform pedigree. There is a preference for the New Zealand model to the extent, at least, of advocating a basically unified 'core company law' aimed primarily at small rather than public companies (albeit perhaps with an opt-out regime for closely held companies, with their own distinct Table A constitution); the South African Close Corporations Act is felt to raise too many problems of transition for companies which wish to outgrow their close status. Looking to Canada, several of the issues in the Dickerson Report[38] resurface in the Review: for

---

[34] Besides the comments above in the text accompanying *supra* n.31, see D Faber, 'Reforming Shareholder Remedies' in B A K Rider and M Andenas (eds.), *Developments in European Company Law Vol. 1* (London, Kluwer International Law, 1996) 119, an overview by the Law Commissioner with particular responsibility for company law, writing in a personal capacity. See also J Freedman, 'Reforming Company Law' in F Macmillan Patfield (ed.), *Perspectives in Company Law: 1* (London, Kluwer International Law, 1995) 197 on the piecemeal nature of British company law reform.

[35] See Report No 246, *supra* n.3, paras 6.84–6.86 and Consultation Paper No 153, *supra* n.3, paras 11.30–11.40: the present law is outlined but substantive change is deemed outside both projects' terms of reference. 'Effective' ratification will be an outright bar to a derivative action.

[36] See text accompanying *supra* n.7.

[37] *The Law Applicable to Private Companies*, *supra* n.6.

[38] R W V Dickerson, J L Howard and L Getz, *Proposals for a New Business Corporations Law for Canada* (Ottawa, Information Canada, 1971).

instance, relaxing incorporation procedures, minimising the burden of formalities, allowing non-par value shares, abolishing *ultra vires* and constructive notice while giving companies unlimited objects, and minimising the formal distinction between public and private companies.[39]

There is of course an argument that the realities of European Union membership and economic ties with Union states mean that more attention should be paid to developments there.[40] This has some force. Factors such as the relative unimportance (in corporate constitutional terms) in UK law of the distinction between private and public companies, apparent lack of business support for a two-tier board, suggestions that European corporate culture is tending to converge somewhat towards the 'Anglo-American' style, and sheer political reality may suggest an ultimate outcome in any case in line with the Review philosophy. However, corporate structures differ widely among EU jurisdictions, and their respective merits will deserve detailed consideration.

Apart from the substantive content of law reform, there is the question of codification. This issue is central to Section B of the Law Commissions' Consultation Paper on Company Directors.[41] As the title indicates—'Formulating a Statement of Duties'—the issue addressed is not reform of the content of these duties but how they are to be set out. Accessibility is the principle: how can directors best be made aware of their obligations, and hence their standards of conduct? Various options are presented, ranging from a comprehensive codification—replacing the existing law—to a non-binding statement of the main duties to be included in various official forms (such as the annual return) or—in addition or as an alternative—authoritative pamphlets setting out duties. The Review also suggests such a statement.[42] While the Consultation Paper is neutral, and responses will be influential, it is worth noting the (now) English Law Commission Chairman's earlier personal conclusions that a non-binding statement was preferable as codification might hamper the law's development and would risk creating further uncertainty and therefore litigation.[43] The paper makes this very point as regards directors' duty of care (where reform has already been achieved through case law strongly influenced by the Insolvency Act 1986[44]; here, however, the paper goes beyond mere restatement to consider

---

[39]   See C Jordan, 'Towards a Commonwealth Model of Companies Law' in F Macmillan Patfield (ed.), *Perspectives in Company Law: 2* (London, Kluwer International Law, 1997) 289. Jordan contributed a substantial comparative legal research paper to the Review: see *supra* n.4.

[40]   For instance Dine, *supra* n.31.

[41]   See *supra* n.3.

[42]   Review, *supra* n.4, para 5.1.22.

[43]   M Arden, 'Codifying Directors' Duties' in R Rawlings (ed.), *Law, Society, and Economy* (Oxford, Clarendon Press, 1997). McBryde's wider discussion of the difficulties of codification is germane: W W McBryde, 'Law Reform: The Scottish Experience' (1998) 3 *Scottish Law and Practice Quarterly* 86.

[44]   The Insolvency Act 1986, s 214(4) sets out the (mixed objective and subjective) standard of care and skill required for directors to avoid potential personal liability for their insolvent companies' debts; this was taken in *Norman* v. *Theodore Goddard* [1992] BCC 14 to reformulate the (previously laxer and purely subjective) common law standard.

enacting a new statutory business judgement rule, but—justifying this (if at all) as reassurance for directors to counterbalance any new statutory duty—it suspends final judgement pending an empirical survey to discover whether they actually feel in need of reassurance.

Companies in Society

The aspect which will attract most public attention domestically will probably be the section on 'the scope of company law'.[45] This centres on the 'stakeholder' debate, the understandable absence of which from the Law Commission's project on Shareholder Remedies caused some disappointment: it is all very well—goes the argument—to assess how efficiently such remedies operate, but the priority should be to analyse what the purpose of companies is, what role they play in society, and (having determined that) whose interests require protection and how.

It is important that the issue has now been formally raised as a factor in law reform. 'Stakeholder' ideas occur in various contexts[46] as a feature of current Labour philosophy. The Review contrasts and discusses two well-known viewpoints: in its terminology, 'enlightened shareholder value' (that is, management acting in the long-term interests of the company will take account of the interests of others who deal with the company—such as creditors, employees and suppliers—because this will better improve returns for shareholders than would a policy of short-term profit maximisation) and a 'pluralist' approach whereby such interests deserve protection in their own right even if they conflict with the shareholders' interests. The Review discusses whether to recognise other, wider, interests (such as preventing environmental damage or encouraging philanthropy), whether management should have discretion or be under a duty to take particular interests into account, and what institutional mechanisms are needed to protect any such interests.

The Review does not reach firm conclusions: much of the discussion is in fairly general terms, and its business is to stimulate debate. It promises empirical and theoretical research on the issues involved. However, it does not seem set on radical change. In line with its objectives and principles, there is a strong emphasis on effective reporting mechanisms as a way to promote transparency in corporate decision-making. It recognises a case for making clear that the 'enlightened shareholder value' approach is consistent with the present law. Beyond that, it realises that permitting (rather than requiring) a pluralist approach risks increasing management autonomy at the expense of accountability; but it is lukewarm on optional, and very cool on mandatory, board representation of non-shareholder interests. In the context of takeovers, legally

---

[45] Review, *supra* n.4, ch 5.1.

[46] And not just company law: see, e.g., in social security, the quite different idea of a new 'stakeholder pension'.

enforceable interest-group rights are seen as 'impracticable and undesirable'. Those who consider such rights as illusory without effective enforcement mechanisms may not be convinced.[47] But it may be unfair to read too much, at this stage in the Review, into tentative remarks designed to elicit debate.

CONCLUSION

The Company Law Review marks a potentially major advance in British corporate law reform. Certainly it will give it a welcome coherence and sense of direction. Whether it will mean a radical change to the current stress on a shareholder-centred model, mediated through market mechanisms, is more questionable. On the contrary, more effective shareholder remedies and information communication might give this new vigour.

It is to be hoped that the Review is not unduly cautious in considering different models for reform. The recent Cadbury and Hampel proposals for self-regulatory corporate governance reform have explicitly assumed the centrality of shareholder value; but we must remember Cadbury's comment that:

> we should not in this country regard the shareholder-driven model as being the only way in which companies can be structured and controlled. At the same time the Continentals will not be able to ignore shareholder rights or Anglo-American standards of disclosure, if they want to tap international sources of equity finance.[48]

Recent European and worldwide developments support this.[49] Some specific problems (such as auditors' and directors' independence) are common concerns in several European countries. At the same time, 'convergence' is a two-way process: for instance, economic realities led some UK-based companies to meet the requirements of the European Union Works Councils Directive even though it did not then apply in the UK.[50] The Review must not miss the opportunity to assess all options in charting the way ahead.[51]

---

[47] See J Kay and A Silberston, 'Corporate Governance' in Macmillan Patfield, *supra* n.39, 49, or more radically, S Wheeler, 'Corporations as Citizens?' in J Gardner (ed.), *Citizenship: The White Paper* (London, British Institute of International and Corporate Law, 1997).

[48] A Cadbury, 'The Response to the Report of the Committee on the Financial Aspects of Corporate Governance' in Macmillan Patfield, *supra* n.34, 23, at 32.

[49] See E Wymeersch, 'A Status Report on Corporate Governance in Some Continental European European States' in K J Hopt *et al.* (eds.), *Comparative Corporate Governance* (Oxford, Clarendon Press, 1998) 1098; 'European Companies Becoming More Open', *Financial Times*, 9 Apr. 1999; 'OECD Code to Safeguard Shareholders', *Financial Times*, 10 Apr. 1999.

[50] Council Dir. 94/95/EEC, 22 Sept. 1994; see N Burrows and J Mair, 'Catching Up With European Social Law' (1998) 3 *Scottish Law and Practice Quarterly* 159.

[51] This chapter was written before the publication of the Law Commission's Report *Company Directors: Regulating Conflicts of Interest and Formulating a Statement of Duties* (Law Com No 261/Scot Law Com No 173, Com 4436, 1999).

Index

Agent managed capital 7
Allopoietic System 44
Anderson, Gary 9–16
Anti trust laws 181
Australia 37–67, 165–7, 171–8, 199
Australian Law Reform Commission 59
Australian Stock Exchange 173–4
Autopoietic theory 43–4, 52, 59

Bankruptcy 65
Berle, A 49–50
Bernstein, Peter 15
Blandi, Joseph 6
Board of Supervision of Financial Business
    (Japan) 184
Bubble Act 11
Butler, Henry 9

Cadbury Report 174, 194, 202
Cadman, Joseph 6
Canada 110–3, 199–200
    taxation 110–23
    investment in USA 113–19
Capital reductions 96–9
Chandler, Alfred 4
chartered corporation 10
Chayes, A 34
Church 1
Closure of Corporate Law 38
Code of Best Practice 193
Collectivisation of shareholders and managers
    18, 31
Combined Code of Best Practice 174–5
Committee for the Rehabilitation of Financial
    Institutions 184
Communication 156
Communitarianism 20
Companies Act (UK) 46
Companies and Allied Matters Act 1990
    United Kingdom 80–100
    Nigeria 191
Companies Registry (UK) 80, 88
Company Law Reform (UK) 193–202
Contracts model 17, 21, 27
Contract theory 58
Corporate affairs commission 80–100
Corporate finance 22
Corporate governance 30, 193, 197, 171–8,
    182–4

Corporate groups 46–8, 47, 56, 118
Corporate Law Economic Reform Program
    Bill (CLERPB) 17, 32, 50, 171–7
Corporate Morality 43
Corporate planning 46
Corporate restructure 58
Corporate veil 53–4
Corporations ombudsman 79–100
Corruption 8

Davies, Joseph 5
Debt and equity 23, 24, 25
Dickerson Report 199
Directors duties 20, 49, 69–76, 172, 177

Directors liabilities to third parties 69–77
    France 71
    Germany 70
    Japan 69, 72–4
    UK 69–70
Disclosure 175–6
Dodd, E 49–50
Dubai, UAE 41

Employee Share Plans 29–30, 50
Employees in corporate law 44–5, 49, 57
Enterprise Bargaining 27
Enterprise Theory 34
Environment 125–42
Environmental audits 132–42
    confidentiality 137
Environmental auditors:
    liability 138, 139, 142
    duty of 140
Environmental Impairment Liability Insurance
    141–2
Environmental management 132
Ethics 52, 62–3, 67
European Company 195
European Convention on Human Rights 195
European Union 195, 200
Export Processing Zone (Nigeria) 191

Foreign Investment:
    US Investment in Canada 119–24
    Canadian Investment in USA 113–9
    Nigeria 187–91
Fiduciary duty 15, 28, 49
Freedom of association 39

Gain seeking 4
General agreement on trades in services 155–67
German Taxation 109
Geschaftsfuhrer 71
Globalisation 155–7
GmbHG Act (Germany) 70, 109
Great Depression 16
Greenbury Report 174, 194

Hampel Code 174
Hampel Report 174, 193, 194, 195, 202
Hartz, Louis 27
Hessen, Robert 10
Hostile Takeovers 150–2
Hurst, W 8, 12
Hybrid entities 101–24
Human Rights 156
    European Convention on Human Rights 195

Implied term of trust and confidence 57–8
Income inequality 33, 34
Incorporation, 8, 46
Industrial democracy 28
Industrial relations 38
Industrial Relations Committee (Australia) 61
Inland Revenue Service 101
Insider trading 179
Insolvency law 47, 58, 65–8
Institutional investors 18, 22, 31–3
International Hybrids 108, 120
Internationalism 155
Internal Revenue Code 103
Investment 113–24, 187–91

Japan 125–53
Japanese Commercial Code 72
Jenkins committee 79–80
Joint stock company 11
    unincorporated 10, 104

Labour Law 37–67
Labour rights 166
Law and economics 22, 27
Liberal National Coalition (Australia) 38
Limited liability 10, 13, 38, 45–8, 102, 199
Limited Liability Company 102–24
liquidation 91–4
Listing rules:
    Australia 173
    United Kingdom 194
Lock outs 39
London Stock Exchange (LSE) 174, 193–4

Macey, J 27
Maier, Pauline 13
Managerial conduct, 26
Maritime Union of Australia 37
Market assumptions 3

Mergers and acquisitions 143–53
Minority shareholders 80–3
Monopolies 7
Moribund companies 94–5
Most Favoured Nation 160–2
Multinational corporations 111, 118, 157, 159
Multilateral Agreement on Investment 155–67

National Farmers Federation (Australia) 41
Neo classical economics 2, 5, 9
Nigeria 79–100, 187–91
Nigerian Investment Promotion Commission 188–9
Nominal directors 75
North, Douglas 2

OECD 162–5
Ombudsman, Corporations 79–100

P&O Ports 38
Parent—subsidiary companies 181
Path dependency 2
Patrick Stevedores 37, 38
Pay for performance 31–3
Payoffs 179
personally managed capital 7
pollution 125–42
Privitisation 28

Representative Directors 74
Rent seeking theory 2, 9, 14–16
Reverse hybrids 108, 117

Securities 81
Securities and Exchange Commission 80–1
Separate legal personality 38, 45–8, 53, 55, 58
Sevoy, Ronald 7
Scheiber, Harry 7
Schmithoff, Clive 79
Sotland 10–15
South Africa 199
Shares:
    cancellation of 180
    buy-backs 180
Shareholders 14, 17–35, 49, 80, 177, 182, 194, 198, 201
Shared governance 17–18
Shareholder centred theories 20, 22, 27–8, 34, 202
State, role of in corporate law 3–16
Strategic insolvency 66
Superannuation, 30
Supermodel syndrome 34

Takeover bids 143–53
Taxation 101–23, 191
Tax avoidance 111
Technology 156

Tollison, Robert 9–16
Theology 1

Unincorporated Joint Stock Company 10, 104
US–Canada Tax Treaty 116, 123
Utilities, 6, 7

Voluntary administration 59, 63, 67

Wallis Committee 23

Waterside workers 38
Wedderburn, K W 79
Window dressing 179
Women:
    as shareholders 14
Workplace agreements 27, 39
Workplace Relations Act 1996 (Australia) 39,
    42, 55–6, 66
World Trade Organisation 160